The Power of Executive Presence for Women

HOW TO GET "IT"

CONI JUDGE, PhD

Copyright © 2015 by Eden Communication Strategies

All rights reserved. This book or any portion thereof may not be reproduced or used in any manner whatsoever without the express written permission of the publisher except for the use of brief quotations in a book review.

Printed in the United States of America

First Printing, 2015

ISBN-13: 978-1979834933
ISBN-10: 1979834938

www.coni.london

CONTENTS

Preface: Everybody's Got Something – and This Is Mine 1
How I Found My 'Something' 2
The Five Facets Approach – Polishing Your Presence One Facet at a Time 3

**Chapter 1: The Cold, Hard Truth About Why
'Good Girls' Don't Always Get the Tiara 5**
How Kate and Angela Missed Out on the Tiara 5
You're Like the Cullinan Diamond 9
Who Wants to be Stuck in Marzipan? 12
Let's Ask Some Very Tough Questions about Getting the Tiara 14
Who Gets the Crown in the End? Not Always the Good Girl 15

**Chapter 2: Why We All Need to Cowgirl Up – And
Get A Blow-dryer to Get the Job 19**
Gathering Interesting and Useful Rocks 19
How 'Blink' and 'Executive Presence' Elevated the Conversation 20
How Anne Found Gravitas 21
What We Can All Learn from an Iceberg 24
Why 'It's Not Fair' Doesn't Help 25
The Holy Grail of Executive Presence Research 26

**Chapter 3: An Excavation into Bedrock OR How to
Start Uncovering Your Authentic Self, Flaws and All 29**
Do You Have Gravitas? 29
The New Alpha-Female Media Archetypes 31

The Importance of Authenticity: The Big Benefits You Get from
Developing a Strong, Compelling, Authentic, Personal Presence 32

Chapter 4: Who Are You Really? Balancing a Personal Presence With Your Professional Presence 37

Can We Really Change? 38

Where to From Here? The Five Facets Excavation and Polishing 42

Chapter 5: How to Polish Your Visual Facet and Look the Part 45

It Starts with Shoes 48

A Quick Tutorial on First Impressions 51

Chapter 6: The Visual Appearance Minefield 55

How Casual Friday Confused Everyone 57

Being a Girl Is Hard 62

Body Image and 'Never Enough' 63

Chapter 7: Visual Conundrums for Professional Women . . . 65

Faking Femininity – The Tomboy Executive 68

Balancing Yin with Yang to Achieve 'Classic' 69

Do Your Own Professional Makeover – or the Top 10 Image Rules
Every Executive Woman Needs to Know and Follow 71

Chapter 8: The Five A's of Appearance for Executive Women 75

1. Attractive to emphasize the positive 75

2. Authentic to who you are 77

3. Appropriate to the environment 79

4. Accommodating to meet expectations 84

5. Aligned with your objectives and your brand 86

Putting the Final Polish on Your Visual Facet 91

Chapter 9: Polishing Your Verbal Facet to Sound the Part 95
Managing Your Voice 97
Managing the 'Mixing Board' for Your Verbal Communication 100
Understanding Your Unique Speaking Strengths 105

Chapter 10: Authentic Speaking Skills 113
Being Assertive: Show Your Teeth but Never Growl 114
Prepare, Prepare, Prepare 117
Listen, Listen, Listen 117
Strategic Use of Small Talk 117

Chapter 11: Creating Aligned Messaging 119
The Triple Filters Test 119
Developing a Narrative 121
Storytelling and Your Corporate Myth 122
The 'Storytelling' Warning 123
Humor: Use with Caution 125

Chapter 12: "Leaderly" Communications 127
How to Have Difficult Conversations 128
Using the Language of Power 128
Putting It into Practice: Sound Like a Leader 130

Chapter 13: Polishing Your Kinesthetic Facet to Embody the Part 133
Kinesthetic Facet: Micro Perspective 135
Kinesthetic Facet: Macro Perspective 135
Why This Matters: The Nonverbals Say It All 136
Being Aware of Your Kinesthetic Presence 138

Chapter 14: The Three S's Every Woman on the Rise Must Master: Standing, Sitting, Shaking 141

    The Simple Act of Sitting. 141

    A Menu of Handshakes 142

    Making a Stand. 145

    Putting It Together: Countdown to Impact 147

Chapter 15: Body Language and Energy. 149

    Body Language Basics 149

    Understanding Energy 151

    Practice Tuning Your Energy. 155

    The Fit Factor: Demonstrating You're Up to the Task. 157

    Train Like an Athlete. 159

Chapter 16: Taking Command – Being Leaderly and Likeable 163

    Commanding a Room. 163

    How to Act Like a Leader 165

    Being Likeable. 167

Chapter 17: Climb the Ladder Gracefully – and in a Skirt and Heels. 173

    How to Be 'Leaderly' Without Being a Bitch. 174

    The Alpha Watches the Pack's Cues. 175

    Creating Physical Distance as a Leader. 176

Chapter 18: Polishing Your Sociability Facet to Build Relationships. 179

    The Art of the Relationship. 180

    Are You a Boss or a Bossypants? 183

    The Art of Saying 'Well Done' 186

    The Trust Equation 191

Top Ten Things Women in Business Should Never, Ever Do............ 125

Chapter 19: How to Be Gracious 195
Mixing and Mingling Made Simple 197
Accepting Gentlemanly Behavior as a Woman 200
Managing Motherhood Graciously...................................... 201
Romance and Friendships 203

Chapter 20: Basic Business Etiquette 207
How to Host a Meeting... 208
Etiquette in the Office – Ten Women You Don't Want to Be........... 209
Technology and Social Media Etiquette in Business 210
Cross Cultural Awareness.. 212
To Gift or Not to Gift.. 215
Handling The Worst Case Scenario 216
Practice: Polishing Your Sociability Presence 221

Chapter 21: The Fifth Facet – Can You Create a Star? 223
A Matter of Mindset.. 224
Mapping the Minefield of Presence.................................... 227

Chapter 22: Understanding Gravitas.................... 227
The Low Hanging Fruit of Gravitas 228
Being Yourself – On Purpose 230
Having Courage to Be You 233
Becoming Mindful... 234
Top Tips for Achieving Gravitas 237

Chapter 23: Polished Politics......................... 239
Proactively Managing the Game Board................................ 241
When You're Under Siege – Grace Under Fire 243
Top Tips for Polished Politics 246

Chapter 24: Positioned for Success **247**
    The Motherhood Conundrum. 249
    Status: One-Up, One-Down or Equal. 252
    Controlling Your Universe. 257
    Drama Free Zone. 260
    Managing the Trust Equation. 265
    Tops Tips to Position Yourself for Success 268

Chapter 25: Navigating The Blind Spot. **269**
    Finding a 'Blind Spot Buddy'. 271
    Nose Blowing and Other Problems 274
    How to Reveal the Hidden Truth to Someone You Think Needs It. 276
    Giving Personal Presence Feedback: When It's Not About You 276
    'She Might Cry' – or Why Women Don't Get as Much Feedback as Men . . . 280
    Why Giving Unwanted Feedback Isn't Such a Great Idea. 281

Chapter 26: Pulling It All Together for the Long Haul. **285**
    How to Get and Sustain Momentum 285
    Cultivating Resilience 287
    The Final Lesson: Vulnerability 291

PREFACE

Everybody's Got Something – and This Is Mine

"Recreate yourself by forging a new identity, one that commands attention and never bores. To succeed you must be the master of your own image rather than letting others define it for you." – Robert Greene, Power

"You will know the good from the bad when you are calm, at peace. Passive. A Jedi uses the Force for knowledge and defense, never for attack." – Yoda, The Empire Strikes Back

I collect Yodas.

On my desk, I have loads of little Yodas. There's a LEGO Yoda, a 'magic question' Yoda, a USB drive Yoda, to name just three. When I'm thinking about someone I want to help, I often find myself rearranging my Yodas subconsciously.

Yoda is wise, but honest. He says, "Train yourself to let go of everything you fear to lose." Yoda tells me to "Always pass on what you have learned." And so I am.

What I have chiefly learned is that I have a gift. It is a very particular gift. I have the gift of seeing very clearly and quickly the flaws in the way a person presents themselves to the world, and understanding what needs to be polished in order for them to shine.

In the wrong hands, this kind of insight could be dangerous. But in the world of Executive Presence I am a Jedi Knight. I use the Force for good, not evil.

We all have something, and this is mine.

How I Found My 'Something'

I really like the film 'Blue Crush.' It's a cool 'surfer girl' film that shows empowered women, but mostly I just like the soundtrack. There's a groovy song called 'Everybody's Got Their Something' by Nikka Costa in the film. It's about believing in yourself and what you have to offer. Add it to your playlist for your next workout – along with 'One Girl Revolution' from the Legally Blonde soundtrack - and feel empowered.

We know that we all have things that we're good at and things that we're not. I have many things I can't do – drive on the wrong side of the road and shift gears with my left hand, cook anything complicated or remember numbers.

But I do have a few things that I can do, so that's where I focus my energy.

When I was quite young, I learned that I'm a good writer. As I began my professional career, I learned that I'm good at helping people grow and develop themselves. I don't get intimidated much when I meet powerful people – not that I don't respect them, but I find them so intriguing that I forget to be nervous. I activate my "Terminator Brain" (as my sons call it) where I start sifting through the person's surface projections and identify the areas that could be adjusted or refined to make them even stronger. As I said, it's a gift. I do it instinctively.

As a specialist in corporate communication, I've worked with top executives in some of the world's biggest companies, with entrepreneurs in start-ups, and leaders in non-profit sectors. I've worked in many industries, such as energy, finance, healthcare, and technology, advising leaders on how to handle communications related to change – mergers, acquisitions, leadership changes, rebranding, IT platforms, and so on.

I take the basics of communication and help them craft strategies to inspire teams, shareholders, and other stakeholders. I was really fortunate to find a good niche at the right time and get opportunities that led my career down an interesting and fulfilling path.

Along the way, I've been an Executive Coach and have worked with women at the helm of important organizations, and women who can't seem to get past the 'hump' or over the plateau and into the executive suite. I've advised women politicians, authors, executives, artists, entrepreneurs, lawyers, television news presenters, reporters, and even rodeo queens.

I've conducted workshops, developed strategies and coached amazingly talented women – and men – who needed me to do two very important things that nobody else had done for them previously:

1. Tell them how they're being perceived, really.
2. Tell them what to do to polish their presence so they get the job they want.

Why am I qualified to advise these exceptional people and why does my approach succeed? Because if I have one skill above any others, it's that ability to see the aspects of an individual that need to be refined to reveal the natural brilliance within. I call these aspects the 'Five Facets.'

The Five Facets Approach – Polishing Your Presence One Facet at a Time

This book is about Executive Presence and how to recognize that it's something you must pay attention to for you to succeed. You may resist this idea because a lot of what we talk about here flies in the face of everything you've always been told and wanted to believe – it's enough to be smart and work hard. Well, it's not. I've known this for some time, since I evolved my corporate communications consulting practice and trained as an image consultant and then realized that 'what not to wear' was only the surface.

New research, coupled with a focus in the US and UK on getting more women as CEOs and on boards of major companies, has revealed that Executive Presence is a key area to address in your strategy to get the job and career you deserve.

So what I do and say may *seem* superficial, but it really isn't. The unpalatable truth is that in the higher echelons of the corporate world, women are held to a higher standard than men. Judgment is swift, and brutal. An authoritative presence counts for everyone at this level. But for women it *really* counts. We have to get it right, the first time and every time thereafter.

What I will say throughout this book may sound harshly judgmental at times. And it is. It has to be – because it's far better to hear it from me in the pages of a leadership book than in your workplace at a moment of crisis.

CHAPTER 1

The Cold, Hard Truth About Why 'Good Girls' Don't Always Get the Tiara

How Kate and Angela Missed Out on the Tiara

More than one executive's career has been lost on a stage, at the podium. It's a terrible thing to witness, and I find it even worse when I see a woman go off the rails – because I know how nearly impossible it will be for her to get another chance.

I can recall two incidents that I found particularly heart wrenching to watch where two talented, capable, smart women crashed and burned before my eyes. In both cases, a lack of awareness of 'Executive Presence' – or the ability to present yourself with confidence, gravitas and grace – was the beginning of the end.

Angela and Kate were both Vice Presidents at Fortune 100 companies – one at a major energy company and the other in finance. Seasoned, tough, with bright futures ahead of them, they were new in their roles and clearly in the queue for promotion. Both had also been given opportunities to speak on high visibility platforms within their companies.

As the communications advisor to leadership teams in both companies, I was pleased that they had been given opportunities to shine in high-level forums. Remember, Barack Obama was just a senator from Illinois until he made a great speech at the Democratic National Convention. It's true that a good speech can set you apart from the pack and be a game changer.

For both Kate and Angela, this was a platform to show their peers and bosses that they could deliver a compelling address to shareholders, analysts, at a flagship conference, before a political committee, or in any other top-tier situation. It was a live 'headroom' assessment that had to be executed perfectly.

Oftentimes we only get one really good chance at bat – and this was it for both Angela and Kate. But both women failed because they didn't understand the power of executive presence. Each woman made bad choices and exposed flaws in one or more of her 'five facets' of presence. Angela was nervous about her presentation and that's probably what led her to lose her better judgment and have one too many glasses of champagne at the cocktail reception preceding the corporate awards ceremony and live global webcast in front of her company's CEO and members of the board.

When I got the message over my headset from an event coordinator that there was a 'situation,' I walked slowly across the ballroom and into the corridor. With only minutes to go before we went live, my only female presenter was drunk and leaning against the wall of the ladies' room stall. I knew Angela reasonably well and had never seen her have more than a glass of wine at a company dinner, so I was stunned.

I got someone to call a cab, sent her home and made excuses for her. I quickly recruited another executive, who happened to be male, to step in for her segment. It was an opportunity lost for Angela. What was worse, a few too many people had observed her state during the reception and gossip was rife. Whereas a man might get a little 'soused' and be forgiven the next day for 'just acting like one of the guys,' women don't have the luxury of swerving off course without greater consequence. Suddenly, this talented woman was talked about as being 'unreliable' and maybe not quite 'right' for the next post. Her potential went from rockstar to rehab.

HOW TO GET "IT"

Angela's error was to expose a huge flaw in her 'Sociability Facet' – her capacity to moderate herself in a social setting. She also completely tanked her Presence Facet by missing a golden window to position herself. What made the lapse of judgment worse, though, was that after the event she didn't take responsibility for her actions or acknowledge the impact her behavior had on colleagues who had to step into the breach. She was semi-apologetic but mostly full of excuses. These may or may not have been valid, I really don't know. What I do know is that I never felt confident to recommend Angela for another speech because I wasn't sure she could represent herself and the company effectively. That ended up limiting her potential to be visible and promotable.

Kate's messed-up moment in the spotlight was less of a wreck than Angela's, but the net effect was equally devastating. I'd seen her in meetings with senior leaders and she was always confident, articulate and intelligent. She was whip smart in her field, while demonstrating great leadership potential. She had poise and commanded respect.

So I felt very comfortable agreeing that she should have a place on the agenda at a senior executive forum, presenting to the top 300 leaders in the division. I'd offered to help her practice her speech in advance, as I do all executives with whom I work, but she declined. Her bosses, all male, and several of her peers – again, all male – did take me up on my offer. I watched them walk through their presentations and reviewed the slides they intended to use, offering suggestions on presentation style, gestures and how to time the speech with the graphics. We talked about what to wear and I reminded them what colors and patterns don't work well on camera as this would be taped and suggested that they wear either a tie with no jacket or a jacket with no tie to establish the right level of formality for the event.

I don't know why Kate didn't want to rehearse – perhaps she was nervous or maybe she just thought it wouldn't be a problem. But I knew it wouldn't go well when I saw her walk into the meeting room five minutes before the start. Her Visual Facet was completely off. Her bright blue skirt suit was too tight, too short, too busty and too garish – it looked like a schoolgirl's uniform gone wrong. Being a little overweight, it only emphasized her size and made her look unkempt. She was not wearing stockings and her make-up was overdone by any standard. Frankly, she looked like a complete mess.

Then she got up to speak – a moment for her Verbal Facet to shine – and instead of the thoughtful, impassioned speech I'd envisioned when I had previewed her slides and speaker notes, she began a rambling, nervous reading that made little sense and made the audience incredibly uncomfortable. Jokes fell flat. As she became more anxious, her speech quickened, the decibel level increased and her pitch rose to a near-screech.

Lastly, her Kinesthetic Facet was completely off. Where she should have been 'big' for a large stage and venue, she was 'small' – limited and narrow. She hid behind the podium, gripping it with white knuckles. Her energy was hectic and unfocused and her anxiety clear.

It was painful to watch. And there was no way for me to fix it. Though it sounds brutal, this was her chance to shine, and she blew it.

Afterward, I approached her and offered to watch her video with her to give her suggestions. I made the same offer to every other presenter, all male. She was the only one who initially accepted, but then canceled meeting after meeting until we never did get together. She asked me to 'send some notes' about my impressions, which I did. But I never heard from her again. Was she embarrassed? Probably. But the only way to improve is to use the tools you have – in this case, me, an expert in impact and corporate communication for executives – to help you improve. By refusing help, she denied herself the opportunity to improve and grow.

Company executives have long memories and when the promotions come around they remember who stands out and who 'isn't quite ready.' Kate and Angela, through lack of preparation and avoidable mistakes, both put themselves in the 'isn't quite ready' bucket. Both women had opportunities to get input and grow — rare for women in the workplace — and both of them failed to take advantage of their moment because they didn't understand just how important Executive Presence is to a woman in business.

You're Like the Cullinan Diamond

In the Natural History Museum in London sits a paste model of the Cullinan diamond. It weighed 1.3 pounds and is one of the biggest diamonds ever found. Legend has it that when the man who cut the gem went to make the initial cleave, he actually fainted from the stress. That's because you only get one go at hacking up a diamond as big as a small melon and not screwing it up.

I love this museum because it's beautiful, but I also love to go and work there near the big fake diamond. It looks like a chunk of rock with no sparkle or dimension or brilliance. It's not until the diamond is cut and polished that its beauty is revealed.

Now, if I wanted to visit the real Cullinan diamond(s), I'd need to go to the Tower of London where they are mounted as part of the crown jewels. But I like the fake paste rock because it reminds me of potential. Natural diamonds are usually formed by high temperature and under pressure at depths of up to 190 kilometers or 118 miles under the Earth's mantle. A diamond takes billions of years to be formed before volcanic eruptions force it to the surface where it can be mined.

The process of cutting a diamond is violent and dramatic. Before any tools are employed, it must be planned carefully, with every flaw considered and mitigated to maximize value. The cut must be designed to retain the most carat weight and color, while enhancing the salability of the stone. Sometimes the quality of the cut must be sacrificed to keep the carat weight higher, depending on how either will impact the value and salability.

The key is that the diamond cutter must be completely pragmatic in their assessment of the stone itself. You can't pretend there isn't an inclusion or ignore a variation in the color just because you don't like it.

The same goes with Executive Presence. You have to be completely honest with yourself to recognize your strengths and weaknesses, and make a plan to enhance one set of qualities while compensating for the other.

The process of changing a rough stone into a faceted gem requires knowledge, tools, equipment and technique. The stone is cleaved into its separate pieces before being bruted or 'girdled' to give it the basic shape. Two diamonds are set against each other to grind and create the desired shape because they are equally hard and can make the cut.

Then the stone is polished, whereby the facets are cut onto the diamond through a process of blocking, faceting and polishing. Only then is it cleaned with acid and examined for final quality.

Only then is its value realized – after being pressurized, vulcanized, cleaved, cut, ground, acid bathed, and set. It's not an easy transition from rock to brilliance.

The word 'facet' is loaded with meaning for me. Coming from the Latin *facies*, its root means 'face' or 'form.' On one hand, it is literally one of the polished surfaces of a cut gem. But it also means 'a particular aspect or feature of something.' It's an aspect or a dimension of an object or, in my work, an individual.

We are a lot like diamonds in the rough. We all have our experiences, beliefs, education, background, culture, heritage and all the other things that, in combination, make us unique and individual. We all have our own pressures to survive and our own flaws with which to cope.

We all choose surfaces project ourselves and who we are to the outside world. We may do this intentionally, but without always considering the consequences. In business, considering how each of our facets is refined and polished to reflect our best qualities requires some analysis, planning, and strategy. Just like the diamond cutter analyzes, plans, and strategizes to maximize the brilliance of the stone and minimize the flaws, we can maximize our own brilliance and minimize our own flaws to project our best self to the world in which we live, and work.

The Five Facets are the surfaces we use to present ourselves. This is the model I use to frame my work with clients to ensure they're making a plan to project their unique brilliance, to demonstrate their value and to be recognized.

Collectively, these Five Facets comprise your Executive Presence, or how you present yourself:

1. Visually. This is your appearance, facial expressions, dress and 'artifacts,' eye movement and eye contact. It's also your online image and your social media identity, which people use to form an impression of you with nothing other than what they read/see.
2. Verbally. This facet reflects your tone of voice, speech patterns, accent, vocalizations, speaking and listening skills.
3. Kinesthetically. Not an intuitive descriptor, but nonetheless critical, this facet encompasses gestures, posture, body language, personal space, smell, touch and energy.
4. Sociability. Particularly important in corporate cultures, this encompasses behavior that's accepted or unacceptable, offensive or non-offensive, cross-cultural awareness and an overall social ease and etiquette. This also is reflected in your social media behavior.
5. Presence. The 'X-Factor,' the instant click and *gravitas* that real leaders project. It's developed and managed very strategically by understanding semiotics or symbols, using juxtaposition

to draw or deflect attention, manipulating the environment, understanding power structures, and being shrewd in your approach to get the job you want and deserve.

For you to shine, each Facet needs to be reviewed, the flaws mapped, the plan created, and the strategy implemented.

Who Wants to Be Stuck in Marzipan?

If you're a woman in business and you've made it to 'the upper middle' – that 'clay layer' that some call 'marzipan' and others call 'plateaued' – you know that this isn't where you want to stay. You've busted your ass to get the degree or you learned from the school of hard knocks and you're still standing. You've fought to get in the door and you've worked hard to keep your spot. You've made compromises in your personal life. You've sacrificed. You've poured your heart and soul, your energy and passion into getting the prize – a top-tier job with a 'C' in front or a seat on the Executive Committee or a place on the Board of Directors.

Then you look around as the pack thins and you see who's getting those rare, few slots that come open. The data all predicts that it will probably be a man. He will likely be younger and less experienced than you. He may have even worked for you or as an equal at some point. You worked just as hard as he did. You may be smarter, have better ideas, or even a better track record in your performance.

So why did he get the crown, while you're still looking around at marzipan?

Good question. And one with an answer that you're probably not going to like. It's because he looks and acts the part – he's seen as a 'safe bet' and you're possibly still seen as a 'maybe' for a bunch of subconscious and illogical reasons that nonetheless influence the decisions being made. So, more often than not, he gets the seat and you have to look on from the sideline.

HOW TO GET "IT"

For every 'train wreck' story, there are dozens of wonderful success stories about women who rise to the challenge and hit the mark. Alexis was a new Vice President at a top technology company who I recommended to speak at an industry flagship conference in front of thousands of senior leaders in her field. Introverted by nature, Alexis is also an established, published expert in her discipline.

So when another, more senior executive had to cancel, there was a perfect window for her to step in. Because she had never given a speech at this level, Alexis was understandably nervous. We worked together to craft her narrative and rehearse her speech. We videotaped her in advance so she could see her body language and adapt to overcome subconscious detractors in her presentation style. She was naturally soft spoken, but she practiced projecting her voice to a level that felt comfortable for her, while still audible to the audience. We talked about her energy and the need to bring it up so that she could engage and connect with the audience. We reviewed who specifically would be in the audience so she could ensure her messaging was on point and relevant for them. We talked about tactics for identifying key leaders to network with before and after the speech, to make the most of the opportunity. We also reviewed wardrobe choices and I explained she was going to have to wear some make-up, which she normally eschewed.

On the day, she was brilliant. She did not come across as a dynamic, go-getter evangelist type, but 'naturally' confident, measured, compelling, and – crucially – authentic to her. She demonstrated grace, handled questions flawlessly, and projected a capable, forward-thinking presence that led others to think of her as more of a leader with greater potential. She has since been promoted to a higher role and has serious potential to reach Executive Committee level.

Let's Ask Some Very Tough Questions about Getting the Tiara

Why aren't there more women CEOs? Why aren't there more women on Boards of Trustees? Why do men get promoted to Executive Committees while women remain stuck on the VP plateau?

Is it because men are smarter? Of course not. Is it because they work harder? No. Is it because we have babies and go 'off the path' for maternity leave and diapers? Ask any woman without a child, and she'll tell you that no, a maternity leave was not the bump in the road for her.

The issue starts with a tiara. The type we've seen on every princess from Cinderella to Kate Middleton. Dr. Deborah Kold and Carol Frohlinger from Negotiating Women, a US firm that coaches women in leadership skill, coined the phrase 'Tiara Syndrome' to define the issue.

'The Tiara Syndrome' is basically this: women believe 'being good' will be rewarded. We say to ourselves: if I work really hard, stay late, arrive early, sacrifice my lunch hour and my weekends, then I'll get promoted and the tiara will be laid upon my head. If I don't have babies, or do have babies but take a really short maternity leave, or do have babies and take a maternity leave but have my laptop in the recovery room – then I'll get the nod. If I get another degree, take another seminar, or invent the world's best widget, then they have to see my talent and I'll be rewarded.

Tiara Syndrome is a close cousin to 'Diana Syndrome' (coined after Princess Diana, it's basically the need to be nice and beloved by everyone, all the time, without fail), 'Smart Girl Syndrome' (the need to always know all the answers that magically appear in your mind without ever having to learn them because you're just, well, 'smart') and 'Imposter Syndrome' (where you feel like you're faking it and just about to be found out). Sorting out all these competing voices is a job in itself.

So, back to Tiara Syndrome – essentially we must be head down, focused and 'being good,' we beaver away, certain that we'll get the prize in the end. After all, we were raised on Disney films where the bad guy loses and justice prevails and the right girl gets the tiara (and, usually, the prince).

Then, when that guy at the desk next to us who has less experience, less intelligence and less skill actually *gets* the open spot and the crown, we scratch our tiara-less head and say "Why didn't I get the promotion – is it because I have ovaries? Should I have taken up golf? Did I not spend enough time being a peacock and bragging about who I know and where I went to school?"

Well, yes… sort of. At our core, women are generally wired differently from men and we grow up with a different set of rules. We don't naturally promote our accomplishments or ourselves because that would be immodest and inappropriate. We expect our work to stand on its own.

(Before you open your laptop to send me a 'corrective' email, please know that I realize this is a sweeping generalization. Not every woman thinks or acts in a certain way, but research and evolution do show us that there are trends and norms, and it would be foolish to discard these insights for the exceptions to the rule.)

In general, we know that being too modest and believing that diligence alone will get you promoted without having to shout about your successes is the downfall of many a potential tiara-wearer. Although wider cultural change to address self-confidence and assertiveness in girls would be necessary to truly fix the problem, the time for you to start is now – with your own career. Women who actively cultivate their careers and own the word 'ambition' succeed.

Who Gets the Crown in the End? Not Always the Good Girl

The trouble is, all the achievements, hard work, and talent may give you 'potential' but they don't get you into the big chair, even if they get noticed.

Ultimately, the crown goes to the person (usually male) who looks and acts the part.

Who's that? He's the guy that rehearsed his speech/presentation and made sure he was prepared to deliver before he got up in front of his peers and boss. He's the guy who sucks up just enough without being smarmy. He's also the guy who looks like a leader, sounds like a leader, acts like a leader, and knows how to play the game.

He knows how to work the Five Facets – Visual, Verbal, Kinesthetic, Sociability and Positioning – to be the CEO, on the Executive Committee, and in the office nearest the nice coffee machine instead of being stuck in the cubicle with the view of the copy machine.

Does this mean you need to be a man? Must you wear a suit and act like a dude? Absolutely not. <u>You don't have to be a man, but you can't be a girl</u>. 'Girls' don't get the job; they get the coffee. It's harsh, but it's true.

Every day, every meeting, every moment is a job interview for the big role.

Before you get the door plaque that says CEO, others need to be able to visualize you in that role. They need to 'see' you in their minds' eye navigating at Board meetings, giving analyst reports, leading shareholder meetings, conducting employee town halls, facing down the reporters, giving hard feedback, making big decisions.

Remember 'A League of Their Own' with Tom Hanks? When the girl starts tearing up and he, as the gruff coach, says 'There's no crying in baseball!'? Well, there's no crying in business, either. Act like a girl – even one time – and you've limited yourself because they'll think you're not up to the task.

What does a 'girl' act like? Well, as I write this I'm sitting in my neighborhood coffee shop and watching a table of young women who've just gotten off school. I'm in England, where school uniforms are usually required, so they're all dressed 'smart' in their jackets, skirts and knee socks, but there

HOW TO GET "IT"

is absolute girl behavior running amok. Can you visualize this with me? Anything teenage girls do when they're in a gaggle – gossip, talk too loudly, talk at a pitch only dolphins can hear, wear skirts too short and shirts unbuttoned too far, act a little crazy, cry, over-dramatize, and generally behave giddily – this is all stuff most of us have outgrown by the time we get to the workplace if we want to be taken seriously. We know that if we behave like a girl in the business world – even just once – we are tagged and marked as 'girl' for a mighty long time, and diminished in the process.

We all started someplace. Think back to your career beginnings, and how what matters is what others could see in you. This holds true even more so as we rise up the ranks. Some people can walk into a house and see potential – others want to buy the final product and simply move in. In business, if the senior leadership can't see you doing it, they won't take a risk on a 'fixer upper' because the stakes are too high. The bold choice may come from a different sector or have a unique skill set, but he – or she – will have one thing for certain: 'gravitas' or 'executive presence.'

CHAPTER 2

Why We All Need to Cowgirl Up – And Get a Blow-dryer to Get the Job

Gathering Interesting and Useful Rocks

I've achieved a measure of success in my career because I work hard and I love what I do. I think one of the personal attributes that has contributed to my success is that I'm a gatherer of rocks, literally and metaphorically. Travel is one of my indulgences and so wherever I go in the world, I pick up a small, unique, interesting rock and I bring it home. I have pretty little jars and chunky glass cubes full of these rocks and shells and gifts of the earth. They form a record of where I've been.

Why is this relevant? This habit extends to collecting ideas along my path that are in various stages of being refined and polished. I gather these 'rocks' from all sorts of places – neuroscientists, psychologists, researchers, corporate trainers, thinking partners, and generally people who are a whole lot smarter than I am. Sometimes I find these rocks in my personal life – looking to solve a problem dealing with one of my children, I may come across a useful tool. Or it may come to me sideways, when I least expect it, at the gym when I hear about an interesting concept.

As I gather new rocks, I try sharing them with my clients. Some of the new rocks shine; others land with a thud. Over time, I've gathered enough shiny rocks and found a formula and an approach that works to help women, and men, make the necessary changes to get off their plateau and reach the next level, or the level beyond.

How 'Blink' and 'Executive Presence' Elevated the Conversation

Two very useful things have happened to help me in my work in recent years.

First, a brilliant writer, Malcolm Gladwell, wrote a book called *Blink* that you must buy and read today. In this book, Gladwell brought together a lot of great research on the subject of how we use 'thin slice judgments' to make decisions about all sorts of things, including people. Some of this was research I'd seen; some of it was new to me and therefore exciting. But the best thing was that it was engaging, very readable, and it lent a new sense of authority to this topic which, frankly, had been a bit 'airy fairy' previously.

Before *Blink*, the closest I could come to explain what I did and was passionate about was to call myself an 'Image Consultant plus Executive Coach' – sort of a 'What Not to Wear' meets 'My Fair Lady' but with more. Not a particularly descriptive, concise or compelling job description, but it was as close as I could get to articulate my job.

The next great breakthrough came in 2012 when the Center for Talent Innovation (CTI) produced a report called 'Executive Presence' that, for the first time, outlined these amorphous concepts like 'gravitas,' underscored the importance of communication, and linked in hard truths about appearance – particularly for women and minorities.

What did they find? That even though there are just as many talented women as men 'swimming in the pool,' only the men seem to survive and be the ones standing at the end. In both the US and the UK, there are more women than men who jump into the water at the beginning of the career pool. Yet, over time, more and more women fall behind and the men advance. Some of them get stuck in the marzipan layer just one level below the top, where, according to CTI, the proportion of women to men has fallen from the starting point of 53% to just 34% in the US.

In the UK, it's worse, with the race starting at 57% female but only 24% making it to the marzipan. Is this because women simply don't want to be the top dog? Well, no. The CTI surveyors found that 91% of women wanted to be promoted, compared to 75% of men in the UK.

This is revolutionary work that has made people stand up and recognize that there is a problem – and it's not ovaries. It's that women need to address these issues of presence to bring their own best selves to the forefront and get the corner office, the seat at the table, the tiara on their head.

How Anne Found Gravitas

Let me share an example of Executive Presence in action, with a very happy ending. In 2005 I met an amazing woman, Anne Ewers, who was the head of the Utah Symphony Opera. Anne was lovely, talented, smart and very good at her job. But there was something missing. It was that extra punch of 'gravitas' that she needed to push her to the next level.

After being introduced by a mutual friend, Anne came to me after she received feedback from colleagues and board members that her image wasn't as 'polished' as it could have been and didn't represent the USO brand. Anne was very reluctant to begin the process and concerned about becoming a 'Stepford Clone,' in her words.

At our first meeting, it was clear that what was happening on the outside was very different from what was happening on the inside. This articulate, intelligent, capable woman who led an internationally acclaimed artistic association looked matronly and dowdy. Her energy was erratic. Her tone was a bit chaotic.

I explained my approach and we worked facet by facet to reveal her best self. We threw out the old jacket from her ex that was still lingering in the closet and bought her a gunmetal grey leather coat. She learned to mix and match her wardrobe so she looked appropriate and still felt authentic when rubbing elbows with some of the world's wealthiest people. She worked on controlling her energy and tone to pitch it appropriately and learned to rein it in when needed and amplify when necessary. She worked on her public speaking skills, already very good, to hone herself to a level of excellence where she could absolutely shine. We polished her social skills so she felt confident in any situation, an area where she was already strong.

We discussed particular situations and strategized how she could use her strengths to get the results she wanted – whether it was asking for multi-million-dollar donations from donors, giving interviews with the media or influencing the musicians' unions to negotiate the optimal contract. Eventually, she applied these skills to interviewing for and getting a great new role as CEO of an even more prestigious organization.

Ultimately, we honed her appearance and communication skills and gave her a new sense of gravitas – where she was showing grace under fire, acting decisively, showing integrity, and projecting vision. Her reputation grew and her career flourished.

Anne subsequently appeared on local news programs explaining the tremendous difference the Five Facets process had made. Anne said, "Finding a new you is always difficult; however, Coni was quietly persistent. Her expertise and gentle approach won me over. She was incredibly sensitive and supportive, very clued in to my needs and who I am. She gave me the courage to try new things. She didn't try to change who I am, but rather enhanced the core 'me.'"

According to Anne, "It's amazing what Coni and I were able to accomplish together. People are constantly stopping me in the streets all agog about my hair, my clothes, the new 'me.' I've never felt so elegant – I'm still 'me,' but enhanced. What's been best about this entire process of transformation is that not only do I feel younger and prettier but I feel more connected with who I really am. My new image represents not only myself, but also my dedication to my position. In my field, image is important and now I have confidence that I'm projecting the professional, sophisticated image that truly represents myself and Utah Symphony and Opera in the best possible light."

In 2007, Anne was promoted to president and CEO of Philadelphia's Kimmel Center, home to eight resident arts companies, including the Philadelphia Orchestra, Opera Company of Philadelphia and the Pennsylvania Ballet. When she received the appointment, she called me and said, "You know, I could never have done this without you. Before we worked together, I would never have had the confidence or been able to project the image to get this job. Now I look the part to get the large donations we need from major donors and do this job well."

I was so proud to work with Anne and help her. I'm inspired by every one of my clients and what they achieve and how they do such hard work to improve and grow. Change is hard work, not for the faint of heart. It requires bravery and dedication to unflinchingly look at yourself, identify where you need to improve and then go about doing it instead of making excuses.

The women who make it to the top don't make excuses or lament that life isn't fair. And they don't back down. They don't bemoan that the system is flawed or wrong. They look at it, take it at face value, decide what *they* want personally and professionally, and then they accept and do what's needed to get to their goal. From the inside, they inspire and teach and advise other women to do the same.

The blame game or 'let's pretend' doesn't work for anyone. Being from Utah, I grew up around farms and ranches. 'Cowboy up' is an often-used expression for 'get up when you fall and deal with your damage.' My mom used to tell me to 'cowgirl up' whenever I would verge on whining. I still hear her voice today when I'm tempted to make an excuse or divert accountability. That's because real women step up and take the reins. If you fall, you don't make excuses or ignore the reasons why you fell – you own it and you Cowgirl Up.

What We Can All Learn from an Iceberg

When I teach my workshops on Executive Presence, called the 'Power of Presence,' I put up a photo of an iceberg as a metaphor to explain the concept. The image shows that about 20% of the iceberg is above the waterline and the rest is deep in the ocean.

This is similar to your personal presence. What is reflected or shown above the waterline is how you're seen or perceived. Others use 'above the waterline' to judge you and make all sorts of decisions and interpretations about who you are, your personality, your values. They make up their minds about what's underneath the water – which is 80% of who you really are – based on the small sliver they see above.

Ideally, then, we would work to ensure that our presence – how we project ourselves in the way we look, speak, and act – is carefully crafted and developed to reflect who we are, what we're capable of, and showcase our talent and potential. A compelling presence is, above all, *intentional.* It's not left to chance. It is also authentic, genuine and believable if it's to be truly impactful. Your strategically refined personal presence should also align with your strengths, passion, and who you are as a person. Lastly, it should be aspirational – not content to just remain stagnant on your plateau waiting for the tiara. An effective personal presence strategy reflects who you aspire to be as your desired best self.

Where professional women tend to go astray is in underestimating how important the 'above the water line' really is to their success. We may be strategic about our goals for the future, plan our retirement and finances, invest years in education and continue to update ourselves professionally but then have absolutely no strategic plan for how we present ourselves.

HOW TO GET "IT"

Why 'It's Not Fair' Doesn't Help

One interesting side effect of my work is that when I approach the topic from a logical, strategic perspective, I often set off a minefield of 'it's not fair' and 'this shouldn't matter.' In the grand scheme of what it takes to succeed, presence and appearance is a very touchy topic. Oftentimes, my work is relegated to the 'What Not to Wear' corner as a sort of 'Pretty Woman' makeover. I myself have sometimes downplayed the importance of my work and my message in the face of the other huge issues facing women in the workplace.

Dr. Elisabeth Kelan, Professor of Leadership at the Cranfield School of Management, is a lecturer, writer and expert in gender and diversity studies. I met her working on a project for GE, and she has become a terrific touchstone in helping me keep perspective on why Executive Presence matters and also why this is hard work.

According to Elisabeth, "Appearance is a tremendously sensitive area because earlier generations of women have fought hard to be recognized in the workplace and for the choices they made. To suddenly say it all comes down to looking at dress appears superficial, so it takes a leap of faith to consider this as an issue to develop as leaders. Presence and appearance is a strategic tool for communication that we shouldn't 'throw away' because we think this 'visual stuff' isn't important."

The Holy Grail of Executive Presence Research

This underscores why the Executive Presence study by the Center for Talent Innovation (CTI) is so revolutionary. They are the first to bring credibility with real data and definition to this amorphous and tension-fraught issue.

The CTI study found that to get to the executive suite, you have to 'look the part.' Being intelligent, a hard worker, performing, and having a sponsor are all essential.

After interviewing nearly 4,000 college-graduate professionals in large corporations, CTI's findings were stunning:

- 66% say 'presence' is key to career growth
- 'Presence' accounts for 26% of what it takes to get promoted – beyond skills, intelligence, experience, etc.

A further 18 focus groups and 50 interviews revealed that Executive Presence depends on getting three things right: appearance, communication and gravitas – what they call their three 'pillars.'

According to the study, executive presence *always* matters, "[It] will not earn you promotion after promotion, but *lack* of executive presence will definitely impede your ability to get as far as you want to go." How you're perceived has now gone from something that's interesting to a skillset that's mandatory.

I recently met with a senior recruiter for CEO and Board level positions to discuss this topic. In our conversation, she told me about a woman who had great potential – super smart, qualified, talented, and a high performer. Yet, they couldn't place her in a senior role. Why? Not because she lacked qualification or was inarticulate. The problem was her hair. Seriously. I'm not making this up. The woman in question - let's call her Amy - would come to work and to meetings with wet hair quite frequently. Maybe she had been to the gym? Maybe she got caught in the rain? Who knows?

The point is, her colleagues and her boss weren't listening to Amy in the meeting and thinking 'Wow, isn't that an amazing idea Amy's just had? She's so great!' No, they were thinking 'Can she not get out of bed five minutes earlier to dry her hair?' 'Why is her hair wet?' 'Does she need a hairdryer?' 'Does she not know her hair's wet?' It made Amy seem lazy, sloppy and out of place. Who is going to put a CEO in front of a shareholder's meeting with wet hair? The bar isn't that high in this case. We're not even talking *styled* hair, here, as in a real, from-a-magazine style – we're just talking *dry*.

HOW TO GET "IT"

So, some poor guy drew the short straw and was told to talk to Amy about it.

It went something like this: "Amy, so, I need to talk to you about your hair."

"What about my hair?" said Amy, a tad warily.

"Well," said the now very uncomfortable short-straw drawer, "it's just that having wet hair at work sends the wrong signal. You know, it's sort of unprofessional. So, you might want to do something about that, maybe."

Did not go well. Uncomfortable for everyone. I imagine the person would rather have been giving Amy the worst performance review in the universe about being late, not delivering on objectives, or needing to further her qualifications than having this conversation about wet hair.

But Amy had a choice: accept or reject the input. At this point, Amy unfortunately went on a rant about how it wasn't fair, she was going to sue them, who cares about her hair, etc.

Question: Is Amy going to make CEO?

Answer: Nope.

It matters. In this case, Amy's appearance combined with her attitude and resistance to feedback or input has now kept her in marzipan – at best – forever. The tale will be known throughout the corporate mythology and she will be 'the one with the wet hair' forever and ever.

Is that what you want? Do you want to be 'right' or do you want to get a blow dryer – and get the job?

CHAPTER 3

An Excavation into Bedrock
OR How to Start Uncovering Your Authentic Self, Flaws and All

Do You Have Gravitas?

'Gravitas,' according to CTI, is the "undeniable heart of executive presence." It's where the rubber hits the road and you show what you're made of as a leader and a woman.

I remember one defining 'gravitas' moment came when I was 30, supporting the Chief Information Officer of a large company. I was facilitating a global webcast when the sound technician forgot to turn off the leaders' microphones during a break. We were in a conference room in London and the leaders were bantering and chatting, when I got an instant message from a remote site that said 'Do you know we can hear you?'

In hindsight, this was my first real screw-up (I wasn't the sound tech, but it was on my watch and therefore I was accountable) and my response was decisive and swift. I got the situation under control and dealt with it firmly and professionally. I apologized and didn't wait to be told what to do, nor did I ask my boss what he wanted me to do about it.

Instead, after the meeting was finished, I took the top guy from the production company aside and was quite direct in my comments – I think I said something like, "On day one of 'so you want to be a sound guy' they teach you the difference between a live mike and a dead one. This is not rocket science and this will have serious consequences for me, and therefore for you. I want a transcript of every word that was said during that 'dead' time in my hands within one hour so I can assess the risk and report back to my boss. I don't expect to receive an invoice for this meeting. How you handle this will determine if you ever do business with this company, and me, again. So I'd fix it if I were you."

Basically, I showed my teeth without being rabid. Enough to be taken seriously, but not enough to be labelled as an 'unreasonable bitch.'

What I didn't realize was that the CIO had overheard my conversation, until another VP told me. He was impressed that I was graceful and activated quickly in the moment, and then took up the sword behind the curtain at the right time. Up until now, I had been the young, blonde American who was competent, a little brash and could write. Now, I achieved gravitas because I showed I could handle a crisis, I could bark when I needed to – and appropriately – and I took responsibility instead of making excuses.

Let's think back to the earlier example of Angela, the tipsy executive who missed her moment on the stage. Where she missed the boat, I actually had to use that moment to flex my own gravitas and Executive Presence. I was responsible for this major corporate awards program, sort of a company 'Oscars' with very senior executives, and a drunken executive didn't let me off the hook for it being delivered successfully.

When I found out about the 'Angela Situation' I had to step up. I think of the swan image – above the water must be graceful and controlled, even if there's an ugly mess going on underneath. So I forced myself to walk slowly when I went to the hallway to assess the situation. I remember it vividly – just a calm, focused energy as I looked at this very senior woman and said, "You're ill. You have food poisoning. You are going to go home. Now."

I then got on my headset, found out where another second-tier executive was who owed me a favor, and told the crew to change it to his name on the teleprompter introductions. Then I walked back into the main room, directly to him, and said, "You're going on for Angela. Just read what it says on the prompter. I owe you."

And then I gave the 'go' signal and we were live.

When these things happen, I just get calm and centered and I think, "Cowgirl Up. You can do this. You've done harder things before. You haven't had a lobotomy – so make it happen." This is gravitas and you never know when you're going to have to channel it and deliver.

The New Alpha-Female Media Archetypes

Beyond the real world, the presence issue is also playing out on our televisions. Television programs with very strong, feminist, female characters such as *Scandal* and *House of Cards* have elevated the conversation on gravitas and workplace fashion to a fever pitch. Each week, fashion bloggers post what shoes, handbags, dresses and even glasses are worn by Kerry Washington's character Olivia Pope and Robin Wright's Claire Underwood, as if these clothes are the most important thing in the world.

And in a funny way they are. When Kerry Washington was featured on the cover of *Vanity Fair* magazine in August 2013, the accompanying article featured three full paragraphs to describe how "Olivia's fashion choices are carefully calibrated to reflect Washington's conception of the character."

On the character's wardrobe palette of pastels, Washington says, "I felt that the way Olivia is written, so much of what comes out of my mouth is stuff that people don't want to hear. People come to Pope and Associates [the character's agency which specializes in 'fixing' problems in Washington, DC] on the worst day of their lives. I'm giving them the hard truth. Olivia is a person who is really smart about the performance of identity – she tells people how to dress for court or for a press conference. So she herself would make a similar decision about her aesthetic. And if I were somebody who spent the majority of my time saying things that were harsh and difficult to hear, I would want my visual aesthetic to be something soft and feminine, warm and easy to be around. So that's where that comes from."

The section ends with the writer of the piece observing, "You get the feeling that, somehow, none of this ever occurred to Clark Clifford," an ultra-connected lawyer and presidential advisor who was the face of fiefdom. This statement, a throwaway sentence, really, illustrates just how uncomfortable we are in discussing the issue. After three lengthy paragraphs, the author feels compelled to say, "But I digress, let's get back to something really important," even after the actress declares that appearance and gravitas *are* important and used strategically as a device by the producers and the character herself.

The Importance of Authenticity: The Big Benefits You Get from Developing a Strong, Compelling, Authentic, Personal Presence

Having a plan to create a strong, authentic and compelling executive presence gives you a leg up over your competitors for the big job because it:

- Increases your visibility and value when it matters and with the right people
- Increases your confidence because you know you're on the right path and projecting yourself intentionally
- Enhances your credibility because you're consistent, focused, and you deliver as promised
- Differentiates you and sets expectations about what others can expect from you when you're in the next role, and the next
- Influences and attracts others who are drawn to authentic, positive energy
- Creates trust and emotional attachment as people begin to know they can depend on you.

HOW TO GET "IT"

Authenticity is the bedrock of an effective presence strategy. When I started working with Anne, the CEO I discussed earlier, her initial fear was that I was going to turn her into a Stepford Clone. Over time, she overcame that fear when she realized I wasn't trying to 'turn her into' anyone other than herself.

Most of my clients are quite senior already. They just need a bit of a push to help them get to the next level. That's why it was so refreshing when Elisabeth Kelan asked me to work with Sierra, a young PhD candidate at King's College London who's working on a study about women on boards, as a 'pro bono' project.

When we met the first time, Sierra was panicked that I was going to tell her to (1) cut her hair (waist length, Rapunzel-like and blonde) and (2) change her glasses (quirky-cool 'geek' glasses with black frames).

I arrived at the meeting early, as I always do for an initial client meeting, and sat where I could see her enter the café and lock in my own first impressions. I noticed the hair and the glasses immediately, of course, but what was most apparent as 'presence detractors' were her energy and general disarray.

As her presence coach, I don't want to turn Sierra into a Barbie doll. I want to help her succeed. So the first step is to get a read on how she's presenting herself to others and identify the facets that need polishing. This was the Five Facets scorecard I gave her at our first meeting:

- Visual: Messy, sloppy, writing on her arm
- Verbal: Aggressive and buoyant, nice tone, very smart
- Kinesthetic: Boisterous, puppy, flushed skin
- Sociability: Fine
- Presence: Scattered, young, energetic

Not bad, but not great. Definitely not who you want to send into an office environment to meet with a C-level executive for a research-gathering interview. The good news was that Sierra was eager to learn, an open book, and whip smart. She lacked the scar tissue that a lot of senior women bring with them and was completely open to feedback. Sierra didn't just embrace feedback and change; she actively sought it and tackled it.

To create a compelling presence strategy for Sierra, we had to ensure it ticked the following boxes:

- Intentional, to deliberately convey what we wanted
- Authentic, genuine and believable
- Aligned with her strengths, passion and who she is 'under the surface'
- Aspirational, to reflect her desired best self.

The main thing I look for in the initial meeting is cohesion. You can only be as polished as the flawed Facet – so if you're letting yourself down in the Visual Facet, your other four Facets don't shine as brightly, either.

If one Facet is significantly flawed, it confuses the audience. With Sierra, her Visual Facet was the easiest to address. I did not make her cut her hair, but I did explain why it needed to be pulled back neatly so that it wasn't a focal point. I also did not make her change her glasses. Why would I? They are perfectly appropriate for a woman in her twenties and they give her a distinctive, memorable quirk. They are a 'signature' and I love them on her.

Sometimes the simplest 'fixes' are obvious and just require awareness. When I met Sierra she had written a note on her forearm in pen, which was visible when she pushed up her sleeve. First meeting, first thing I told her was not to do that again, ever. I did it in a joking way, but made the point. Easy. Together, we took something from her blind spot into her awareness and the last time I met with her she told me that she has never written on her arm or hand again since I made her aware of how it would

HOW TO GET "IT"

be perceived in the professional world. It was ironic that she hadn't taken this out of her blind spot already, as she told me that it had been commented on before. Embarrassingly, she had written a note on her arm prior to an interview with a major headhunter, but the writing had smudged and looked like a curse word. Not optimal. And easily avoided.

With Sierra, the other Facets took more time and effort and we slowly refined and polished each of them, and continue to do so as she grows and her role expands. I love to have coffee with Sierra and hear how she's doing and think with her about how she can progress and evolve.

CHAPTER 4

Who Are You Really? Balancing a Personal Presence With Your Professional Presence

Sometimes leaders get confused about Presence work because it feels a little bipolar – like they're projecting one image at home and another at work. If we keep authenticity in mind, this isn't a problem. Where it is key, however, is to make it clear that you are obviously different at home from how you are at work.

I worked with an amazing female CIO, rare in the corporate world. She was a bit of a geek, which is not a problem because geeks are chic. But she was very confused about how to project herself in her corporate world, which was very formal and straight-laced, as opposed to the technology world where jeans and T-shirts are de rigueur. So, we agreed this was largely a visual issue as her other four facets didn't change between the two environments. And, appealing to her natural strength in compartmentalizing, we came up with three uniforms: home, tech-work and office-work. We then defined each environment ('tech-work' would be a meeting in Silicon Valley that was not board level, 'office-work' was at headquarters or with board level executives).

Her uniform list was something like this:

Tech-work: Sweater dress with boots, skinny trousers with flats and a button-up top untucked or a nice sweater, an interesting necklace, roomier handbag.

Office-work: Tailored dresses with scarf or jacket, skirt suits, pant suits, heels, structured handbag.

Home: Casual clothes and jeans, date-night clothes.

Why would someone need a 'home' uniform? Well, because she did. Initially, I tried just addressing the 'tech-work' and 'office-work' uniforms, but she could not let go of 'What do I wear at home?' After we defined these three uniforms, she had a formula that she could work with – and when she shopped she was clear about which environment she needed to dress for and how to complete the uniform.

Reconciling that who you are at home isn't the same as who you are at work may seem obvious to some, but it's quite challenging for others – particularly if you define yourself as your job. You may have a hard time thinking objectively about your presence as something to manage and craft with intention and purpose, and still feeling authentic.

My advice is to accept that this may not be comfortable for you and do it anyway. Practice it and you'll feel more and more authentic and understand the differences with less complexity and more confidence over time.

Can We Really Change?

Change is hard. What if you delve into your Five Facets and find out you need to change something significant about yourself – whether it be drying your hair, fixing your teeth, or writing on paper instead of your arm? What if you're embarrassed by what you learn about yourself?

HOW TO GET "IT"

'The Emperor's New Clothes' is an old fairy tale about the charlatan tailors who sell the Emperor a suit of invisible clothes. As he walks nude down the street, everyone bows and exclaims at the beauty of the clothing. Except for the one child who blows the charade by saying 'But he doesn't have anything on!' We can't change unless we acknowledge when we're wearing the Emperor's New Clothes with complete honesty.

I find change starts with knowing two things: 'current reality' and 'desired state.' I always start my coaching relationships by asking the person to write down three adjectives that describe how they want others to see them – if there was a neon sign over your head, what would be the three big flashing words? This is your 'desired state.' Usually this is easy for people. We all know how we want others to perceive us.

What's harder is the next question, what are you projecting currently? Without excuses, varnish, or any other façade, write down the three words you think are hanging on the neon sign over your head at work right now. This is your 'current reality.'

This only works if you are truthful and honest with yourself. It won't work if you make things better or worse than they actually are or start analyzing how you got here. It really needs to be a reflection of how you're presenting yourself from a position of non-judgment, acceptance and even compassion.

We are polishing the final stone, keeping in mind that the raw stone has its flaws. That doesn't make it bad or wrong. We focus on what we want to create in the early stages without worrying about how we get there.

So, ask yourself: how do I want people to view me? If your career really matters to you, what job do you want? It's okay to just want it because you want it – you don't have an obligation to actually achieve it or to justify why you want it. But it does need to be aspirational and reflect your very best, ideal self.

If your vision for your presence is inspired from the inside, you will automatically be authentic. If you approach this journey from a sense of curiosity, aspiration, and compassion, you'll achieve it.

Elissa is an amazing woman who survived a childhood in a polygamist cult, where she was married to the leader at a very young age and subjected to repeated physical and mental abuse. This courageous woman escaped and built a new life. She wrote a moving book about her ordeal and experiences.

I was asked to work with her because her book was about to hit the global platform and she had a significant presence issue that was going to potentially prevent her from succeeding. Basically, when you knew her story you had a vision of what she'd look and sound like, and I want you to visualize this person in your head now. Can you see her? Depending on your exposure to polygamy, having watched 'Big Love' on HBO or the other polygamy reality shows, you'll have a vision in mind.

It probably doesn't mesh with Elissa today. Instead of being a little mousy, conservative, or understated, she went to the other extreme when she escaped the polygamist lifestyle. She'd never had a chance to dress 'fun,' wear make-up, practice making fashion choices and learning from mistakes. She'd never been allowed to be verbal with her elders and learn how to moderate her speaking voice. She didn't know how to behave 'normally' in social settings.

Elissa had, not surprisingly, overcorrected by wearing a lot of bright pink, sparkly, tight-fitting clothing and teetering high heels. Her verbal style was very fast and peppered with a lot of self-conscious laughter. She was a little awkward socially. She was also one of the most courageous, sincere, authentic people I've ever met.

When we began working together, her biggest fear was that people would judge her or not believe her story. Again, not surprising as she'd been brainwashed from birth to believe that going against the leaders of the sect was tantamount to assassinating the Pope.

Teaching her how to dress, refining her speaking style, and giving her a brush-up on etiquette was easy. What was much harder was giving her the confidence to know that she simply had to let her authentic self shine through and people would know she was sincere, trustworthy, kind and truthful. It was impossible not to know that about her as soon as she opened her mouth and told her story.

Once we brought her vision of her authentic self into focus, the rest came through naturally. She went on a book tour, including being featured on *Oprah*, and was great. Her book, *Stolen Innocence,* went on to be on the *New York Times* bestseller list.

So, what does this mean to you, on your way to the C-suite? It takes courage to acknowledge your current reality because it can come from a lot of strange places and experiences accumulated over a lifetime. There are specific, sometimes subconscious, reasons that have caused us to choose these surfaces to project ourselves to the world. Looking at the root causes of why you don't want to wear make-up, or why you wear tops that reveal your cleavage even knowing that it's inappropriate, or why you can't resist picking at your cuticles or talking over other people is a scary place to go for most of us.

Once you do go there, you can see and then refine the rough bits. Before you embark on this expedition and excavation, you need to have confidence that your authentic self will be enough to see you into the office and career you want for yourself. *You* are enough and you don't need to create a fake You to get there. Your real You, with a little tweaking and refining, is more than good enough. So have faith in her and the bravery to look at yourself objectively.

Where to From Here? The Five Facets Excavation and Polishing

> *"One secret of success in life is for a person to be ready for their opportunity when it comes."* – Benjamin Disraeli

Executive presence matters to every woman. As you move up the feeding chain, you have more latitude for self-expression, but it still matters. No matter how cool you are, you still have to make allowances and adapt – even Vivienne Westwood and Lady Gaga curtsy when they meet the Queen.

Many of us look at women who are at the top of their game and think they got there because they were genius, lucky or just talented. And while that may be partially true, we also can be fairly certain that those women did not get there by accident or coincidence. They made smart choices, used strategies and took action. They 'risked their significance' in the words of Dawna Markova, author of *I Will Not Die an Unlived Life* and one of the mentors and exemplars for me. To make change, you have to risk and you have to be open to seeing the unflattering and uncomfortable things about yourself to achieve your goals and seize the opportunities in front of you.

Success doesn't come easy and changing your Executive Presence and the way others perceive you is very hard work. It's important to remember that it's about making progress, rather than doing everything perfectly. If you put in the effort and stick with it, you'll see reward.

When you're considering your own presence according to the Five Facets: Visual, Verbal, Kinesthetic, Sociability, and Positioning, start by becoming aware of your flaws and strengths to pick the right facet to polish. Ask yourself the following questions:

1. *Which aspect of my life do I want to focus on now?* This may be personal or professional. Oftentimes, my clients come to me for professional work on their career, but we end up addressing

HOW TO GET "IT"

issues with their presence in their personal life. It doesn't matter, really. What does matter is that as you're learning, you choose something that is important and really matters to you. So it may be a specific situation (I want to give a good speech) or a person (I want my boss to be impressed by me) – as long as it is important.

2. *Which facet do I think is the most challenging for me?* As you've read the book thus far, which one makes you cringe, squirm, palpitate or otherwise want to avoid? Odds are, that's the one you need to focus on. You can also think about feedback you've been given in past performance appraisals or in situ. If you had to 'sort' that feedback, like laundry, into one of the five baskets, which basket would be the fullest?

3. *How will I reveal my blind spot(s) in this facet?* Be specific. I want you to write down the name of the person you're going to ask to be your blind spot buddy on this facet or the five people you're going to ask for quick feedback. I want you to commit to a date by when you'll ask for this feedback. I want you to write down exactly what you're going to say or write to these people to ask them for this feedback. No excuses. No wiggle room to let yourself off the hook. Be brave.

4. *What do I think I can stop, start or continue doing to improve in this facet?* It may be that you are at some level aware of issues, but you're not recognizing it and bringing it into the Arena yourself. There may be reasons why you're avoiding it, and we don't need to dive into those now. It's just enough to do your own inventory.

5. *How will I know if I'm making progress? What will success look like?* Your boss will give you more responsibility. You'll get great feedback forms from your speech. You'll be asked to give a TED talk. You'll feel more joy at work. You'll stop feeling 'less than' in meetings. Whatever it is, be specific.

CONI JUDGE, PhD

My hope is that this is more than reading another business self-help book for you. I'd like it to be the start of a conversation about how you can reveal your best self and get the job and career you want. The truth is there is no one who can tell you exactly what to wear, say, do and be to get the job. The task we all face every day is simply to be the best we can, try our hardest, and get better. We can do that by noticing what works and what doesn't. We can do that by helping other women notice, too. And if we come from a place of sincerity and genuine support, we all get the tiara in the end.

CHAPTER 5

How to Polish Your Visual Facet and Look the Part

I'm not the first woman to be fascinated by gems, but I am a bit of a magpie in my affection for shiny stones. Elizabeth Taylor, second to Queen Elizabeth II in epic jewelry ownership, famously said, "I adore wearing gems, but not because they are mine. You can't possess radiance, you can only admire it."

The act of refining a raw stone into a precious jewel that radiates light has always fascinated me. In its rough form, a diamond is a lusterless crystal that resembles a chip of broken glass. To be transformed into a jewel, it must be cut into a particular gem shape and then polished, facet by facet. In the hands of a master diamond cutter, the stone can be transformed into something spectacular.

A diamond cutter cannot approach every cut in exactly the same way, because every stone is unique. His work begins with an examination of the stone's crystalline structure – its 'inclusions.' He looks, he assesses, he plots and plans, and then he decides what specific cut will bring out the maximum brilliance and potential of that particular stone.

Like a precious stone, you, too, are unique. I don't view our inclusions as flaws, but we have the raw materials we were born to work with – our genetics and upbringing – and then we have our personality and our experiences; the choices we have made, the education we have received and the goals we pursue. For each of us, this is the raw stone, the things that make you 'you.'

When I work with clients to polish their 'facets,' I try to follow the principles of the master diamond cutter. I see her as a completely unique raw stone and my job is to help her become her best self – according to her own definition, not mine.

To explain the way I work, I've come to use the metaphor of the raw stone being polished. We all present ourselves to the world through five specific surfaces that we have created, intentionally or unintentionally. Together, these are what I refer to as the Five Facets of Presence:

1. Visual – how you look
2. Verbal – how you sound
3. Kinesthetic – how you stand and interact
4. Sociability – how you act
5. Presence – how you bring it all together to form the 'wow' factor

Of these, I find the visual facet the most important and the most challenging to work on because it's so emotive. We know it's important because of countless studies, including research by Harvard Medical School and Massachusetts General Hospital, that found people assess your competence and trustworthiness in a quarter of a second (250 milliseconds)– based solely on how you look.

Visual appearance is also a potential minefield of deep-seated beliefs, fears, and insecurities. If I tell you that your voice isn't as strong as it might be, you might consider that a fair observation; if I tell you that your choice of clothes is unflattering to your figure, that might begin to feel like a personal attack.

HOW TO GET "IT"

How we look is deeply personal, particularly for women. Even if we outwardly regard it as the least important aspect of how we present ourselves, we still know that we are being judged to a considerable degree on our appearance.

The CTI study claimed that appearance is a key element in determining if someone has 'it' as a leader. This is the final filter, where good grooming and physical attractiveness, by whatever standard, finish off the whole package.

Women, in particular, are judged on appearance. Yet as women we also receive less feedback on it than men do when it's having an impact on how we are perceived: just 32 percent of women in the study said they had received feedback on their appearance from a superior, compared to 47 percent of men.

This lack of feedback puts us at a disadvantage when it comes to understanding what we can do to improve our standing in the workplace.

As if that weren't bad enough, wait, there's more: professional women are also often judged for actively working on their appearance. The woman who is seen to do so can be considered vain by colleagues or more focused on her looks than the job – even though the way we look is a major determinant in whether we are chosen for promotion or a specific career path.

Somehow, then, there is this completely unrealistic expectation that our success in this facet should be effortless and invisible; women should just automatically and without effort look 'right.' If we work at it, we set ourselves up to get it 'wrong'; and thus to experience the feelings of shame that accompany falling short of the required standard, whatever that is.

If we're seen to be too trying too hard to please others with our appearance, we can be accused of selling out to succeed, of lacking authenticity. What are we to do? Can you be authentic *and* actively cultivate a strategic, professional appearance? Do you have to sell out to succeed? Questions like this create even deeper pools of shame and self-doubt.

I say it's time to take appearance out of the shame spiral for professional women and my goal is to discuss it in practical, strategic terms as an element that you can control to help you get ahead and achieve your professional goals. Your other option is to ignore this facet and continue to do as you've always done. If that's getting you where you need and want to be and you feel confident in the way you present yourself visually, then you probably don't need this book.

But if you do have a niggling voice that wonders if you look okay, or if you've ever felt like you missed out on getting the rulebook for how to dress and wear makeup and be a woman in business that looks the part, then maybe it's something to cultivate and control.

Rather than ignoring the impact of appearance and visual presentation as superficial and unimportant, use it as a weapon in your professional arsenal. Together, let's assess your Visual Facet head-on, leave shame or bias at the door, and help you polish and refine your image to move ahead and get the job you deserve.

It Starts with Shoes

For me, like many women, every morning starts with the shoe dilemma. *Marie Claire* did a survey of readers in 2011 that found working women choose their outfit for the day based on their shoes. I'm not sure how scientific this is, but this resonates as a valid hypothesis for me and my female friends agree. So I say let's roll with this idea.

Personally, I start by thinking about the day ahead and analyzing the situation like the Terminator assesses the battlefield:

- What meetings are on my schedule? Will I be standing and giving a presentation or mostly sitting at a conference table or a desk?

HOW TO GET "IT"

- What conversations am I having with whom? Senior leaders? Specifically, conservative men, fashionable women, conservative women? What industry are they in? What types of shoes will they likely be wearing? Have I met them before and already established myself, or is this a first meeting?
- What modes of transport will be required? Planes, cars, trams, subways, buses, walking? Do I need to lift things like suitcases?
- If I do have to walk, what terrain will I traverse? Cobblestones, grates, pavement, echoing corridors? Do I have to walk far, far-far or really far?
- What's the weather like today? Rainy, snowy, sunny?
- What's the state of my feet? Sore from yesterday, pedicure perfect and viewable or must be obscured?
- How long will I be required to wear these shoes today? Is this an 8-hour day or an 18-hour day? It makes a difference.

After I've chosen the shoes that I think will satisfy the mission for the day, I have to put on the 'What will they think?' filter. Are the shoes too sexy, too flashy, too stylish, too frumpy, too old, or too new?

Does this even matter? Well, yes — because each person I encounter today is likely to look first at my face and hair, and then at my shoes. Then he or she is going to decide what they think about me. And remember, Harvard says he or she will do this snap assessment in only a quarter of a second.

If I choose the wrong shoes, despite being comfortable and practical for the day at hand, I may give the impression of being unkempt and therefore unprofessional; too sexy and therefore unprofessional; too casual and therefore unprofessional. In my mind, all roads lead to unprofessional.

Am I being paranoid?

Possibly. But I don't think so. This week I had two executives, Jeremy and Sandra, independently and spontaneously share with me that they had misgivings about Iris, a woman who's recently been promoted to a leadership role. Each expressed concern about Iris' lack of skill and capability. Why? It started because she wore a pair of run-down, old, unpolished, cowboy-style boots to the office on a day when she was giving a presentation to her new leadership team and in a corporate culture where most of the other women wear heels or ballerina flats and the men wear brogues or otherwise shiny shoes. She also wore some type of jeggings, I was told. Interestingly, neither of them mentioned anything about the top that Iris wore that day. Possibly they never took their eyes off of the boots to look up.

Iris' scruffy boots sent a visual signal about her that confused her colleagues, and this turned into 'She's not professional,' 'She doesn't have what it takes,' and 'I just don't think she's taking this seriously.'

Iris likely had no idea when she chose those boots to wear that day that it would make a difference to her career. Maybe she wore her most professional blazer and blouse or a brand new sweater and thought that was professional. She probably thought she left the meeting and everyone was impressed by her slides and the quality of her thinking. Instead, her colleagues, peers and boss were looking at her boots.

Is this fair? Probably not. But if you think about how we as a society use shoes to define and stereotype one another (think Crocs, Birkenstocks, cowboy boots, and so on), it's really not surprising.

I've found that playing it safe is more important than expressing my individuality with my shoes, especially during the first meeting. That's because, while I have a lot of beautiful shoes, I don't want my shoes to be the talking point when I've left the room. I want people to talk about my ideas, my contribution, and how I add value, not my five-inch red heels.

So I wear black pumps with a four-inch heel. That's a little high for some, but it doesn't feel like a sell-out to me. I still feel like 'Coni' in those shoes. I also carry in my bag a pair of ballet flats (I'm wearing them now, actually) that are easy to slip on for cobblestones and still look smart.

Men don't have this problem – or, at least, their margin for error is much smaller with shoes that, let's face it, look pretty much the same. Or so I thought: recently, I helped my 50-year-old brother buy dress shoes to wear to a family funeral and I was stymied by his aversion to 'square toe' dress shoes. We had to go to at least six stores before we found a pair he liked – and he hates shopping, so this was not his idea of fun.

What I learned from my shopping trip with my brother is that shoes matter more than I thought to men in the professional world. They, too, use the shoe test to judge one another.

Shoes. Not too sexy, not too frumpy, just unnoticeable, appropriate and able to traverse many miles.

A Quick Tutorial on First Impressions

'Impression Management' is another buzzword in this evolving and somewhat amorphous field of visual image for women. Researchers at the Cranfield School of Management in London have adopted the term to describe how one must strategically manage appearance and first impressions. While I prefer Executive Presence because it extends beyond the first impression to a longer term strategy, I think we all agree that the first impression is critical.

We now know that you only get one chance to make a first impression within 250 milliseconds.

However, it's worth having a quick chat about exactly *how* we make an impression on others and how we quickly form impressions of other people. You can read Malcolm Gladwell's *Blink* for more detail on the subject, but here's the quick and dirty version:

A 'first impression' is actually the process of forming a judgment about another person based on a very small amount of information – called a 'thin slice.' The ability to form thin slice judgments was embedded in our early caveman ancestors who needed to immediately know if the person at their cave entrance was there to steal their fire or share their fire. They didn't have time to meet, discuss, weigh the evidence and decide how they were going to proceed with the relationship.

We are much the same today. In fact, the ability to form thin slice judgments is embedded in our adaptive unconscious, a part of the brain that functions on a very primal level.

The most interesting thing about thin slice judgments is not just that we make them, but that once they are formed we rarely change our minds – even when we get more data about the person.

Let's think back to Iris, the woman who wore the worn-down boots to an important meeting. Once her colleagues saw the boots, they formed an opinion, dismissed Iris as 'unprofessional' and they stopped listening for the most part. They may have paid attention to parts of her presentation and certainly took something away from the meeting. But in their minds, she is still lacking something and nothing that she could have said or done, no matter how brilliant, would have changed their minds.

They didn't do this because they were being mean or cruel. They weren't even aware that they were doing it, actually. When we encounter someone for the first time, we form an impression almost instantly. We immediately take a snapshot impression and take in seven different factors in a particular order:

1. Gender
2. Age
3. Ethnic background or skin color
4. Bearing (how they stand, move, posture)
5. Appearance (face, hair, clothes, artifacts)
6. Eye contact (hostile, submissive, open)

HOW TO GET "IT"

7. Speech (tone, pitch, rate, accent)

Based on our own experiences and our cultural biases, we use this initial scan to assess the person and form an interpretation about them. Some of the biggest decisions we make have to do with their personality and what we perceive of them, including:

1. Is the person friendly or hostile?
2. Is he/she intelligent or not too bright?
3. Is he/she likeable or not?
4. Is the person competent or scattered?
5. Do I trust this person?

These five aspects relate to the 'Big Five' personality studies that are the basis of personality profiles such as Myers Briggs, DiSC, and others. Interestingly, your true Myers Briggs score has very little bearing on what others perceive of you. Even if profile indicates that you are an extrovert, others can still perceive you as unfriendly or introverted. It is important to know, therefore, not just what personality attributes you *have*, but what personality attributes you *project*.

After we complete the initial scan and make our interpretations about the person, the final step is positioning. Based on what we believe about this person from a very small amount of data, we will decide how to position ourselves in relation to them. Depending on our assessment, we can choose to be:

- Open/receptive
- Neutral
- Wary
- Hostile

With Iris, the team saw the boots, were confused by the signal, and decided to be a little wary. She's new to the team and somewhat unproven, so in this window the group is looking at signals to indicate whether she is part of the tribe — whether she is worthy and capable.

The issue that Iris faces now is that, once we determine our positioning, we then filter every future encounter with that individual from this point of view. In effect, we go about the relationship not with an intention to learn more or gain insight, but to prove our first impressions to be true by collecting evidence that supports our gut instinct.

Theoretically, it took a few seconds for Iris to make a negative impression and now it's going to take a lot of work — up to seven meetings, depending on which expert you believe — to dispel it. Who else did she meet that day? She may have seven opportunities to engage with her team and repair the damage — assuming she is even aware that there is damage to repair and that she doesn't have further blunders along the way.

But what about the people she met that day who saw the boots, formed an opinion, and with whom she has no further chances to reconnect? It is very rare for someone to give us the opportunity to meet seven future times if they have formed a negative impression at the beginning of the encounter. Therefore, it is important that every impression results in an open or at least neutral response from the other person so that we can build a positive relationship.

Making an impression isn't a choice; it's inevitable. The impact we make depends on the surfaces we choose to represent our values and our individuality to others.

CHAPTER 6

The Visual Appearance Minefield

As the most emotive of the facets, the way we present ourselves visually is deeply personal, especially for women who tend to relate their visual facet to their body image.

In my book *Beauty Rehab: Your guide to feel beautiful, sexy and confident in 28 days*, I discuss why beauty and appearance is a massive area for women. You only have to look at some of the reported figures on the money women spend on their appearance in the United States alone: $38 billion hair industry, $33 billion diet industry, $24 billion skincare industry, $18 billion make-up industry, $15 billion perfume industry, $13 billion cosmetic surgery industry. And these industries are growing every day.

For women, we are bound by specific community expectations around our appearance. We may view appearance through the sub-lenses of age, race and ethnicity, but in each case a set of expectations exists.

Why? Some leading thinkers think it relates to the money at stake for retailers, that they have to continue to manipulate our appearance expectations to keep us spending money. This is a valid point and, indeed, industries from automobiles to home décor need to continue to develop new trends to keep consumers spending. After all, retailers have the most to benefit from selling lipstick as a salve to insecurity.

I don't believe this is the ultimate driver, however. I believe our desire and need to belong, to 'make sense' of others, to place them so we can orient ourselves — these drive much of our obsession with appearance. We choose surfaces to project ourselves because of what we want to say and what we want others to think about who we are. This desired projection is influenced by our past and changes with age and exposure to different cultures and environments.

Appearance is really about defining who we are for the rest of the world and declaring which 'tribe' we belong to for others to see and understand.

Simone White sings a beautiful song, 'Bunny in a Bunny Suit,' that was also used in an Omega watch ad featuring Nicole Kidman. The poignant lyric touches on how appearance and façade interrelate with who we are inside. In particular, the singer imagines herself 'pretending' to be who she is. It is as though in her appearance and dealings with the external world, she can never be anything more than a facsimile of her true self; and this facsimile, that she constructs deliberately, is a shield that protects her — thus she is a 'bunny in a bunny suit.' What the world sees is very like her, but imperceptibly different.

We are all alike in this respect, even if we don't display that level of self-awareness. The surfaces we choose to project ourselves to the world serve as a shield against judgment, as armour against intrusion, as a signal of our values, as a reflection of our emotions, and as a symbol of our belonging.

This is not a superficial conversation; it is the beacon that we send out to tell people who we are, what we believe and what we want. It is very like us, only different.

How Casual Friday Confused Everyone

Life used to be relatively simple in business wear. Men wore suits, which are designed to project power and dominance. And women wore dresses because that signaled being 'dressed up' for work.

Then, in the 80s, a film called *Working Girl* redefined the female professional dress standard, and women began to emulate men by wearing skirt suits. Eventually, this evolved into a woman's suit with trousers.

This went on for a while. Women settled into a bit of a uniform for working just like men had their uniform, the suit and tie. It was relatively simple. It signaled professional, capable, smart, trustworthy, and competent. It was easy to understand and practically universal. Sometimes, for comfort's sake, women would wear trainers when walking from the train or subway to the office, and then they'd change into their basic black pumps with a two to three inch heel.

In the mid 90s, I was working with a company called National Semiconductor and commuting each week from Salt Lake City, Utah, to San Jose, California. I was responsible for communication and a member of the leadership team, working mostly with the General Manager of a global division. In San Jose, the world was run by EEs – electrical engineers – who were creating new iterations of computer chips and job hopping from company to company.

Apple was going through an identity crisis. Intel was rising. The dot-com revolution was looming. Guys in California didn't wear jackets to work every day. They wore shirts – sometimes with a tie, sometimes without – and slacks. It was a warm climate with sunny, open campuses, and they would walk between buildings and eat lunch outside at picnic tables. It seemed like working on a Hollywood set and the engineers would 'hop' from company to company and take their increasingly casual dress code with them.

I had three children in the 1990s – '93, '95, '97 – and so I was largely wearing maternity skirts and blouses for that decade, trying to find a 'uniform' that projected professionalism while I was hugely pregnant and uncomfortable. In the 1990s most maternity wear included bows of some type, so it was no easier then to be professional and pregnant than it is now.

Unexpectedly, technology changed the corporate dress code dramatically. I mostly remember technological innovations in my work according to each of my sons' births. In 1993, when I had Connor, we were just able to transfer files by computer and use email. The internet was still coming of age. To earn extra money on the side, I was writing help screens for the first online grocery shopping service. In 1995, when I had Ryan, my second son, the internet was more common, though still the homeland of the 'geeks' I worked with in Silicon Valley. By the time I had Alex, my third son, in 1997, I'd moved to Chicago, was working for a consultancy, and companies were exploring internet retailing. We were developing the first intranet sites and using webcasts to communicate information with employees.

This is when the dress code really changed. The geeks in California had gone from the fairly loose corporate style to 'Casual Friday.' Sometimes used as a way to raise money for charity (if you paid a few dollars you could wear jeans to work! And help raise money for a good cause!), Casual Friday went from once a month to once a week to every day. The dotcommers now had their own companies and their own offices and their own uniform – jeans, T-shirts and Converse.

Following the trend of power and change, the rest of the world slowly migrated and followed suit – or lack of a suit. A lot of guys just couldn't let go of their dress slacks, so they found khaki Dockers – long accepted as weekend-appropriate menswear by those in the know. Eventually, Dockers and a blue shirt without a tie was the new norm, at least in America. Men had found a new uniform. They felt comfortable with it. It signaled a new standard of power.

HOW TO GET "IT"

This caused a new dilemma for women. When we wore khaki trousers and a blue shirt, we looked like Girl Scout camp counselors. So we started searching for a new uniform and things got a little wonky. A pencil skirt and blouse seemed about average. But some women wanted to let their personality shine. This evolved into more and more casual dress – it was sort of like the school uniform was being retired and the dress code was becoming a free-for-all.

A lot of the female role models were coming from the Pacific Northwest, the land of the Birkenstock and no make-up. So, was it okay to not wear make-up to work anymore? How about hosiery? A bra? There were no more rules and anything was acceptable.

The only problem was, while our rules relaxed, our sense of judgment did not. We still held others to a standard of what was visually acceptable, even as we started thinking about wearing sandals to the office on a Wednesday.

In the CTI study, they asked men and women what they thought the biggest appearance blunders were for women. The top four, according to both men and women, were: no bra (ranked as most heinous by women), unkempt hair (considered the top transgression by men), too-tight clothing and having a visible panty line.

When I read the results, I understood how we, as women, could get confused about the bra thing. There was the 'feminism = I don't need to wear a bra' confusion going on and so maybe that was a throwback. I could understand the too-tight clothing. In an era of reality television, sex sells and tighter clothing has become more common, though still inappropriate. I can also understand the VPL, a long-time eyesore that goes hand in glove with 'too tight' clothing.

What was sort of shocking to me was that unkempt hair is even *on* the list, let alone in the top one or two for both genders. I don't see many women with what you might call unkempt hair in the offices where I work, on the train into the city – any city – or walking around town.

I think that 'unkempt hair' is more than 'don't wear dreadlocks to the office.' It is also a default signpost for 'bad grooming.' In fact, the CTI study found that more important than being physically attractive (which can actually be a detriment if a woman is 'too pretty'), being slender, or wearing expensive clothing, good grooming is what matters most to both genders in the professional world.

Makeup is another conundrum. In 2010, Procter & Gamble funded a study at Harvard that found women who wear a little makeup – think polished, not plastic – are considered more likeable, trustworthy and competent. I have three faces – weekend, work, evening. Yes, even on a weekend, I wear makeup.

My weekend face is minimal: under-eye concealer because I'm prone to dark circles, mascara because I have blonde eyelashes and need contrast, powder to even out my skin tone without being heavy handed and cover any spots, and nude SexyMotherPucker lipgloss by Soap&Glory. It takes me about five minutes to perform this task and another seven minutes to blow dry my hair.

Is this necessary? Can't I take the weekend off? Sometimes the universe gives us an example. Today happens to be a weekend and I woke to find I was out of milk. I like milk with my coffee. So before I took a quick walk to the corner store to get milk, I took 7 minutes to put on minimal makeup, comb my hair, and put on jeans, sandals and a clean and non-wrinkled T-shirt. And… I ran into a client who was on his way to some sport thing. We exchanged greetings, commented on the weather, confirmed we'd see each other again at a meeting in a couple of weeks, and off we went our separate ways.

HOW TO GET "IT"

I am really glad that I took that seven minutes. I don't want this man to see me without makeup or in my sweats with the paint splatters and holes walking down a public road. Ever.

My thinking is this: just like you never regret only having two cocktails instead of four the next day, you never regret looking reasonably appropriate when you're in public.

Some women really don't want to wear makeup and consider it a waste of valuable time that they could spend elsewhere and they get quite agitated on the topic.

In a *New York Times* article about the P&G/Harvard study, Deborah Rhode, a law professor at Stanford University who wrote *The Beauty Bias*, was quoted as saying, "I don't wear makeup, nor do I wish to spend 20 minutes applying it. The quality of my teaching shouldn't depend on the color of my lipstick or whether I've got mascara on."

Professor Rhode's book is important work, detailing how appearance unjustly affects some workers. While she doesn't want to be labeled as a "beauty basher," she says "I'm against our preoccupation, and how judgments about attractiveness spill over into judgments about competence and job performance. We like individuals in the job market to be judged on the basis of competence, not cosmetics."

I understand where she's coming from, you may be surprised to hear me say. But I think there's a realism missing and a faulty assumption. First, I don't like that smart women don't always get the job because of the way they look. But rather than put my head in the sand and pretend it's not happening, I'd rather do something about it. As I can't change the mindset of every human on earth, all that is left is for me to inform and advise.

Second, who takes 20 minutes to put on makeup? Even my most glamorous evening makeup only takes 15 minutes, maximum, and that's if I pluck my eyebrows and try to wear fake lashes. So, honestly, is five minutes too much to be seen as likable, trustworthy and competent?

Good grooming for a woman means being clean and polished. It means wearing a little make-up and having an actual hairstyle. It means not wearing clothes with stains on them. It means not wearing the dirty old boots to give a presentation. It's a key part of how you get ahead.

Being a Girl Is Hard

So why *do* women wear the old boots, no make-up, no bra and no hairstyle without understanding the consequences?

It comes down to fear of being judged in a different way. Brené Brown, in her books on shame and imperfection, talks a lot about appearance based on hundreds of interviews with women from all demographics. Brown says that often, when it comes to appearance, women feel forced to choose between bad or worse:

- Be thin, but don't be weight obsessed.
- Be perfect, but don't make a fuss about your looks and don't take time away from anything like your family or your partner or your work to achieve your perfection. Just quietly make it happen in the background so you look great and we don't have to hear about it.
- Just be yourself – there's nothing sexier than self-confidence (as long as you're young, thin and beautiful…).

The problem is that this makes us feel powerless and shameful about our appearance – whether we're trying or not. After we feel shame, we are then likely to blame others or disconnect from them. When we're disconnected, we can't be powerful or engaged with others, both are which are necessary to be a leader.

Brown has found that appearance and image is an almost universal shame trigger for women, the strongest of all the triggers in her research that includes parenting, money, addiction, sex, ageing, and religion. Her work on building resilience to shame is breakthrough in my view and what I would consider required reading for an aspiring female executive.

Body Image and 'Never Enough'

Now we enter into the 'never enough' trap. Being female can be daunting and an A-type personality wants to do things the 'right' way. It is possible to over-polish your surfaces and overcompensate. The perfectionist voice says, 'Look perfect. Do perfect. Be perfect. Anything less than that is unacceptable.'

Body image is a minefield of issues for women. According to researchers at the Dove Institute, more than 90 percent of women experience shame about their bodies. Body shame is so powerful and often so deeply rooted in our psyches that it actually affects why and how we feel shame in other categories like age, sex, and religion.

When we talk about body image, we're talking about how we think and feel about our bodies, which has little to do with our actual appearance. It is our image of what our bodies are, often held up to our image of what they should be. Rarely do these two images match.

This is my own, personal trap. My mother was always overweight and always on a diet. As long as I can remember, I have been afraid that I will be overweight. I gained over 70 pounds with each of my sons – and at 5'5" that's a lot of weight for me. So, after losing it three times, I started to fixate on making sure I didn't gain it back. I exercise and I watch what I eat. But if I gain more than three pounds, I start to get very agitated. I think about it a lot. I feel guilt for eating the biscotti with my coffee. It's ridiculous, and I know it, but it's still real to me and it causes me stress.

Every female executive I've ever worked with has, at some point, talked with me about her body image and weight. And the advice I give them is this: the key to body image is to own yours. You know that you are not alone. You are now aware of this 'issue' – whether it is an actual physical issue or if it's only in your own mind – and you must own it. The great thing is that if you own your story, you get to own the ending. If you own your surfaces, you own your choices, and you own your ending.

If you own your body image, the distraction of the ideal image loses its power and it is no longer that loud voice in your head. If you can't accept your body and own it at this weight, then you need to change yourself. Diet. Exercise. Invest in your body like you invested in your education. Give time to your fitness like you give time to your personal development or networking. Hire a trainer. Hire a nutritionist. And don't lie to them or cancel on them – make that time a priority. Make the time to exercise. Pay attention to what you eat.

If you can't do this, then you have to let go and accept yourself at this weight, with this body, and move forward. Dress for your body shape to feel confident. Look your best, no matter your weight, and let it go.

CHAPTER 7

Visual Conundrums for Professional Women

We've already discussed the 'be perfect but don't be seen to be trying to be perfect' conundrum. The visual facet is rife with mixed messages and catch-22s that seem to exist only to trap women.

Knowing these dichotomies is the starting point for dealing with them. And why do we need to understand and manage these conundrums? Because, according to CTI, your visual impression counts for 73 percent of your overall presence, and mistakes are rarely forgotten.

Like Iris and the scruffy boots, no matter how many times she wears perfectly appropriate shoes to the office, they will never forget the one time she made a misstep.

According to CTI, some of the conundrums women face are:

- Be appropriate but still be authentic
- Be attractive but not sexy
- Be chic but not trendy
- Don't be too old but don't be too young
- Be in shape 'within reason.'

It's a daily balancing act. It requires a degree of self-awareness and blatant dispassionate perspective to see where you are and acknowledge when you're close to a line in the sand. It's up to you to shift the balance and stay inside the zone of acceptability.

Every woman is prone to fall out of the zone, no matter how smart she is. One of my favorite clients was Dawna Markova, writer of books including *I Will Not Die an Unlived Life* and *Open Mind*. She's a neuroscientist, a researcher, and an amazing person. I've known Dawna since 2002 when she lived in Utah. Since then, she's lived in Napa Valley and now resides on a Hawaiian island. Together, we've gone through her closet and shopped tirelessly for comfortable shoes and the perfect black sweater. At heart, she is something of a hippy and talks about 'energy' as comfortably as she talks about synapses. She is earthy and comfortable in her own skin. Every time I speak with her, I come away awed by her insight and general brilliance.

So, a few years ago I asked Dawna to fly to Germany and give a keynote speech at a leadership conference for the top 300 finance executives of a very large, very conservative blue-chip company. She was talking about innovation and inventive thinking. She had her team design a great presentation using the latest technology. She had interviewed key leaders in the company to get a sense of their issues and concerns. She had brought with her customized materials for the attendees highlighting her key points and giving them tools to discover their own inventive thinking.

As the preceding speaker was finishing his comments, I was standing next to Dawna in the wings waiting for her cue to go on. With about five minutes to go, she suddenly turned to me and said, "I think I should not wear my shoes."

It took me a second to process what that meant, exactly. "Not wear your shoes? Do you want a different pair of shoes? Do those hurt or something?" I said.

HOW TO GET "IT"

"I think I would feel more comfortable if I was barefoot," she replied.

Now, because I know Dawna well, I felt comfortable being very direct in my response.

"No way. You're wearing your shoes."

"But, really, I do think I would feel better without them," she tried again.

We now enter the 'authentic' conundrum. Dawna's authentic self is barefooted. She is connected to the Earth and loves to feel its energy through her toes on the ground.

The problem is that she's about to go on stage in front of an audience of 300 executives, roughly 85-90 percent male, who are wearing 'casual' dress – khakis, blue shirts, and brown leather shoes. She's wearing a lovely jacket, blouse and trousers that are just 'artistic' enough to show her character without being distracting. Her shoes were nice – I can't even remember what they looked like, so they must have been perfectly fine.

So, is it selling out for Dawna not to go onstage shoeless? Should I have said, "Sure, if you feel comfortable, that's what you should do. Be confident and it will be fine!"

Of course not. Because as soon as she's that 'authentic' she becomes 'inappropriate.' In no way is it appropriate as an adult woman to go onstage as an authoritative presenter in a hotel in the middle of Munich in front of a bunch of bankers without wearing your shoes. That is *not* appropriate.

Would they have listened to a word she said? How much of their attention would have been consumed by thinking about why she wasn't wearing shoes? They would be thinking: 'Was it to make a point? Did she forget? Does she have a weird foot disorder? What's going on?!'

In the end, Dawna wore her shoes. I doubt anyone noticed her shoes. She gave a great speech and the feedback was stellar. If she'd gone onstage without her shoes, I don't think the outcome would have been the same.

Fortunately, she had a sounding board and, wisely, she listened.

Faking Femininity – The Tomboy Executive

Closely related to the issue of appearance and shame is the idea of being 'feminine.' Men in power like women who are feminine – particularly men of an older generation who are used to thinking about women in a context like mother, wife, sister, daughter, or niece.

Feminine, according to Brown, is a woman who is nice, pursuing a thin body ideal, showing modesty but not calling attention to her talents or abilities, being domestic, caring for children, investing in a romantic relationship, keeping sexual intimacy contained within one committed relationship, and using her resources to invest in her appearance. Basically, a woman who is willing to stay as small, sweet, and quiet as possible, and use her time and talent to look pretty. Her dreams, ambitions and gifts are unimportant.

This clearly doesn't jibe with a woman who has opinions. It doesn't work for a woman who is not petite or 'small.' And sometimes women decide to throw out all concept of being feminine – including make-up and heels – because they don't fit the desired norm and they are tired of being rejected for it. They choose to opt out entirely – sometimes quietly, sometimes sullenly, and sometimes angrily.

Whenever I talk to groups of women or write about this feminine dichotomy, I know I'm going to get grief on this subject. There will be women who are angry about what I have to say. When someone doesn't want to wear a bra or make-up, she has her reasons, and they are deep and connected to something visceral inside her psyche, I find. Otherwise, she wouldn't be so annoyed with me.

And I think she has a right to be annoyed. Just not at me. I am, unfortunately, the messenger in this scenario — and we know what typically happens to messengers bearing bad news. My message is this: if you do not wear a bra, if you do not have a hairstyle, if you do not wear some make-up, if you do not nod to some of the feminine ideals, you will not be the CEO. Ever.

Balancing Yin with Yang to Achieve 'Classic'

I love *Game of Thrones*. It's a great show with amazing female characters in power. The two queens, Danerys and Cersei, are blonde, beautiful and balance power and femininity. When I think about the issue of feminine idealism, I think about a character in the book and series, Brienne of Tarth, a woman who is nearly seven feet tall and who is scorned, rejected and pitied for her lack of feminine and social graces, despite being a kick-ass warrior, honest, loyal, and determined.

Not to be a spoiler to anyone who hasn't read the books, but unless the guys at HBO do something way off script, Brienne will not be a queen. She is a great warrior and one of the few truly moral characters in the entire series. But to be a queen, she'd have to have a makeover first. She would have to wear some make-up. She would need to wear clothing not made of steel. She would need some serious counterbalancing.

The concept of Yin and Yang comes into play here. In a nutshell, 'Yin' is feminine and 'Yang' is masculine. If you think of them as being on either side of a see-saw, your objective as a woman in business is to balance perfectly in the center, which is 'Classic' — neither too Yin nor too Yang.

The foundation is your physical self — your height, weight, coloring, features, and demeanor.

- Women who are on the extreme Yin side of the spectrum are *delicate* — they are petite, small-boned, have finely textured skin, fair hair that is softly curled or tousled. They are youthful and graceful.

- Women who are on the extreme Yang side of the spectrum are *dramatic* – taller, with stronger bone structure, angular features, darker coloring, slightly coarser skin, sleek hair, and a bolder energy. They move purposefully and are mature.

So, going back to *Game of Thrones*: physically, Brienne is clearly Yang. She has fair coloring, but otherwise she's completely Yang. Danerys is the most Yin of the trio, being petite and fair. In real life, the actress has dark hair – so by making her blonde, they've made her more Yin. Cersei is balanced in the centre – though physically rather tall and with angular features, she is also blonde with soft hair.

Another layer to the spectrum is one's personality traits:

- Very Yin personalities are gentle, idealistic, a little shy, friendly, informal, warm, fragile, and desiring to follow and please.
- Very Yang personalities are more assertive, forceful, independent, firm, decisive, direct, daring, formal, cold, sophisticated, closed, desiring to lead and protect.

All three of our *Game of Thrones* characters have strong personalities that could be considered Yang, though Brienne and Danerys show a gentler side that is more Yin.

Now that we have their personality and physicality plotted, we would label Brienne as very Yang, Cersei as quite Yang, and Danerys as about level and slightly 'romantic' on the Yin side of the scale.

The tipping point now is clothing and styling. If you are physically Yin and have a Yin personality, you need to dress more Yang to be taken seriously. Conversely, if you are physically Yang and have a Yang personality, you need to dress more Yin to not be intimidating.

Thus, we need to plot clothing and style on the scale and use it as a tool to shift the balance:

- Yin clothing: softer, curved, rounded lines and shapes, small patterns and shapes, soft colors, pliable fabrics, lighter weights, finer textures, unstructured and untailored.
- Yang clothing: harder, angular shapes and silhouettes, solid lines, larger shapes and patterns, bold colors, dark colors, firmer fabric, heavy weight, coarse texture, bold contrasts and tailoring.

In *Game of Thrones*, Danerys used to wear soft, floating, ethereal fabrics. Now she wears a jewel-colored tunic that is severely cut and a bone/claw choker around her neck – that's a lot of Yang styling to show she's serious and a queen to be reckoned with. If I was making over Brienne, we would have to introduce Yin into her wardrobe and style in an authentic way – to bring her back to Classic, we would need to overcorrect.

I am aware of my Yin/Yang balance every day. I'm average height and more Yin in appearance – so I wear more Yang clothes and accessories to level at Classic. If I were to wear soft flowing dresses in pastels, I'd look like a little girl.

Gloria, a CEO I worked with in Chicago, was very Yang – brunette, tall and imposing. We had to intentionally introduce Yin to her style through softer cuts in her jackets and lighter weight blouses with less structure so that she wouldn't be intimidating and cold.

Do Your Own Professional Makeover – or the Top 10 Image Rules Every Executive Woman Needs to Know and Follow

Everybody Loves a Makeover! As you can imagine, I've watched more than a few makeover shows and read many similar magazine stories in my lifetime. But makeovers never seem to stick. Have you ever watched an episode when they go back and visit the made over person afterward? Usually she's gone back to her roots and undone all the 'making over' that was so carefully planned by the experts.

The question is why? The answer is because they didn't address the key issues about why she was choosing those surfaces to project herself to the world. Is she continuing to go back to her own mental image of ideal or did she really just not understand how to replicate the look when she was on her own?

So it's with trepidation that I offer an instant makeover for you, because I can give you ideas, but without understanding your current choices, it may or may not stick.

However, I think we can make some headway if you can open your mind and commit to follow my *Top 10 Image Rules Every Executive Woman Needs to Know and Follow:*

1. Dress for your actual chronological age. Too young and you appear girlish, too old and you appear matronly. Skirts should never be shorter than your middle finger when your arms are down and palms facing your thighs. Clear everything else out of your closet, now.

2. Don't wear clunky shoes. Clunky shoes are… clunky. Chunky heels don't look good on anyone. The same goes for ankle straps most of the time. Do a 'shoe review' and throw away any shoes that are worn out or not flattering.

3. Only wear sweats to the gym and pajamas to bed. Ever. There is absolutely no excuse to wear them in public, even at the grocery store at 2 a.m.

4. Hair and make-up should be subtle and natural. Only have a hair color that occurs in nature. Go easy on the hairspray – most women use twice as much hair product as they need. Update your hairstyle. Color your hair unless you are going to commit to grey. Make-up should be simple and professional, but don't be seen in public without any make-up at all. If you're clueless about make-up, go to a make-up counter at a department store, look

HOW TO GET "IT"

for a sales person who has what you think is appropriate make-up, and have her show you what to do.

5. You can't go wrong with an A-line skirt and blouse. A too-high neckline makes you appear heavier and look constricted. So in general, V-necks are best with no cleavage revealed. If you have larger arms, go no shorter than ¾-length sleeves. Go buy a couple of good skirts and blouses that you know fit you well and you can wear when you need to impress.

6. Trousers must fit well. Beware trousers that are too long or too short with pleats and front pockets. In general, get flat front trousers with a moderately low rise (1" below belly button) and a slight flare at bottom to make you look longer and thinner. Have the pockets stitched shut to avoid gaping. Try on every pair of work trousers you have and take a picture of yourself in them. Do they honestly fit you well? If not, throw them out.

7. Wear your real size and avoid the 'too-tight' faux pas. Your clothes should skim but not be like skin. You should be able to 'pinch an inch' for a proper fit. Get your clothes tailored. It's cheap. It makes things fit you properly. It makes you look thinner. If you're hoarding too-small clothes that you'll 'fit into someday,' throw them out.

8. The most important thing you wear is what's underneath. Invest in well-fitting undergarments, including a properly sized bra, seamless underwear, and Spanx. If you haven't been fitted for a bra within the last two years, or if you've gained or lost a lot of weight recently, go for a fitting and buy new bras and undergarments.

9. Carry nice handbags. Bags should be reasonably sized. It's much better to carry a small handbag *and* a briefcase than to carry a behemoth bag. Just be sure that you avoid looking like a pack mule by carrying both bags on one shoulder. This isn't good for heavy bags or long distances, but in general, if you can't carry

both of your everyday bags comfortably on one arm, then you're carrying too much! That sends a signal of disorganization and makes you appear overwhelmed.

10. Draw attention to your face as much as possible. Wearing monochromatic neutrals with splashes of color or contrast has the added bonus of making you look thinner. One interesting, complementary-colored piece of jewelry – a pin, pendant, earrings – or casually tied scarf is enough.

CHAPTER 8

The Five A's of Appearance for Executive Women

Every day is an opportunity to make an impression. Every meeting is another arena to fight in and gain ground in your path forward. You need to be prepared for battle and have your armor and weapons at the ready.

Your daily pre-work checklist should ensure your visual appearance covers the Five A's:

1. Attractive to emphasize the positive
2. Authentic to who you are
3. Appropriate to the environment
4. Accommodating to meet expectations
5. Aligned with your objectives and your brand

1. Attractive to emphasize the positive

'Attractive' doesn't mean 'gorgeous.' Attractive means appealing and pleasant. We all have our issues, and, as we've discussed, the primary trigger for women in terms of its power and universality is how we look. Still.

So, it's important to define attractive for Western or Westernised culture. The 'ideal' female shape is average height (between 5' 3" – 5' 7"), slim but shapely, and evenly proportioned between hips and chest, with a smaller waistline. If you are outside those bounds, your objective is to do what you can to approximate it visually.

This does not mean that you aren't allowed to have a real body. There are three basic body shapes – ectomorphs are long and lean (like Julia Roberts), endomorphs are round and prone to weight gain (like Oprah Winfrey), and mesomorphs are muscular and athletic (like Cameron Diaz).

Depending on your actual body shape, you can use clothing to create a visual illusion that your body shape is closer to the ideal hourglass or inverted triangle than reality. Fit your body shape first, then create structure to give yourself the desired effect. Use solid blocks of color to make yourself appear taller and slimmer.

You should also emphasize your best features. I defy you to find a woman who does not have an attractive feature, no matter how self-critical she may be.

When I work with a client, we look at her body from an 'inventory' standpoint – what are her strengths? Just as we have our strengths in our professional skillset, so we do in our appearance. It would be foolish to ignore that you're a great mathematician or brilliant strategist or naturally intuitive problem solver. Know your appearance strengths – whether it be your eyes, your body shape, your hands, your hair – and use them.

This is not about being sexy or manipulative. This is about being attractive. We are attracted to attractive people; for you to get into the big chair, people need to be attracted to you.

Three quick tips for female leaders to emphasize the positive:

1. Pay attention to your grooming details and make sure your hair, nails, teeth and skin are impeccable.

2. Hair is the simplest way to look more attractive. Invest in a hairstyle that is natural, has movement, and reflects current styles.

3. Without doubt, eyes are usually a person's best feature. You can inspire trust and confidence by wearing colors that emphasize or match your eyes: blue and aqua for blue eyes; green or purple for green eyes; green or burgundy for dark eyes. This brings attention to your eyes; it makes them appear more vibrant and, therefore, makes you appear more trustworthy.

2. Authentic to who you are

Age and ethnicity are absolute – you can't change them. To attempt to do so significantly is inauthentic. Now, don't get me wrong, I believe in Botox. But I also know that too many facelifts won't work at the boardroom table. Pretending to be someone you're not won't work.

It's hard to balance on the line and to be authentic in a culture that wants you to fit in and 'people please.' If we've worked hard to make sure everything looks 'just right' on the outside, the stakes are high when it comes to being our authentic self.

You do not have to sell out to succeed. You can be your authentic self and make it to the top. The key is to modulate and see your appearance like a soundboard mixer hears a piece of music. You don't have to obliterate the saxophone, but perhaps it doesn't need to dominate.

Start by defining your current executive style. How would you describe your true, most authentic style? Here are some personality adjectives to get you started – choose two or three that define you:

- Studied
- Relaxed
- Authoritative

- Approachable
- Friendly
- Sophisticated
- Active
- Casual
- Formal
- Gregarious
- Energetic
- Thoughtful
- Calm
- Earthy

How do you reflect that personality in the surfaces you choose? How do you think others see you? Think about the clothes you wear, your accessories, your hair, your grooming — does it mesh with that personality? If you consider yourself to be 'gregarious' but you wear formidable clothing, there's a disconnection between who you appear to be and who you are.

Maybe it's time for a style shift. What would you want to project at work? You'll note that each of these adjectives is perfectly fine, and none of them would be wrong to project in the workplace, as long as they're balanced and not over the top. Too much of any one of these isn't a good thing for a woman on her way to the top of the food chain. You need to be a little of all and able to choose what you want to project with purpose and intention.

How can you bridge from your current reality to project more balance? If you're too formal, adding more color and softer fabric will help. If you're coming across as too 'earthy,' find ways to introduce structure with a refined hairstyle or accessories that are on the polished end of your spectrum. You don't need to fake it — you just need to push to the very edge of your boundary intentionally to give the perception of balance.

Authenticity also comes through in our eyes and facial expressions. Again, things that can't really be faked unless you're a professional actress.

Three quick tips for female leaders to project authenticity:

1. Women tend to be over-rehearsed with eye contact. It's been drilled into us to hold the gaze of the person we're communicating with. If you want someone to trust and like you, your eye contact should be held for about two seconds at a time, accompanied by a smile and/or relaxed facial expression. It's long enough to see their eye color, and no longer than needed – otherwise, you're staring them down.

2. Being authentic means being interested. Even if you are genuinely interested in what someone is saying, you may inadvertently project uninterest by blinking your eyes. Blinking tends to increase when we're bored or uninterested in an activity or a conversation. Before an important meeting use eye drops to make sure your eyes are moist and reduce the frequency of blinking to send the signal that you're paying attention.

3. To be less threatening, women have learned to smile and nod, sometimes to excess. Humans can spot a forced smile because the mouth doesn't turn upward and the smile is lop-sided. Take a picture of yourself 'fake smiling' and 'real smiling' and see if you can spot the difference. Be aware of your fake smiling. Do you do it a lot to cover up what you're feeling or to feign interest? If so, practice letting your face relax, notice when you're triggering the fake smile, and retrain yourself.

3. Appropriate to the environment

Now that you know how business casual confused the universal rules of business dress, you need to know how to correct for it.

When I conduct executive presence workshops, I often show a slide that has a photo of then Vice President Dick Cheney sitting among a group of men in dark wool overcoats wearing a khaki-colored puffy coat – the kind you get for free from a company with a logo embroidered on it. He was representing the United States of America at a formal ceremony at the former Dachau concentration camp and he looked like an idiot. Why, why, why? Was there no one to lend him a wool coat? Was he really that cold that he couldn't suck it up and wear something else? Did he just not realize he was dressed for a football game and not a formal event?

Be smarter than Dick Cheney. When you're deciding what to wear and how to accessorize, do your own 'Terminator' scan and consider your day:

- Where will you be geographically? I mean, in the world. Are you in Europe, North America, Asia? It matters.

- Will you be inside or outside? Does that mean it will be cold or hot? Will it be rainy?

- What time of day is the event? Morning, afternoon, evening? Unless you have an audience with the Queen, don't wear a tiara before noon.

- Who's going to be present? Your boss? Key leaders or clients? Delegates from the United Nations? What will they be wearing?

- What's the purpose of the function or meeting? If it's a serious subject and you're presenting in public, the color palette should match the tone. Don't give bad news wearing a yellow dress, for example.

- What is the industry and company culture? This can vary widely. If in doubt, go for neutral – your classic A-line skirt, V-necked blouse with long or ¾ length sleeves, 2-3" heels, hosiery, and an interesting accessory or scarf.

- And, most importantly, what impression do you want to make? Envision the three words you want them to think when they see you. Is that the impression you're making?

HOW TO GET "IT"

So, after all that, how do you decide what to wear? If you're still unsure, there is a handy, practical system to help you choose what to wear and when that covers the majority of industries and cultures. Judith Rasband, a pioneering thinker in image consulting for professional men and women, created 'The Impact Scale'.

Judith understood before most people that how you dress affects how you feel and act, and how others react to you. She also understood that you can only be as 'elevated' as your lowest element. It's essentially the lowest common denominator of style — if you're wearing an evening dress (high) but with sneakers (low) you don't average at medium. You settle at low. No matter what else you do, you can pile on diamonds and emeralds, the sneakers will still drag you down to low. This is why Iris' boots brought her down. Even if she was wearing an expensive, designer, perfectly tailored suit, the boots drag down the entire look to the lowest level.

On Judith's scale, there are four 'levels' of impact. What you wear has a causal relationship with how you feel and how others perceive you, so you consider your objective and dress accordingly, keeping in mind that you'll need to adjust for the situation, like the weather and culture as we've already discussed.

The Style Scale is particularly relevant for women, who, without a uniform or guide similar to men, are often left to their own interpretation of the rules.

Level 1 is 'Sporty': Be cautious with Level 1, which is wearing untailored, collarless T-shirts or hooded tops and jeans, cargo pants, sweats or shorts, open-toed shoes/sandals or athletic shoes, backpack, vests or parkas.

You want to wear Level 1 for weekend or non-work situations, like if you're working at the office alone without visitors, at an offsite retreat involving physical activity, or doing a job that day that involves physical labor. If you're going onto a factory floor and you're going to have to wear an orange jumpsuit and steel-toed boots, you should dress at Level 1 underneath.

When you're dressed at Level 1, you feel and behave more as a friend – casual, light-hearted, and active. You convey agreeableness and a sense of being easygoing. You also convey a 'temporary' status at Level 1. You don't project weight or gravitas. The upside is that you're comfortable; the downside is that you may appear sloppy and unprofessional.

Level 2 is 'Casual': If you want to rise up the ranks, you should be conscious of how much time you spend at Level 2, which is characterized by wearing a collared shirt/blouse or sweater with trousers or casual skirt, flat or thicker-soled shoes, and an unstructured handbag. There is no 'third piece' like a jacket, scarf or sweater at Level 2. You'd wear Level 2 for work situations such as corporate retreats, training sessions, some 'business casual' situations, when working in the back office, or when meeting with stakeholders (like clients or employees) who work in very casual environments.

When you're dressed at Level 2, you feel and behave more as a counsellor. You convey approachability, flexibility, co-operation, and a more relaxed character. The upside is that you come across as friendly and engaging; the downside is that you can easily be *too* casual and it's difficult to command respect.

Level 3 is 'Professional': This is the easiest to pull off. At Level 3, you are wearing a tailored day dress or a softly tailored jacket, sweater, or scarf with unmatched trousers or a skirt and flats, boots or heels. This is appropriate for less formal occasions, including most meetings, if you're the presenter at a 'business casual' event, less formal office visits, sales calls, informal networking, or other public facing activity.

When you're dressed at Level 3 you feel and behave like an advisor – confident and knowledgeable, still with a relaxed manner. You convey accessibility, influence, capability, receptiveness, consistency, and reliability.

HOW TO GET "IT"

The upside to Level 3 is that you're professional but still approachable; the downside to Level 3 is that it requires skill to match and co-ordinate separates fashionably so there is more margin for error. Buying separates that are from the same collection or designer is a safe bet if you're uncertain.

Level 4 is 'Expert/Authority': This must be mastered by any woman who aspires to the C-suite, boardroom, or corner office. When you're wearing Level 4, you are wearing either a tailored matched suit that includes a jacket/skirt/trouser, or a simply structured day dress that is perfectly tailored and a refined shoe with a heel and appropriate hosiery.

The key to Level 4 is dark/light contrast and structured fabric and lines — the principle behind the man's suit. If you're opting for a dress, it must be of a substantial fabric and be impeccably cut to be considered appropriate.

You would wear Level 4 for the most formal business and public occasions, including meetings with or presentations to authorities/senior executives, customer visits, legal situations, and media presentations.

When I give a workshop, no matter how casual the environment, I dress at Level 4 or a very slight dip below if I don't wear hosiery. I do this because Level 4 makes you feel and behave as a trusted expert — more powerfully, confidently, credibly, orderly, focused, and well mannered. At Level 4, you convey the most gravitas and presence, which makes others perceive you as having more credibility, persuasiveness, attention to detail, trustworthiness, and stability. The upside to Level 4 is that you are seen as very authoritative; the downside is that you can come across as excessively stiff.

What if you're a 'creative type'? Let's say you're in advertising, beauty, marketing, the arts. Or what if you're in a casual environment like construction, an oil rig, or a tech start-up. Does this mean you don't have to follow the rules?

The short answer is, no. You need to understand the rules and adapt them to suit your situation. Being a graphic designer doesn't mean you get to be sloppy and wear a T-shirt and jeggings every day. If you're meeting with a corporate client, you need to understand that you need to modulate. If you're a graphic designer in a global company, you need to fit that culture more than you need to fit your role or industry.

Rarely have I heard a valid reason why a woman can dress at Level I every day that wasn't really a justification for 'I don't want to bother dressing up' for whatever reason – comfort, cost, or effort. The reality is, if you want to be in the corner office, you need to know when to dress to impress and how to do it. Otherwise, you'll always be the quirky, arty woman who may get the window cubicle but won't ever get the power chair.

Three quick tips for the female executive to be appropriate:

1. Make sure your clothes are always clean and pressed, no matter what 'level.' No spots, rips or wrinkles.

2. If you're in doubt as to what's appropriate, dress slightly more formally and conservatively than you expect others to be dressed.

3. A beautiful scarf is a savior. Invest in the best quality scarves you can afford in colors that complement your hair and eyes. It can elevate or 'conceal' a casual outfit. It can become a wrap if it's cold or a headscarf if necessary. It can emphasize your eye color and bring attention to your face.

4. Accommodating to meet expectations

Being accommodating is really about showing respect. How you look translates into how you regard other people. If you put no effort into your appearance, the implication is that you don't respect the people you are with. You also signal to others that you lack emotional intelligence or the awareness that you may be making others uncomfortable with your visual choices.

HOW TO GET "IT"

Earlier, I wrote about Sierra, the PhD candidate with Rapunzel-like hair who had notes jotted in pen on her forearm. These were obvious visual conflicts that were interfering with her desire to project herself as being a capable, intelligent, trustworthy interviewer of senior executives.

With Sierra, I needed to help her find a way to meet expectations whilst remaining authentic. People expected her to be young – she was a PhD candidate after all – but they also expected a level of seriousness and professionalism that reflected her university. So showing respect while remaining herself became our objective.

Community values will also inform our expectations of how others could or should present themselves visually. I grew up in Utah, a conservative and highly religious state. When I moved back to Utah from London in 2004 and started working with Intermountain Healthcare, one of the largest employers in the State and formerly owned by the Mormon Church, I knew what was expected from a visual perspective. The Mormon culture, in which I was raised, is very modest when it comes to dress for women and men. When I worked at the Intermountain offices, I made sure that I wore clothing that accommodated their values.

Essentially, you never want to make anyone uncomfortable, male or female. Dressing too sexily may gain attention from some, but it will also make others uncomfortable. Wearing a provocative emblem or symbol may represent your values or beliefs, but you should also consider if it can and should be adapted to meet others' expectations.

In my workshops I show a slide with two pictures of the noted English fashion designer Vivienne Westwood. Westwood was one of the originators of the Punk movement, and the first photo is of her wearing one of her original 'straightjacket' tops with an obscene Mickey Mouse image on the front. The second is of her wearing a dress suit and curtsying to meet Queen Elizabeth II. Even Vivienne Westwood, or Lady Gaga for that matter, dresses to meet expectations when they meet the Queen.

Ask yourself what do others expect from you? Think of the three most important work environments for you currently – say, in the home office, at a production facility, or at a showroom. What settings are you in most regularly that are relevant and necessary for your success?

Now, consider who is the most important individual in each environment. Think of a specific person that you know by name. What does he/she expect from you? What does he/she value?

Thinking back to Judith Rasband's Style Scale, which level is most accommodating for each environment? What would your 'uniform' be when you're working in that environment and with that individual to achieve the relationship you want?

Three quick tips for the female executive to accommodate:

1. Always have a nice quality pen. To be completely bereft of a pen is accessory suicide because it shows a lack of preparedness.
2. Don't show cleavage or thigh while you're on your way to the top.
3. Look like a lady, as you would expect a man in business to look like a gentleman. This means making sure the people around you are as comfortable as possible. Leave the piercings out and cover up the tattoos when you're meeting people who you know will be made uncomfortable by them. Wear clothing that shows respect. Consider how you look and how it makes others feel.

5. Aligned with your objectives and your brand

The fifth A is to be Aligned. The way you look should not only reflect who and where you are, but where you want to go.

One of my clients, Leila, was a television reporter who was doing a story on me for the morning news. The idea was that we would broadcast live

HOW TO GET "IT"

at regular intervals from her apartment throughout the morning and do a closet clearout.

Simultaneously, a beefy man from a local closet store was installing a new system of racks and shelves so that the before/after would be even more stunning. Basically, Leila got a new closet for free – good for her. If I could get a free closet, I would too.

We did a superficial purge for the purposes of the program, picking out a few really tragic items that she tried on for fun, and we agreed needed to be let go and put into bin bags to be sent to a charity shop. She had dozens of pairs of cargo pants that were cropped, and no skirt suits. She had dozens of pairs of flip-flops, and few court shoes.

She was a 35-year-old woman with the wardrobe of a 16-year-old girl. The final segment showed us making a checklist of the new wardrobe items she needed to buy. It went well and was a generally pleasant morning, until the camera switched off.

As the crew was packing to leave and I was getting ready to go, Leila started opening up the plastic garbage bags and retrieving the 'discarded' clothes.

"What are you doing?" I asked, confused.

"Oh, just putting these back," she replied.

"Okay, well they're your clothes of course, but I do think you need to think about letting them go. Like this top." I pulled out an official Boy Scout Uniform blue button-up top that she'd bought at a charity shop and, when worn, pulled against her cleavage as she does not have the body of a twelve-year-old boy. There is no appropriate place on earth for a grown woman to wear a boy's Boy Scout shirt (sorry, Madonna), especially not a news reporter in the public eye.

Leila got defensive of the Boy Scout top. She justified the reasons why it was harmless to keep the top. Then she pleaded with me to keep the top.

It was like watching someone go through the stages of grief over a Boy Scout uniform.

By now the crew was long gone and she and I were alone in her chaotic apartment, strewn with bags and clothes. This is when she had the Big Reveal and opened a cupboard under her stairs, where she had a *dozen* bags of clothes she bought from charity shops that she was sure she was going to "do something with."

I was gobsmacked. I did not see that plot twist coming.

Though it was only 11 am, I thought this called for a drink. We made mimosas and sat at her kitchen table. Ignoring the bags of elephants literally in the room, I talked to Leila about her goals and her work.

She had settled into being a 'fluff' reporter, she said. Now, though, she was tired of doing the puff pieces, celebrity news, interviews with sports mascots and covering cheerleading competitions. She wanted to report hard news. She wanted to be an anchor. She thought it was the top brass being "sexist" and she wasn't getting hard assignments because she was 'too pretty.' These may or may not have been valid points; I don't know. But what I did know was that based on what I'd seen her wear on that morning's telecast, I wouldn't have put her in the anchor's chair, either.

After letting her wallow and whine for a while, I asked her, "If you got called to go in now to anchor tonight's newscast, what would you wear?"

She thought for a minute and said probably her red leather jacket.

"Okay, let's try it on," I said.

We got out the jacket and looked at her reflection in the mirror. "Do you think a 50-year-old housewife who lives in a small town wants to hear about war and economic collapse from a woman wearing a red leather jacket?"

HOW TO GET "IT"

It was a breakthrough. We shifted the conversation to talk about her aspirations and how she needed to define a personal brand that showed her bosses she had the goods to do the Big Desk job. As long as her wardrobe was full of clothes for the puff reporter, the serious reporter had no room to emerge. We also uncovered that she was dressing too young in an effort to not look too old, because television is an industry that eschews age. The irony was that by trying to look young, she had ended up not looking serious – and therefore not being taken seriously.

She needed clothes for her future, not her past. It's an old adage: dress for the job that you want, not the job that you have. In Leila's case it was true. She smartened up her wardrobe and made the changes. Eventually she re-edited her demo reel and was able to get a more serious news job in a bigger market. She threw away the Boy Scout shirt and bought a woman's blouse.

Ask yourself: What are your brand headlines? Does your wardrobe work to meet your personal and professional goals? What can you do to refresh and renew?

"Well, I think that a red leather jacket would look great," you might be saying. "That is just the fresh edge the news needs!"

And I would agree with you – but on the right woman at the right time in her career. At the beginning of your career or when you're in 'proving moments' and under scrutiny to make a move up the ladder, you need to play by the rules. If you're just not a leather jacket gal, you'll look as if you're trying too hard to look young. But as you progress and establish your brand, you earn more latitude. In fact, you should at that point expand your brand to include distinctive elements, and maybe the red leather jacket would work well.

For me, it comes back to shoes. I have six-inch red patent leather Mary Janes that I love to wear. I don't wear them on the first day with a client or even in the first few months, and I definitely wouldn't have worn them at the beginning of my career. But now, I'm in my mid-40s, I've paid my dues, I'm on the consulting side, and if I want to wear my fancy red shoes, I do. It also fits with my brand – bold, strong, fun.

As women on the rise, we are typically compared to and often in competition with other women. This dynamic is worthy of its own book. The former US Secretary of State Madeleine Albright said it succinctly: "There is a special place in hell for women who do not help other women." There is an even lower rung in hell for women who sabotage other women.

On your way to the top, look up to other women who have made it. If there are no women in your company who've reached the upper echelon, look more broadly to the rest of your industry and even to related industries. What do these women do? How do they present themselves? What is their brand?

In your own company, be respectful of other women, especially those who outrank you. Don't outdress the women above you. Learn from them. Emulate them. But never outshine them: you'll have your turn soon enough. And I hope you'll then look at the women around and below you, and help them rise as well.

Three quick tips for the female executive to align her objectives with her appearance:

1. Do you need to exude power or to intimidate? If you're going into a situation where you need all the power you can get, dress more formally and expensively than you think the other people will and use bold artifacts, such as a heavy pen or expensive-looking folio. Use your choice of shoes to send power signals as well – high heels, power-colored, perfectly polished.

2. Do you need to establish immediate rapport? To forge a relationship with someone, seek to match their formality of dress while still being professional. You can also use artifacts that are equal to or slightly below the other person's in expense

and status to create a sense of equality. Having a significantly better phone, watch, shoes or bag than the other person can be perceived as threatening. To bond, you need to look nice – but not too nice.

3. Identify a 'trademark' style piece for yourself. Madeline Albright had her brooches, Sheryl Sandberg has her dresses, Michelle Obama has her sleeveless tops. For me, it's my scarves. I have a collection of lovely, stylish scarves that I wear either draped around my neck or knotted on my handbag. What go-to piece do you love in your wardrobe? What makes you feel confident? What do you get complimented on? Answer those questions and you'll figure out what your trademark should be.

Putting the Final Polish on Your Visual Facet

For many days I worried about Iris of the scruffy boots. She isn't my client; I really don't know her that well. But I'm reminded of the G K Chesterton quote: "We are all in the same boat, in a stormy sea, and we owe each other a terrible loyalty."

I feel I owe Iris, and every woman, a terrible loyalty to help her see where she's unknowingly and unwittingly gone astray and help her get back on course.

So I went back to the female executive, Sandra, who had told me about the boot debacle, to see what could be done. I thought that Sandra had a better relationship with Iris than Jeremy and appeared to have more emotional intelligence. Sandra is also slightly more senior than Jeremy and I thought she'd carry more weight with Iris.

I invited Sandra for coffee and we discussed the project and a few other topics before I brought the conversation around to Iris. I asked Sandra how Iris was getting on with the team, now that she was settling in.

"Well, I think she's trying. I'm not sure, really. She does have good things to say, but I'm not sure she's ready for this position or if she's been promoted too soon," said Sandra.

"Has she worn the boots again?" I asked.

"Oh, God, no. Thank heavens. That was just bizarre," she replied.

"Do you think she knows how others saw her that day, that the boots were an issue?" I responded.

"Well, I don't know, really. I doubt it."

By the end of the conversation, I'd reminded Sandra of when she was coming up in the world and how hard it was to get it 'right.' I'd also encouraged her to take on the task of Iris' success for herself – as a sort of personal mission to be an undercover 'Executive Presence Godmother.'

I encouraged her to give Iris five questions to self-assess her Executive Presence Visual and create a Visual Facet strategy – under the banner of 'I thought you might find this interesting. I'm always looking for ways to develop my own Executive Presence and am sharing this with other women who I see who have potential to rise to the top ranks, like you.'

I hope Sandra does step up and help Iris. I hope Iris is able to set aside her ego, insecurities, and potential fear and actually listen to what Sandra has to say. I hope Iris is brave enough to look at her visual presence head on and make some changes that will help her repair the damage done and reposition herself for success. And, mostly, I really hope Iris throws away those boots and never wears them again.

Let's assume that you're Iris and you've just had a conversation with Sandra. Now you need to do the work and figure out how you're going to polish your appearance and visual presentation to project confidence, competence and gravitas.

HOW TO GET "IT"

Here's your homework. To create your own Executive Presence Visual Facet Strategy, ask yourself

1. What is your ideal visual projection of yourself? Come up with three specific adjectives that you would want to have in neon above your head if you could.

2. How are you projecting yourself visually right now? Consider all of the elements that form your visual appearance: hair, skin, make-up, weight, clothing, shoes, accessories, jewelry, nails, age, wealth, hair, teeth, smile, etc. Be specific and ruthlessly honest.

3. How will you reveal your blind spots around your visual appearance to understand how others perceive you? Are you going to ask someone to help? If so, name that person specifically. You can also take photographs, video, or do other self assessments. On my website, www.coni.london, I offer a diagnostic tool that you can use to ask others to give you feedback, and my guide to 'Revealing the Blind Spot' to help give and receive feedback.

4. What will you do to polish your visual presence? Name one thing you will stop doing, one thing you will start doing, and one thing you will continue to do that's working already.

5. Lastly, how will you know if you're making progress? When will you check in to see if you're improving? Who will you ask to give you input? What is your milestone – a promotion, an invitation to a team or group, a speaking engagement?

Your visual presence is unique to you and it can be a powerful component in your career progression if you choose to address it objectively and strategically.

As I did at the beginning of this book, at the end of every lecture or workshop, I put up a slide with a quote from the architect and designer Le Corbusier: "Color is unique to our being. Maybe each of us has his own."

I believe this is true. You have your unique color that is specific to you. Your job is to let it shine, have it recognized and, once given the opportunity, back it up with the skills and value you bring to your organization and your profession.

If you've done the work to understand how you present yourself and polish this facet, you'll feel more confident — which is the core of projecting gravitas and the key to getting the job you deserve.

CHAPTER 9

Polishing Your Verbal Facet to Sound the Part

In 2000, the film *Gone in 60 Seconds* opened worldwide. Starring Nicolas Cage and Angelina Jolie, it was a fairly unremarkable remake of a 1974 film, mostly remembered for featuring some of the world's most iconic classic cars. If you look up the film on IMDb, you'll find a plot summary and a complete list of all the cars featured in the film.

What you won't find, unless you really dig around, is that *Gone in 60 Seconds* was a groundbreaking film for women's voices.

Up until 2000, when the film's trailer came out, no woman's voice had been featured as the 'voice of god' in a movie trailer. The words 'In a world…,' 'In a time…,' 'There was a man…' had always been voiced by sonorous, undulating male bass voices.

In the *Gone in 60 Seconds* trailer, voice-over actress Melissa Disney was the first, and so far only, woman whose voice was used to introduce a major film release, purring "Hello, boys" as muscle cars screech across the screen.

In a world where the release of a film trailer is often an event in itself, so much so that it's often preceded by a teaser – a 30-second squib that trails the trailer – only one small woman's voice has ever been heard in a cinema near you.

CONI JUDGE, PhD

In her 2013 comedy, *In a World,* writer, director and actress Lake Bell opens up the bizarre sub-genre of the much-mocked art form and shows how the female voice is an instrument that must be wielded carefully, with the tagline 'Speak up and let your voice be heard.'

Bell's character goes through her own transformation, eventually scoring the voice over for a *Hunger Games* style trilogy and opening her own voice coaching business. Her aim is to rid the world of 'sexy baby' voices and empower women to be taken seriously – because who wants to have a lawyer who sounds like a Kardashian?

As women in business, how we speak is as important as what we say, a point illustrated beautifully in *The Iron Lady* where British Prime Minister Margaret Thatcher famously spends hours with a voice tutor doing 'humming' exercises to lower the unpleasantly high pitch of her speaking voice.

The CEO and Chairperson are the face and the voice of an organization. Their voice needs to be measured, appealing, resonant, and authoritative. Voice reflects emotion, is persuasive, and attracts or repels.

In this section, we'll focus on the Verbal Facet of your executive presence:

1. Managing Your Voice/Paralinguistics: How you come across as a communicator and present yourself through your voice, speech patterns, and vocalizations.

2. Authentic Speaking Skills: How to develop your speaking skills and listening skills – critical for creating a connection with colleagues and stakeholders.

3. Creating Aligned Messaging: How to use corporate mythology and storytelling to create a message platform aligned with your personal brand.

4. Leaderly Communications: How to have difficult conversations and speak with power to make real change.

HOW TO GET "IT"

Managing Your Voice

The study of the voice is called 'paralinguistics' — basically, this covers how you present yourself through your tone, speech patterns, and vocalizations.

Paralinguistics is important for both men and women. Men are deemed more masculine, powerful, and authoritative based on the timbre of their voice. Consider, would Darth Vader be as impactful if he had a higher-pitched voice?

While voice matters for men, it is even more important for women. Women tend to be more specifically judged on voice traits than are men, possibly because the voice is another dimension of attractiveness. An attractive voice equals an attractive woman. In *Her*, the futuristic film featuring Joaquin Phoenix and Scarlett Johansson, we never see Johansson as a character — we only hear her voice as she portrays an operating system. But what a voice it is. An entire, completely developed and compelling character exists in voice only — attesting to the power of not just what you say, but how you say it.

Johansson has a lower tone and register. She has a slight lisp that is appealing and distinctive. Her raspiness is also considered sexy. Think back to Kathleen Turner in the 1980s and how her raspy voice became one of her signature acting hallmarks. Marilyn Monroe's distinctive voice, too, was considered a large part of her sex appeal.

So, the paralinguistic features of a voice can be part of creating an attractive personality. Like the visual facet, this doesn't need to be sexual, just appealing. On the flip side, the female voice can also be a disruptive factor in a woman's executive presence by making her unattractive.

According to Toastmasters, experts on the topic and a terrific source of further information, leaders should strive to develop a voice that is:

- Pleasant, conveying a sense of warmth

- Natural, reflecting your true personality and sincerity
- Dynamic, giving the impression of force and strength – even when it isn't especially loud
- Expressive, portraying various shades of meaning and never sounding monotonous or without emotion
- Easily heard, thanks to proper volume and clear articulation.

'Nails on a chalkboard' is a phrase commonly used to describe a female voice, and rarely used to describe a male voice. The shrillness of the feminine voice at volume, under pressure or when expressing irritation can lend itself to comparison with the most irritating noise we can imagine.

Maybe it goes back to being scolded by their mothers or female teachers, but men react negatively to female vocal characteristics. Some of this is also more apparent when we look at how women and men speak differently from a paralinguistic standpoint.

In high school, I joined the debate team in my first year. I'm naturally more introverted, so being on the podium was a challenge for me. The issue was that my otherwise normal voice became a soft mouse squeak as soon as I tried to debate my colleagues. My debate coach, Mr. Hadley, drove the mouse out of me over the next three years until I became a confident speaker and learned how to use my voice like an instrument. I believe this was one of the most valuable lessons learned in my youth that has contributed to my professional success today.

Later, in university, I paid my way through school by getting a scholarship to be the news director for the university radio station. This meant I had to 'gather' and read the news every morning (pre-internet, this actually meant buying the morning newspapers and reading the articles I liked). I also had to take on a radio shift as a DJ once a week. I chose the Sunday morning shift because it was quiet and I could do my homework while I changed records and CDs. My show was the 'new age' segment, so there were eight-minute tracks called 'Song of the Whale' which made studying even easier.

Radio was a great learning ground for controlling my voice. I learned that I could manage it by 'acting' like a DJ. At first it felt artificial to me, but over time I got used to it. Because I was doing the new age segment, my voice had to connect with the music and be smooth, melodic, and relaxing. I learned to adjust my voice to fit the purpose and see it as a tool that I could manipulate and work with to achieve an objective – in this case, do a good job and keep my scholarship.

Learning to manage voice is key for every professional woman. I think it's even harder now when I see young girls who mimic the Kardashian nasal 'babytalk' and I wonder how they'll manage in the corporate world: babygirls don't give analyst reports.

In the corporate world, there are several conundrums women have to contend with in order to manage their verbal presence:

- Be feminine, but speak with strength and presence
- Lower your pitch, but don't speak too low and sexy
- Don't talk too fast, but don't talk too slow
- Show energy, but don't over emote.

How do you balance these dichotomies but remain authentic? To start with, you must be aware. Often awareness of your voice, how it's perceived, and how it impacts your presence is enough to get you to pay attention and start making corrections. If you have significant speech issues, it's worthwhile finding a coach who specializes in vocal issues to help you refine your voice.

Managing the 'Mixing Board' for Your Verbal Communication

Just as you should assess the environment for what to wear and your visual presence, you need to assess the environment for your verbal presence. How you speak at home is different from how you speak at work. But work settings are not entirely uniform – you face different situations and environments from day to day. As you address your verbal facet, consider the venues in which you're speaking. Is it public or private? Is it a big audience or a small group? Is it inside or outdoors?

Within the specific environment, adapt your voice like a sound engineer manages a soundboard, by responding to the feedback you get from the audience and dialing it up or down as needed.

Beware, too, of the deadly paralinguistic traps that lie in wait to undermine the authority of women in business:

1. High pitch. This is obvious – women have higher-pitched voices than men. But it can be a fine line between sounding feminine and shrill. Typically, our voices get higher when we're emotional – excited, energetic, enthusiastic, upset, agitated. Women's voices also tend to rise at the end of sentences, which can make us though we are questioning our own statement as we make them and undermining our authority.

The higher your natural pitch, the less weighty or serious others perceive you to be. To mitigate this, you will need to focus on slowing down your speech and practice speaking in your lower registers – particularly in emotional situations where your credibility depends on you remaining calm. It can make you squirm, but it's worth recording yourself in a regular conversation and listening back to your own natural speaking voice. Are you speaking from your nose, your throat or your chest? Speaking from the chest gives your voice more depth and makes you sound (and feel) calmer and more credible.

HOW TO GET "IT"

Famously, upon becoming leader of the Conservative Party in 1975, Margaret Thatcher was advised by, firstly, a television producer and then by the actor Laurence Olivier that her high-pitched and sharp-toned voice made her sound shrill. She had voice coaching to lower her pitch and slow her delivery so that she sounded weightier.

There's nothing good about shrill. Shrill gets ignored. Shrill gets cut off. Shrill gets perceived as hysterical — a word rooted in 'hysteria,' a condition thought to be caused by the uterus and therefore unique to women. Shrill is the opposite of controlled, poised, and capable. We vote for politicians with lower voices because we associate a deep voice with power, authority and strength. The UK electorate voted for Margaret Thatcher as Prime Minister in 1979 and the rest is history.

Pitch is in the muscles and in the breath. If your voice is too high, practice relaxing your neck and shoulder muscles and breathe. Tension and restricted vocal cords cause the voice to get higher. If your voice is naturally high, correct it with a slower pace, no filler words, and speak very linearly.

2. Slow pace. Often women are criticized for 'talking a mile a minute' — but in reality, we tend to speak more slowly than men. Or at least we do on certain topics, such as money, strategy, and process. That's because when we address serious 'business' topics we hesitate. We slow down and seem to be reticent, indecisive, or even plodding. We betray our cultural lack of a sense of entitlement with our speaking style, and this in turn makes decision makers impatient to hear what we have to say.

Conversely, men confidently and assertively increase their pace of speech on business topics, yet slow down on personal topics. These may seem clichéd generalizations, but they also reflect a culturally ingrained manner that men and women learn at home, in education, and in the workplace.

When we talk about people, emotions, or other topics that are more engaging, women speed up and our pitch rises. When we talk about 'business' topics, we slow down too much and become hesitant and uncertain.

Gravitas comes from a voice that exudes calmness, certainty and authority. This comes from knowing what needs to be said – word for word, if necessary – when it comes to conversations or presentations on business issues.

There's nothing wrong with silence, either. Use pauses strategically. Rushing to respond signals that you're overeager, while pausing before your reply to a question signals that you're thoughtful, self-confident, and makes the other person listen more closely. (Try counting to three before you respond – even if you know the answer!)

3. Increased inflection. This is often referred to as 'prosody.' Men's voices are typically naturally more monotone, while women's voices are more expressive and have a greater range of inflection – we're 'sing-songy.' Men tend to prefer to listen to a monotonic voice; women tend to respond to voices that are expressive. If a man is more emphatic or inflective in his language, he tends to be perceived as more feminine and therefore less powerful.

Flattening tone is important for women when delivering business information, particularly on serious topics like budget cuts, layoffs, and other 'bad news.' In these situations, stay away from the 'top zone' and keep your voice in the middle tone-zone.

This doesn't mean you should be monotone. We convey a lot of the meaning in our conversation through prosody and it's quite hard to listen to someone who has only one note. But if we have repetitive prosody, where we end every sentence on a high note, we go back to the issue of sounding weak and quizzical instead of decisive.

4. Not being heard and understood. Vocally, women have significant obstacles merely in being heard and understood. The first is volume. Greater volume indicates greater passion and emphasis. But speaking softly will also get people to play closer attention in the right context. In speeches, you can usually adjust your volume to be heard. Don't be afraid to speak loudly. In one-to-one conversation, you can also adjust your volume quite easily.

The biggest problems for women come in groups and meetings where most women's voices are softer than the average male, giving men or people with louder voices the opportunity for interruption by literally talking over us. If you're soft-spoken, try some defensive tactics to make sure you're heard, like sit more centrally at meetings (literally making you the center of attention). Rather than wait for a moment to chime in, if you find it challenging to speak up, plan ahead to have your topic included on the formal meeting agenda.

The opposite is the 'loud talker.' Are you a loud talker? If you are on high volume all the time you're imposing your sound on people, which is inconsiderate. Americans are often criticized for speaking too loudly and I actually agree. Living in England for almost a decade has made me more attuned to volume. I can hear an American a mile away on the tube, bus, or even shopping. We speak loudly, and a female voice on level ten is off-putting. Notice your volume and adjust.

Articulation is another key to being understood. Enunciate your words, particularly if you have an accent that your audience isn't used to hearing. As an American living in the UK, I have to constantly adjust my accent to flatten it and adapt so that English people have an easier time understanding me. I say 'mob-isle' instead of 'mob-le' and my cadence mirrors the English accent. In the UK, as in other cultures around the world, accents matter, and while you don't need to have a posh accent, you need to consider the ramifications of your accent with certain audiences and how you can adapt it while maintaining authenticity. You don't need to sound elite, but you shouldn't sound uneducated.

Also make sure you're pronouncing words correctly. I recently attended a workshop where the educator, an expert in using a personality-profiling tool for corporations, repeatedly said 'pacifically' instead of 'specifically.' The first time I thought it was just a flubbed word. The second time I thought maybe it was me. The third time I wrote a note to my colleague that said "Is he saying 'pacifically' instead of 'specifically' or am I nuts?" In this case, it would have been awkward to correct him, but those blind spots are killers. Make sure you're getting the feedback you need to fix these simple mistakes.

5. Overusing vocalizations, fillers and non-words. We all use non-words – those pesky 'ums' and 'uhs' creep into everyone's language from time to time. We tend to 'um' and 'uh' more frequently when we're unprepared or not confident on the topic. As long as it's not invasive or distracting, a normal amount of filler is expected and can be managed by using pauses.

We also all have a 'pet word' that we go to when our brain is processing – 'you know,' 'like,' 'so,' 'actually,' are all examples of common pet words. Finding out your pet word is important as it can quickly go from innocuous to annoying to obstacle. Ask a colleague or friend to listen to you when you speak and point out the words that you tend to use to start sentences or between thoughts. That's your pet word, and your job is to notice it and try to eradicate it completely. It's going to slip in naturally, so if you work to eradicate it completely, you have a chance of mitigating it to reasonable.

Harder to correct are other vocalizations, such as sighs and laughter. We sometimes laugh when we're uncomfortable or caught off guard. While this is an issue for both men and women, for women this tendency brings them closer to the dreaded 'giggle.' Gigglers are around the water cooler, not in the boardroom.

Swearing is another issue. I curse like a Marine, particularly when I play golf. Every year, my resolution is to stop swearing so much. It's my bad habit and I'm aware of it. Women are more likely to be judged negatively for swearing than for not swearing (the 'I need to swear to fit in' defense.) If you're not priggish or judgmental of others who swear, your choice to not use bad language is unlikely to even be noticed. The other benefit is that if you ever do swear, it will be more effective because people will realize you are genuinely angry. One 'f-bomb,' when you've never used it before, will go a long way to make your point.

> **Top Tips:**
>
> 1. Your voicemail greeting is another way of making an impact. Listen to yours. What does it say about you? Practice a greeting that projects the impact you want to make.
> 2. Before you talk to anyone important, try a vocal warm-up recommended by experts: breathe deep, and go through these six sounds: ahhh, ba ba ba, brrrr, la la la, rrrrr, and weee awww.
> 3. Get a vocal coach if you need one. Local acting companies, Toastmasters, or speech therapists (they're not just for kids!) can help you deal with real problems in your speech that may be holding you back.

Understanding Your Unique Speaking Strengths

We all assume that all minds think in the same way. Dawna Markova's research identifies six unique patterns of thinking, each with its own way of learning and communicating. One of the ways Dr. Markova helps people communicate is by understanding how they take in and express auditory information.

So part of how you present yourself verbally is related to how your brain is 'wired.' You may have been told you're a 'visual' learner or an 'auditory' learner – that's only part true, according to Dr. Markova. We all listen and express information verbally; we just approach it in different ways.

First, what do we mean by 'auditory'? Essentially, it's using your ears and your mouth as the telephone of your mind. It's processing sounds and words by listening to conversations, music, stories, sounds and it's expressing yourself through sound and/or words. When it comes time for us to listen or to speak – to engage our auditory channel – our brains respond in a particular way, depending on how we're wired. That auditory channel will either stimulate our conscious mind, subconscious mind, or unconscious mind.

For me, when I'm listening or speaking, my unconscious mind is stimulated. For my eldest son, Connor, auditory stimulates his conscious mind – which is the opposite of how my brain works. My second son, Ryan, is stimulated subconsciously by auditory stimulation. If we don't understand and address these different perspectives, it can easily lead to miscommunication, hurt feelings, and missed opportunities.

In her groundbreaking book *Open Mind,* Dr. Markova breaks it down like this:

Coaches/Communicators. If speaking and listening triggers your conscious – or 'focused' – mind, like Connor, you typically:

- Learn most easily by discussing and listening – so lecture-based classes or meetings are easy for you to follow and stay engaged
- Can immediately access names and what was said – sort of like having a 'court reporter' in your mind
- Speak logically without hesitation over word choice
- Describe abstract ideas using complex language
- Speak constantly and intensely most of the time
- Feel energized and alert by speaking, it revs you up
- Speak naturally and can easily talk to anyone
- Organize yourself by talking about what needs to be done
- Like telling people what to do.

HOW TO GET "IT"

Storytellers. If speaking and listening triggers your subconscious – or 'sorting' – mind, like Ryan, you typically:

- Use talking to help you sort your thoughts
- Like to hear both sides of a story
- Usually like to tell stories and use metaphors to explain things a lot of the time
- Can listen to what people are saying, but also tune into your 'inner voice' or dialogue
- Sometimes hesitate slightly to find the right words
- Can pay attention to the whole conversation but also hear the details.

Connectors. If speaking and listening triggers your unconscious – or 'private' – mind, like me, you typically:

- Don't like to speak about details to groups of people
- May forget names, acronyms, and it can take time to find your words
- Dislike having people talk over you or fill in your words
- Are sensitive to tone of voice and can be offended by sharp words, yelling, loud talking
- Like to zone out to your iPod and find listening to music very relaxing
- Sometimes talk in circles until you find the point
- Often find it easier to walk and talk
- Need silence or a space to find your words.

When I work with a client, male or female, I focus on their verbal patterns to figure out which pattern I believe they use auditorially. While I don't always explain to them how this science works, I do adapt the way I speak and engage with them depending upon how they are 'wired.' I also adapt the specific advice I give them about their speaking or verbal skills to reflect their thinking pattern and also their own personal habits and strengths.

Both men and women need to address their verbal facet, but women face some particular issues. In this section, let's look at three very different women with different thinking patterns, and how I coached them to improve their verbal skills based on Dr. Markova's insights.

Madeleine – the Coach/Communicator

As a senior executive in a telecoms firm, Madeleine hit every conversation head on. I would often find it hard to get a word in edgewise because her verbal style was so aggressive. This meant she was heard in the boardroom – which was an advantage in her company – but it didn't always translate well with staff.

My coaching for Madeleine was that she needed to first be aware that not everyone responded to her direct way of speaking – and that she needed to take more breaks to let others chime in. Sometimes she needed to be silent to be 'mysterious' and then her words would have more weight. If she was talking non-stop, the relentless wave of words turned into sounds that turned into background noise.

She also had to be cautious about interrupting others. Interrupters may feel they are engaging in conversational turn-taking appropriately, but rather than coming across as interested and engaged, Madeleine could be seen as controlling. Madeleine's boss was female and, in general, women tend to respond more negatively to being interrupted than men. Based on Madeleine's descriptions, it also seemed that her boss was more sensitive to auditory stimuli and likely more prone to be offended or put off by Madeleine's verbal style, so I coached Madeleine to be aware of interrupting her and look for nonverbal clues that signaled when she was coming across too strong.

With her staff, I encouraged her to make sure she used visuals when she gave feedback or guidance, to recognize that not everyone responds to verbal stimuli as effectively.

I helped her recognize when she was turning others off by talking too much or too aggressively. I encouraged her to force herself to ask questions and listen to answers – being quiet didn't come naturally, but by consuming most of the air in the room, she was denying the ability for others to ignite and ideas to grow.

Her advantage was that she had a great memory for what was said and a quick recall of facts and information that she could use in meetings. She was also great at giving formal speeches and presentations – that was her power zone. As long as she remembered to not talk over others during the Q&A portion – to be a good listener – she was dynamite in front of an audience.

Sarah – the Storyteller

Sarah was an executive at an insurance company and a member of several non-profit boards. Her auditory style meant that she was in a sorting, somewhat 'neutral' mode auditorially. These are the easiest clients to coach when it comes to verbal ability because they are typically middle of the road – good speakers, good listeners. With Sarah, she was a good natural storyteller, which made her very human and likeable. She could naturally sense when someone needed to speak and was good at slowing down her own verbal pace to let him or her find the right words.

The main area for Sarah to work on was her tendency to ramble when telling a story. Sometimes she'd get 'in the flow' and not realize that her audience had checked out and was seeing her as long-winded. Once she realized that was an issue, she was easily able to recognize signals and adapt and remind herself to get to the point. It was helpful for her to have notes before going into a presentation so she'd be sure to stay on topic and to refer to if she needed to be reminded of facts or data.

Another issue Sarah had was that her stories could sometimes veer into describing others in less than flattering terms. This is a tricky area because of what psychologists call 'trait transfer' – where what you say about someone else tends to bounce back and reflect on you. So when Sarah would tell stories about her couch-potato son and his junk food habit, or her former boss who would skive off work every Friday, it could actually reflect that *she* was lazy to the listener. I coached Sarah to try and tell stories about positive traits in others as much as possible. So when she told stories about her last boss who was a great leader and attentive to detail, *she* was seen as leaderly and attentive.

Courtney – the Connector

A news presenter, Courtney had a job where verbal impact was everything. Her voice and her way of speaking were very important to how she presented herself. It's interesting to find people who are stimulated unconsciously – or are quite sensitive to verbal stimuli – who are in jobs where they are effectively on stage all the time.

For Courtney, the issue wasn't when she was delivering the news. In those situations it played to her strengths because the script was already written and she just needed to read and deliver, managing her voice. The issues came when she had to speak off the cuff or in meetings, where she found it very difficult to speak up and would often gear herself up to speak, just at the moment when the conversation turned to the next topic and the opportunity was lost. Then she'd feel offended by a colleague's cutting her off and take it personally.

She was a concise speaker who needed that space to find her words. Unfortunately, others who are more verbally aggressive tend to consume the time and so Courtney had to force herself to 'push in' and be heard. As women rise up the ranks, the group will naturally defer and give her space and time to weigh in. However, until you're at the point where your approval is required, you have to force your way into the conversation.

HOW TO GET "IT"

My steer for Courtney was to prepare for a meeting just like she would an interview – with objectives and specific questions written down. We set a goal that for topics where she wanted to be heard, she would force herself to be the third person to speak – not too early out of the gate but still allowing time to speak and be heard – even if she had to interrupt someone else.

I also encouraged her to use email or 'walk and talk' to have tough conversations when necessary, and to avoid having sensitive conversations via conference call where she only had tone of voice and no visual information to help balance the conversation.

CHAPTER 10

Authentic Speaking Skills

In each of the five facets, authenticity is fundamental. Fake doesn't work anymore. Over processed is a turn-off. So you would think that we are getting better at balancing being polished with being our authentic selves. Or are we?

As part of a question and answer portion of the 2007 Miss Teen USA pageant, Lauren Upton from South Carolina was asked: "Recent polls have shown a fifth of Americans can't locate the U.S. on a world map. Why do you think this is?"

In a lovely southern drawl, Upton responded: "I personally believe that U.S. Americans are unable to do so because, uh, some, uh, people out there in our nation don't have maps and, uh, I believe that our education like such as in South Africa and, uh, the Iraq, everywhere like such as, and, I believe that they should, our education over here in the U.S. should help the U.S., uh, or, uh, should help South Africa and should help the Iraq and the Asian countries, so we will be able to build up our future [for our children]."

Clearly not her shining moment and it's understandable that her nerves got the best of her. Unfortunately, in this networked, cammed-up world our mistakes live forever.

Within hours Upton's quote went viral and became YouTube's most viewed video for the month, ultimately logging over 78 million views and spawning countless parodies. Upton was also the dubious winner of the 'stupidest statement of the year' but interestingly was also classed as the second most memorable quote of the year by the Yale Book of Quotations. Though she later went on the *Today* show and gave a better response, she will always be known as the "uh, the Iraq" teen beauty queen.

What can you learn from a southern beauty queen? The camera is always on. When we talk about authenticity, it doesn't mean you can check your brain at the door. She was authentic, to be sure, but she was unprepared and her flub was immortalized.

Being Assertive: Show Your Teeth but Never Growl

Speaking out is an important part of being seen to be leaderly. There are times when you have to be direct, blunt or aggressive to make a point. The key is to moderate your verbal impact so you don't come across as over the top and veer, once again, into 'shrill' territory.

In her book, *I Thought It Was Just Me,* researcher Dr. Brené Brown talks about the challenges of speaking out for women. There are so many mixed messages and expectations when it comes to being strong vocally, it's no wonder we get confused.

Being authentic, according to Brown, is to be natural, sincere, spontaneous, open and genuine. Yet when she explains the narrow band of expectations of women through which we need to filter what we say and how we say it, the act of being authentic seems daunting.

Brown's research has found that professional, authentic women in our culture are expected to fit in a bandwidth all the time, characterized by ten factors:

1. Don't make people feel uncomfortable, but be honest
2. Don't sound self-righteous, but sound confident

HOW TO GET "IT"

3. Don't upset anyone or hurt anyone's feelings, but say what's on your mind
4. Don't be offensive, but be straightforward
5. Sound informed and educated, but not like a know-it-all
6. Sound committed, but not too reactionary
7. Don't say anything unpopular or controversial, but have the courage to disagree with the crowd
8. Don't seem too passionate, but don't come off as too dispassionate
9. Don't get too emotional, but don't be too detached
10. You don't have to quote facts and figures, but don't be wrong

I've worked with female politicians at all levels – local, state and national, and staying in this range is a nearly absurd challenge! Walking this tightrope every day is tiring, but the first step is to even acknowledge that it's there.

After you distinguish that this reality exists, you can figure out how to position yourself. You don't need to be in the middle all the time – in fact, you shouldn't or you'll be seen as pandering and insincere. But you do need to be aware when you're reaching an edge and stop, read your audience, and then decide how best to get your point across.

Karen, a politician running for a gubernatorial election, had a series of debates with her opponent – a traditional, conservative white male. His strength was in his data, not in his heart. So our strategy was for her speeches to fit right in the sweet spot of these ten verbal factors to maximize her authenticity, and therefore her likeability, trustworthiness, and competence.

For Karen, speaking and listening stimulated her 'sorting' mind – so it was relatively easy to coach her to use storytelling as long as she stayed focused. There were, however, five weaknesses that we had to mitigate for her to succeed:

1. Filling the void. Silence isn't a bad thing. She needed to let pauses and silences run their course instead of rushing in to fill gaps in her opponent's speaking. That also lent more weight to her own words.

2. Over explaining. It's good to be comprehensive, but people also want to know just enough detail. She had a tendency to get into the minutiae on topics where she was particularly knowledgeable and passionate. Recognizing when people were tuning out and cutting herself off required discipline.

3. Staying on point. As she would find connections between topics, she could interrupt herself and go on tangents. This jumping from topic to topic meant that she never seemed to get to the point and the connections she was making in her mind weren't obvious to the listener. They couldn't catch up or understand where she was going. So she needed to resist that urge and stick to the point. I encouraged her to keep a pen and paper at the podium so she could make one-word notes for points she wanted to raise later on, as some of the basis for topic-hopping was that she was afraid she'd forget the point that she wanted to make.

4. Conveying warmth. Karen had a smooth, warm voice when she talked slowly. When she started to speak too fast, the timbre was compromised and she wasn't as effective. We worked with breathing, posture and vocal exercises to manage the timbre of her voice.

5. 'Bitchy' is a fine line. We've established that women are held to a different standard in what we say and how we say it. A man can say something and be seen as 'tough' where a woman making the same point is seen as 'bitchy.' For Karen, the cardinal rules were to never say anything that smacked of gossip, judgment, complaining, excuses, or exaggeration. She needed to make sure her content was meaningful, coherent, succinct and above all, polite.

Prepare, Prepare, Prepare

The key to presenting yourself well in the Verbal Facet is to always be prepared. I advise every client to know what you want to say and have notes. Given Dr. Brené Brown's points above, as a woman you also need to be more prepared than the men in the room, so be three questions deep. In every aspect, think of three layers of questions that might be asked and make sure you have the answers so you're never caught flat-footed. If you are caught out, don't pretend. Say you don't know, you'll find out, then follow up and try not to put yourself in that situation again.

Listen, Listen, Listen

I have become an observer of listening, and I'm always stunned at just how little of it actually occurs. For all the focus on speaking, there's very little on listening. Yet every message needs a receiver.

Do you really listen? Or do you pause in your speaking to think about what you're going to say next when the other person stops talking?

How do you feel when you're actually listened to? Important. Special. Acknowledged. Yet, how frequently do we try to impress others by speaking and pushing *at* them instead of using the power of listening to achieve the same thing?

Notice your own listening and commit to improve.

Strategic Use of Small Talk

Women are at a huge deficit with small talk because men are not usually completely relaxed when chit-chatting with women, largely because they may be filtering their conversation to be 'politically correct.' While this is necessary (and a good thing, really, because I have no interest in locker room talk) it also puts us at a disadvantage because any casual conversation is approached from a position of wariness at best, defensiveness or hostility at worst. Connection in small talk with most senior men requires strategy and finesse for women.

Unable to rely on locker room talk, the next realm of small talk is hobbies and interests – which can be sports, politics, or gossip. This puts women at another disadvantage, especially if we don't share the same interests as men in leadership positions because we have nothing to contribute; and when the conversation turns to gossip, a man is perceived to be strategic where a woman is bitchy.

You're not going to engage in locker room talk, so you need to have something else to talk about. So be able to banter and know the culture. What are leaders talking about? What does your boss talk about with his 'rising star' juniors between meetings or in cocktail party situations? What shows do they watch, what sports do they follow, what politics do they track? Make it a point to know what's going on. This gives you confidence to insert or at least nod appropriately in conversations, and positions you for important bonding.

Why does small talk matter? Because it's a way of engendering trust. If someone understands or cares about the same things you do, you trust them more than someone who is an 'outsider.' It's a short code for 'we're on the same page.'

When it comes time to deciding who gets promoted and who doesn't, trust is a key factor. You need to be visible and contributing to be seen to be fitting in. and so more likely to get the nod for promotion. That means knowing how to engage in appropriate small talk.

CHAPTER 11

Creating Aligned Messaging

To turn the phrase on its head, it's not just how you say it, but what you say. So if you have a great speaking voice, and know how to manage your verbal skills, you still need solid content. This is something every executive, male or female, should do naturally, but shockingly few actually do.

The Triple Filters Test

I had a boss early in my career, Doug, who was just a great guy and one of the best bosses I've ever had. When I was a new parent, Doug told me how he managed bickering among his five children. If someone has a way to manage five kids, you listen! He said that every time his children came to him to tattle or 'tell,' he would stop them and ask: "Is it true, is it necessary, is it kind? If not, go back outside and play."

As my own sons grew, I found myself also using this test – and it worked like a charm. Ninety percent of their 'But Mom!' conversations went out the door. (Another test Doug told me that I have found incredibly useful in cutting off whining and the certainty of absolute disaster was the three Bs: "Is it broken? Are you bleeding? Are you breathing? ... Then shake it off and go back outside and play." But I digress...)

Later on, I heard someone talk about what I recognized as 'Doug's Test' as a common knowledge story called 'The Triple Filters Test.' Sometimes it involves Socrates and other times it involves an Arab scholar, but the truth of the story is the same.

In a nutshell: In ancient Greece, Socrates was reputed to hold knowledge in high esteem.

One day someone came to the great philosopher and said, "Hey, guess what I just heard about this other guy we both know?"

"Hang on a second," Socrates replied. "Before telling me anything, I'd like you to pass a little test."

"A test?"

"Yep," Socrates continued. "Before you tell me what you think I need to know about my friend, there are three filters. The first filter is TRUTH. Do you know what you're going to say is true?"

"No," the man said, "I mean, it probably is but actually I just heard about it and…"

"So you don't really know if it's true or not," said Socrates. "So, now let's try the second filter, GOODNESS. Is this something you'd qualify as 'good'?"

"Well, ummm, on the contrary, no, it's not good at all, which I why I really need to tell you…"

"So," Socrates interrupted, "you want to tell me something bad about my friend, but you're not certain it's true. I may still want to hear this, because there's one filter left: USEFULNESS. Is what you want to tell me about this man going to be useful to me?"

"I don't know. Maybe."

"Okay," concluded Socrates, "if what you want to tell me is neither true nor good and we don't know if it's even useful, why tell it to me at all?"

At the surface, we can see this is a story about filtering the information we spread, but at a deeper level it's also about the information we seek and create. Imagine how different the world would be if we only chose to seek or create information that was true, good, or useful?

Before you say anything, and before you prod the machine to generate information, make sure it passes the Doug Test.

Developing a Narrative

I specialize in change communications – helping present messages to stakeholders to get them to know, feel and do what we want them to know, feel and do on a topic or during a time of transition. One of the tools I use is a 'message house' – it's a common way of structuring messaging in a logical format so that they key points stand out and are supported by specific detail.

It's the same format I learned in high school when I was taught how to write an essay: thesis statement, topic sentences, supporting detail. Same format for structuring a debate: hypothesis, argument, proof.

So, right now, make a message house for yourself. If you were the product, the thing to sell, what would your platform be? Here are questions to ask yourself, and the answers I have for my own message house as an example.

1. The Roof: What is your umbrella message – your overarching headline, purpose, and mission? *I'm an expert in executive presence and passionate about helping women succeed.*

2. Supporting pillars: What are your top three 'pillars' that demonstrate you are well rounded and serious? What do people need to know? *I have twenty years experience working in large companies; I combine leading research with practical application; I get results.*

3. Foundation: What is the underpinning evidence, proof points, support, stories, etc that prop up your pillars? *I have a list of clients from blue chip to start up that is pretty darn impressive; I've worked with really smart people and learned a lot that I bring to the table; I have my wonderful clients whom I've helped and seen succeed.*

That's it. It's not complicated. But you need to sit down and make the case. Prove how you are unique and line up your message.

Storytelling and Your Corporate Myth

In his book *The Language of Leaders,* Kevin Murray, who I count as a friend and one of my most influential mentors, talks about the power of stories for leaders:

> "Stories are the superglue of messages. Great stories have legs and travel far, define you or your organization. Every leader uses stories. We are wired to listen imaginatively. Backed up by facts, stories touch, move and inspire. Let people conclude their own message or lesson – that makes it more powerful."

The stories you tell are the stories people will tell about you. And these stories become myth and part of your legend.

When I was in high school, at around age 17, I worked at Nordstrom, a posh department store with a reputation for stellar customer service. I didn't recognize it at the time because most of my brain at that age was consumed with boys and clothes, but Nordstrom was brilliant at corporate mythology. I remember at my induction training being told a story about a customer who returned a car tire to the store for a refund, and was given the refund in cash by a young sales associate. Nordstrom doesn't sell tires or any automotive supplies. They sell clothes, cosmetics, and accessories. Now, the expected punchline is that the salesperson got in trouble or sacked. Far from it. The story is used as an example of 'what's right' and the salesperson was lauded and promoted.

Why would a retailer want to tell young associates that it's okay to give back money for a product we clearly didn't sell? Because it was a parable – 'the customer is always right' taken to a new level. During peak sale seasons, we were given buttons that said "No Problem" – the definitive script for any situation.

What is your mythology? What stories do you tell? What do they say about you?

I worked with Charlotte, who was a woman on the rise in a manufacturing company. When I did 360 reviews with her colleagues, one of the examples that came up again and again was that she once shut down a production line because she saw a safety issue that a subcontractor refused to address. It was a bold move that was risky, but paid off. It showed that she cared about the safety of people, that she wasn't afraid to make the hard calls, and that she was not to be diminished. When I asked her about the anecdote, she said that she was worried about it at the time, but that it seemed the right thing to do.

How did she move it from an occurrence to a myth? By not bragging about it herself, but by making sure that others knew because they were told. It has to be discovered and shared on its own, not something you propagate yourself. It was also bold and big. Highly visible, the rumor mill took it up quickly and spread it around. Suddenly, she was tough and not to be messed with – good traits for a leader.

The 'Storytelling' Warning

Now let me share an example of a bad storytelling episode I witnessed not too long ago. I was giving a presentation on communication skills to a team of around 15 senior leaders, 14 men and one woman, who worked together. The boss was there along with his top direct reports. As part of the training, we talk about how to engage audiences. A participant raised his hand and asked about how we need to adapt communication to connect with the up-and-coming generation, given that they are used to being connected to devices and have different standards of propriety (e.g. – they don't think it's rude to ignore you in favor of their iPhone).

I answered the question and then we went to a break. At the break, the man came up to me to further inquire and the conversation led to chat about the very popular game 'Candy Crush' that started out as a game played by teenage girls and has now spread virally across the universe, including to my 18-year-old son, who I think is addicted to this game which I find silly. I am, however, impressed by how the game developers have made it engaging by using time-based reinforcing tactics to get more lives and linking it with social media to encourage spread.

As we started the workshop after the break, the participants were assembling and getting settled. The boss was sitting down and asked about Candy Crush. I briefly explained that it was a very popular game and a good model of addictive gaming with the time constraint, and that I was glad of the time constraint because it meant my son had to stop playing for a while when he ran out of lives. I could then push him to go do something productive.

At this point, the woman participant – remember, she's the only woman in the room and on the leadership team – decided to share with the group that she plays Candy Crush – a lot. She then went into great detail about how my son could get around the time constraint in the game by resetting the clock on his phone. She went on and on, ignoring my cues to redirect her and the group. By now, her boss and colleagues were looking at her like she had three heads. It was verbal purging of the worst kind – admitting not only to playing a game called Candy Crush, but also to playing it enough to learn how to cheat at it, and confessing to cheating at a virtual game.

When it comes time to decide who gets promoted to the next chair vacated, what does her boss know about her now? That she is trivial and she cheats. And what story do her colleagues have to share about her? She is now the Candy Crush Girl. Is that the mythology you want?

Humor: Use with Caution

Humor is important for creating common ground. Integrating humor into your speech makes you more likable and helps others relate and connect to you.

The best type of humor self-effacing; showing that you can laugh at yourself not only conveys that you don't take yourself too seriously, it also demonstrates confidence.

There is a line between having a sense of humor and being a 'joke teller.' Men tend to fall into this trap more frequently than women – we all know 'that guy' who tells joke after joke as if he were auditioning for a comedy club slot. In particular, telling a racial or off-color joke shows poor judgment, yet I'm always surprised at how often it occurs. If in doubt, don't say it.

If you're in a group where someone is telling a questionable joke, excuse yourself discreetly. If it's your boss telling the joke, you don't want to alienate him (or her). If he's prone to this type of humor, you may want to 'take a call' when he starts winding up for the story so that you're not culpable when he eventually gets called in by HR or sued. If you can't escape gracefully, give a noncommittal half smile and redirect the conversation to safer waters without being a killjoy.

I personally am terrible at telling jokes, but I do employ humor in my speeches and conversations. I steer away from sarcasm because it can easily be misinterpreted. The other problem with humor is everyone thinks they're funny and we all have our own unique humor. British humor is very different from American humor. The French think they're funny, but it honestly escapes me. So tread lightly with humor and stick to 'safe,' lighthearted banter.

CHAPTER 12

"Leaderly" Communications

From the day you interview for first job, you need to speak like a leader. Leaders don't talk about trivia; they talk about things that are important.

Paige, a VP at a large company, is always getting mired in the trivia. Rather than expecting her team to step up and deliver, her conversations tend to devolve to gossip, judgment, and complaining.

How do leaders talk?

1. Leaders don't speak ill of people who aren't present. This is how they ensure others confide in them.
2. Leaders don't judge. They are Switzerland and neutral in the moment.
3. Leaders never explain or make excuses. They take responsibility.
4. Leaders never complain. They aren't negative – nor are they sunshine, light and roses – they are level.
5. Leaders rarely say 'but' because they know that word negates their previous position.
6. Leaders don't lie. They don't exaggerate or embroider.
7. Leaders give facts, not opinions. If they give their opinion, they express that this is their opinion. Then, facts have weight and opinions matter.

8. Leaders have integrity because they give their word thoughtfully and they always keep their word. If they can't keep their word, they acknowledge it and do what it takes to make it right.

How to Have Difficult Conversations

Leaders have to have hard conversations: firing people, sharing bad results, giving performance corrections.

Before you go into a conversation that you know will be challenging, follow these three steps:

1. Ask yourself: what do I want this person (or group) to know, feel and do?
2. Consider the environment and how the person receives auditory information. Should you walk and talk or use a visual so that you don't overwhelm with words?
3. Are you speaking the emotional truth? This is the most powerful position you can come from – what is absolutely true for you in this moment? You can never go wrong if you speak the emotional truth.

Using the Language of Power

Leaders speak powerfully. To do this, you need to know what type of conversation you're having and what conversation you want to have. There are three basic types of 'languages': explanation, possibility and action. Look to sports as a good metaphor for how we use these types of languages.

1. When we're 'explaining' we're talking from the stands. We talk about 'they' or 'you.' We say 'I think…' or 'it should…' but it's still explaining what's happening from a distance.

HOW TO GET "IT"

2. When we're using the language of 'possibility' you're talking as a coach. You're saying 'we can…' 'let's try…' or 'how about…' You're not touching the ball, but you're influencing and directing.

3. The third language, action, is hands-on and challenging. In the language of action we put ourselves on the field by saying 'I will…,' 'I need…,' and 'I can…' We're moving the ball forward in the language of action and in control.

To get to the language of action, we have to get people to commit. People commit through making requests, offers and promises. I had a boss that used to say he wasn't doing his job if he wasn't making 10 unreasonable requests every day. What requests do you make?

Paige doesn't make requests – she lets people off the hook by making excuses and not holding them accountable. Then she complains that nothing gets done. So, let's deconstruct a simple example. Paige needs to send a report to her boss by the end of the week. She mentions in her Monday morning staff meeting that this needs to be completed and she needs everyone's input. She doesn't actually make a request or get others to make offers or promises, however. So, on Friday at 4 p.m., she's scrambling, sending nasty emails, and generally being unpleasant. Her staff dislike her, the report is late and disorganized, and it happens again and again. Everyone is having conversations from the stands and the ball is on the field, dead.

What should she do differently? It's actually shockingly simple: make a real request and hold people accountable. In the staff meeting she should say: 'I need your three highlights for the quarter emailed to me in a one-pager by Wednesday at noon. Can you all do that?'

The 'Can you do that?' is key because if you don't give people the opportunity to say 'No' they cannot say a powerful 'Yes.' If people say 'Yes,' then they're on the hook. If they say 'No,' you have the option to renegotiate (I can do it by Thursday morning) or commit to commit (I don't know if I can do that by Wednesday, but I'll let you know by the end of the day).

Now, her team has made a promise. It's up to Paige to hold them to it. If they don't deliver the goods on Wednesday at noon, she needs to ask them why. If she is inconsistent, they won't take her seriously and her word means nothing.

Knowing your 'word' and keeping your word is critical. Paige has given her word, implied by not disagreeing with her boss, that she will have the report by Friday close of business. It's increasingly rare to find people who keep their word and it separates the real leaders from the pack.

We seem to have a formula of 'Teflon speak' where the word never sticks. Somehow we have come to allow that making a promise by giving our word, then breaking the word with a good excuse is as good as having honored the original commitment.

Real leaders don't do this. They make promises they can keep, and then they keep them. This demonstrates commitment, builds trust, and helps you climb the ladder to the corner office one solid rung at a time.

Putting It into Practice: Sound Like a Leader

Sometimes just acknowledging an issue is enough to fix it. When it comes to your verbal presence, what's distinctive for you now, that you didn't see before? What will you do to fix it and improve?

Make a plan to refine your verbal presence by asking yourself:

1. What is your strength in this facet? Where you feel most confident, authentic, energized?
2. When have you been 'spot on' verbally – what did it feel like, sound like?
3. When have you struggled to shine in this area – what would you do differently with what you know now?

HOW TO GET "IT"

4. What opportunities are coming up for you where you can practice 'polishing' your verbal facet? What will your action plan be to project your best self in this facet?

5. How will you measure your progress and get feedback on your verbal abilities? Who can you ask or how can you get validation that you're on track?

Your Verbal Facet is an essential part of how you present yourself effectively and persuasively in a business environment. But it's only one aspect of the diamond that you're polishing. Each section in this book covers a different facet of how you present yourself as a woman in business. Investing in your verbal presentation — to sound like a leader — is just one facet that needs to be polished. The other sections in the book cover each facet in more detail, helping you refine and present your best self from every angle.

CHAPTER 13

Polishing Your Kinesthetic Facet to Embody the Part

'Body language.'

'Energy.'

'Nonverbals.'

These amorphous words are frequently bandied about and rarely defined or understood, yet they are key in tackling the third Facet of Executive Presence: Kinesthetic.

For women in business, the Kinesthetic Facet is crucial in projecting a competent, dynamic, appealing executive presence. In this section, we'll explore your Kinesthetic Facet and how you can become aware of your presence on both a macro and micro level – and refine this facet to become a strategic advantage for you.

Understanding 'kinesthetic,' which is defined as learning or activity that relates feeling such as a sense of body position, muscle movement and weight as felt through nerve endings, became a big landmark for me in my study of personal presence and leadership. In the definition I use for my work, kinesthetic goes beyond body position or body language to encompass how we present ourselves 'energetically' – even to include smell as a means of communication. (And as someone who regularly travels on London public transport, I can assure you that smell is a very powerful communicative device!)

The simple things we do day to day, how we stand, how we sit, how we hold our bodies, can change our physiology. This facet is always influencing how others perceive you, but more importantly, it changes how YOU feel about yourself.

I've found it is most useful to look at the Kinesthetic Facet from both a micro and macro perspective:

- <u>Micro</u> to consider the more subtle details and nuances of how a woman projects herself (e.g., body language, posture and gestures)
- <u>Macro</u> to consider a woman's overall energy (is she 'buzzy,' 'draining,' 'distracted'?)

Thinking about this facet is like exercising a muscle that you didn't know you had. To do it properly requires precision and the ability to control the details (micro) without losing sight of the whole (macro).

I've started taking a Pilates class at my local gym in an effort to improve my flexibility and core strength. After the first class, intrigued by the precision of Pilates, I booked the instructor, Kristina, to give me a series of one-to-one courses so I could better focus on my weak areas.

When we're training, Kristina has me focus on very specific muscles and use my brain to think about the different muscles activating or switching off, all the while maintaining complete control. For me, it's as much mental as is it physical and my brain works overtime thinking about what to do and how to do it.

Why am I talking about Pilates? Because I find I use the same type of thinking when I think about the Kinesthetic Facet. I strive to be in complete control of the dynamic with the individual, group or audience and pay attention to what I want to switch on and off, making adjustments to stay in tune with them – just as I focus on certain muscles in Pilates and continually adjust to work the right areas.

Kinesthetic Facet: Micro Perspective

So let's start with what most people mean when they talk about 'nonverbals' – body language. The majority of people in professional circles are comfortable talking about body language because it's considered a common negotiating tactic and a key part of basic presentation skills. When I explain my field of expertise to people for the first time, they'll often say "Oh, I went to a course on that!" and it was something to do with body language. Because of this common baseline of understanding, starting with the 'micro' elements of how to stand, sit, mirror, etc., is usually easy with my clients.

In this section, I'll dive into what I've found are the most useful Micro tips and suggestions to refine your body language, gestures and other details. There is a wealth of work on this topic readily available if you want to explore it further for negotiating, sales and similar situations.

Kinesthetic Facet: Macro Perspective

Where it gets a little more nebulous – or 'airy fairy' as some might say – is in the 'macro' aspect of the Kinesthetic Facet, where we start talking about things like 'energy' and the ability to 'captivate a room.' This is an area that is really not understood and I find a dearth of material on how to manage or understand it.

Being an American living and working in England, I've learned not to toss around the word 'energy' or eyebrows will be raised. In the States, it's still a little strange for some to talk about this area of presenting oneself, and in the UK it's akin to talking about the pending zombie apocalypse.

While it may be awkward or uncomfortable for some, this is still an essential element to understand in one's personal executive presence, and to ignore it simply because it is nebulous and verging on 'mysticism' doesn't help anyone. The reality is, we do bring an energy to a room or conversation, and if you want to rise in the ranks, you must consider this as a relevant topic to understand and manage.

In this section, I treat the micro and macro sides of the Kinesthetic Facet as two halves of a single organism – each side affects the other. To really get it, you need to shift your way of thinking to consider very tangible and understandable elements (micro) and then expand to factor in the more ambiguous components (macro). This may feel a bit strange at first, but stick with me and by the end of the section you'll have a new way of thinking about how you show up as a leader that will set you apart from the pack.

Why This Matters: The Nonverbals Say It All

Understanding nonverbals (any way of communicating without our voice and words) is key for all leaders, particularly for women, according to the Center for Talent Innovation. In their groundbreaking study on Executive Presence, CTI found that the top six communication skills for women at director level or above were:

1. Great speaking skills (60%)
2. Ability to command a room (49%)
3. Assertiveness (48%)
4. Emotional quotient, or reading the audience (39%)
5. Sense of humor (33%)
6. Posture/body language (21%)

Of the top six, three of them – commanding a room, reading the audience and posture/body language – are components of the Kinesthetic Facet and are interrelated.

HOW TO GET "IT"

The first time I heard the word 'kinesthetic,' it was working with Dr. Dawna Markova. Dawna's breakthrough work gave a new framework to understanding how we receive and express information through our senses.

According to Dawna in her book *The Open Mind*, thinking kinesthetically means functioning receptively and expressively through hands, skin and muscles. Experiences are collected through multiple receptors, including feelings, movements, actions, touch, texture, temperature, pressure, spatial awareness, smell, taste and sensitivity to energy. We express ourselves kinesthetically by doing, making, building, driving, touching, moving and participating.

We all react to kinesthetic connectivity differently. Some people are huggers, others aren't. There is no right or wrong, we're just wired the way that we are wired. Kinesthetically sensitive people need more space between themselves whereas people who are less sensitive are comfortable being quite close, even with relative strangers. You also see a difference in stillness. Some people are perpetually in motion, while others have pent-up energy right below the surface, and some are mostly quite still.

Exercise is a positive outlet for energy, and we all find different ways of engaging with physical sport or activity that has to do with our kinesthetic 'wiring.' Some are natural athletes who learn sports easily while others take longer to learn and may find physical activities frustrating and awkward.

I enjoy physical activities that are free form and non-competitive, while others like to use sports as a social networking activity or prefer competitive, organized sports. When I'm at the gym or in a class, I tend to keep to myself and focus while others find it a natural environment to interact and make contacts.

Touch is another kinesthetic trigger point that can be based on your thinking pattern or your culture. Many people are very shy about touch and private about feelings whereas others like to touch and be touched and are quite open in sharing their feelings.

Touch, even by a stranger, can have a powerful impact. In general, when a stranger touches you lightly it has a positive effect on your feeling for that person. In one study, male and female librarians were asked to touch some borrowers for a half second when returning their library cards. Those who were touched responded that they liked the library better than those who weren't – and were also in a better mood.

Research also shows that touch is important for women. When a woman touches a man or woman on the arm it forms a connection and has the single most meaningful impact on being perceived as friendly and likeable, even more than smiling.

Being Aware of Your Kinesthetic Presence

Considering how important kinesthetic presence is to a woman's success, it's surprising how unaware many senior women can be when it comes to their own body language and the impressions they make on others.

At one point in my career I was working at an FTSE 100 company, supporting quite senior executives as a communications adviser. A new female executive, Ceri, was hired from outside the company and had already made a strong name for herself in business through some high-profile connections. Still relatively new to living and working in the UK, I was an American who at that point believed that the British upper classes must be sophisticated and classy and I fully expected this woman to be elegant and something like Princess Diana in a business suit.

So I was stunned when, at our first meeting in her office, sitting in the little coffee table area, she proceeded to fold her leg up onto her sofa, take off her shoe, and start picking at the dead skin on the heel of her foot. Gross. Just gross.

I tried to keep track of the conversation, but all I could see were the dead hunks of skin that she was picking off her foot and flicking onto the carpet. Now, there's a major etiquette issue here – which we can address in the

HOW TO GET "IT"

next section about the Sociability Facet – but I'd like to think about this kinesthetically.

First, my advice as an expert is to never ever ever do that. She conveyed a nonchalance with this absurd body language and action that was disrespectful and downright strange.

I remember being told early on by a great boss that even if I was completely bored in a meeting, I was to always 'sit up straight, pulled up to the table, taking notes and giving the impression that you're listening and you care.' Given that a fair amount of my career has been spent in very technical meetings across all manner of industries where my expertise is needed at the beginning for context and at the end to communicate decisions, it's not always easy to stay engaged and connected on topic. But I do try and recommit to bring my attention and if nothing else, show respect to the engineer, scientist or strategist who put in the effort to prepare for the meeting. One of the most important ways to show respect is through kinesthetic energy and body language.

This really does matter for women. According to CTI, women's executive presence is more susceptible to being damaged by inadvertent body language errors, especially when it's about diminishing or minimizing her stature.

"Executive presence is about perception, not performance," write the study authors. "That is why how you sit, how you stand, and what you choose to do with your hands prompts others to assume your potential regardless of whether or not your body language is an accurate representation of your leadership prowess."

After the impromptu 'self pedicure' moment, I wondered if Ceri even realized what she was doing. I can't imagine someone deliberately deciding to pick their feet in front of another person in a professional setting in the Western world. More likely, she was simply focused on other things and somewhere her brain logged 'there's a patch of dead skin on my foot' and then she just did it without thinking.

We all have things in our blind spots that need to be recognized and dealt with. The blind spot lack of awareness is the reason we absentmindedly rock back and forth during presentations, click pens annoyingly during meetings, or chew on our fingernails without thinking. These ingrained, subconscious behaviors are actually bad habits that linger in our blind spots. The best way to eradicate them is to create awareness – either by self-monitoring or getting an outside source to tell you what your subconscious 'tics' are – and then conscientiously eliminate them.

Kinesthetic issues to look for in your blind spot and make sure you're not doing them subconsciously:

- Hair twisting or playing
- Touching your face (especially nose!)
- Wiggling
- Foot jiggles
- Scratching
- Lip licking or biting
- Picking at skin (dry, scabbed, etc.)
- Adjusting clothes – bra straps, underwear

Questions to ask yourself:

1. Are you aware of your 'energy'?
2. Do you know how to control your energy?
3. Do you take responsibility for your energy?
4. Are you aware of your nonverbals?
5. How will you reveal your 'blind spots' to yourself?

CHAPTER 14

The Three S's Every Woman on the Rise Must Master: Standing, Sitting, Shaking

I thought I knew how to drive until I moved to England. I got my driver's license in the States when I was 16 years old and would drive an average of 100 miles a day when I commuted. So imagine my surprise when I got behind the wheel on the right side of the car and realized that I could not physically manage shifting the gears with my left hand and drive on the wrong side of the road. An automated task suddenly became a huge challenge.

In the course of regular business, what do most of us do? We stand, we sit, we shake hands. It seems basic, but these three building blocks of kinesthetic communication are critical to get right. You may think you know what you're doing, but it's possible that you've just been driving on the 'right' side of the road for so long that you're unaware of bad habits. Let's take a dive into the three S's and start driving in the executive track.

The Simple Act of Sitting

Whether you're sitting behind a table/desk or in a chair with your legs exposed, the guidelines are the same:

- Sit up straight and tall. Particularly if you're behind a table or desk, you only have your upper body to convey all of your body language – so don't waste it by slumping or caving in.
- Avoid 'shrinking.' We'll talk about this more later, but make sure you own your space.
- Don't block your face with your hands.
- Don't pick, twist, fidget. This includes making toys out of things on the table like paperclips, tiny pieces of paper, or pens.
- Keep your feet solid and on the ground, even at a table. Don't tip the chair, don't twine your feet in the chair legs or another chair.

If you don't have a table in front of you, you should convey attentiveness by sitting up and forward (no slouching) with your chin up but not too far. Arms should be on the armrests to own your space. Keep the tips of your fingers together, in your lap and pointing forward – not up or down.

When sitting, particularly without a desk to conceal your legs, be sure to pay attention to your skirt and how much thigh it's revealing. If you find that it's too short, which can sometimes happen at the least opportune times, sit slightly to the front edge of the chair with tall posture, and cross your legs at the ankle and slightly to the side and under your chair to minimize focus on the thigh. Put a notebook or your hands on your lap to cover where your undies might accidentally be visible to someone sitting directly across from you. To avoid looking tense and 'perched,' try not to fidget and keep your shoulders as relaxed as possible.

A Menu of Handshakes

A handshake is a common ritual in business. While sociability is also a component in handshaking (a handshake may not be the appropriate form of greeting in some cultures, which I discuss more in the Sociability Facet section) it is the ultimate kinesthetic connection because it's literally hand to hand.

HOW TO GET "IT"

The handshake matters, and research shows that women with the firmest handshakes are seen as more confident and assertive. Women with confident handshakes make a more favorable impression on others than women with a more 'feminine' handshake, softer or more diminutive.

A handshake can also be a woman's secret weapon. Because men, in particular, anticipate a weaker female shake, a woman with a firm handshake is judged more positively than men with comparably firm handshakes. So where men are expected to have a good shake, a woman rises in estimation when she proves that she's cracked the code. Always put your best shake forward!

Any other form of hand-to-hand greeting – like a fist bump, thumb over thumb shake, or an old school high-five – is not part of any woman's repertoire unless you're on a company sport league. So even if your workplace is very casual and male dominated, for a woman to fist bump a man would signal over trying and be off-putting.

From a tactile perspective, think about the hand's dryness and temperature. You want to be sure it's not sweaty and not cold. If you tend to have sweaty palms, try resting your palm flat on your thigh rather than shoving it in a pocket. I have perpetually cold hands, so before I enter a room, I quickly rub my hands together to warm them up and give them a shake. In a cocktail setting, I make sure to have a cocktail napkin in case my hands get cold and damp from holding a glass.

A 'good' handshake is strong with a complete grip, lasts about two pumps and gives you time to make eye contact, to the point you can see the color of the other person's eyes. That's enough to make contact but not too much so as to be creepy.

Once you master the basics, you can then move up a level to choose your shake based on what you want to achieve:

- **Classic 'Keep Your Distance' Shake:** This is standard for a first meeting. You keep your right arm outstretched, not too high, posture upright. The hand is held horizontally with palm facing left. Maintain a medium clasp of about 50% strength – too firm is over assertive, while not firm enough is passive. Take the hand fully by the palm, not the fingertips. This shake says: we're equal, not unfriendly, but I want to know more. The first time you meet someone, you should hold on for a moment longer than you would normally, literally holding the other person's attention while the opening pleasantries are exchanged.

- **The Dominant Shake:** Use this when you want to say 'I have the upper hand,' literally. Begin in the usual palms-facing form but with your palm slightly bent over. Then, during the shake, subtly turn the other person's hand to put them in a nearly palm-up position with yours palm-down. Still exert only 50% pressure. You need to do this really smoothly or it will seem clumsy and strange. If you are in doubt about your ability to pull this off, don't try it or you'll potentially do more harm than good. Stick to what you know – the Classic Shake.

- **Welcome to My Space Shake:** In this shake you bring the other person in a little closer than in the classic by having more of a bend at the elbow and wrist so your forearm is still parallel to the floor. This is also a strong shake and assumes some superiority as you are the welcomer. It's more subtle, more collaborative, friendlier, and doesn't need as much 'push' as the dominant shake.

- **Welcome to the Clan Shake:** This is the shake we use for our trusted advisers, building on 'Welcome to My Space.' Men do this instinctively with men they trust by bring them in even closer in proximity, but they may be reluctant to do so with a woman because they risk seeming overly familiar. A man may introduce a shoulder touch or semi-hug to a woman he considers part of the Clan. At this closeness, the 'up and down' motion of the shake is more exaggerated. It can convey a lot of confidence, but it's very familiar so don't use it on a first meeting unless you're very certain the person will welcome it.

- **Mano a Mano:** In this shake, your arm is almost parallel to your torso, bringing them in as close as possible. This is the most intimate shake and very masculine. It may include another hand on the arm, or the clichéd 'politician's handshake' where both hands are clasped over the other person's. Women use this rarely and men typically only use this with people they really know and like and who like them or it will be irritating and cloying. For a man, an unwelcome Mano a Mano would be considered potentially threatening to another man.

A close cousin of shaking is cheek kissing. In the Sociability Facet we explore the waters of cheek kissing based on cultures, but the rules in general:

- If in doubt, don't initiate.
- Know what's appropriate in the country you're visiting – one, two or three kisses so you don't get an accidental lip-touch.
- Do not actually touch cheeks. You should be able to fit a palm between your cheeks easily.
- Don't make kissing sounds, ever.

Making a Stand

How you stand projects your energy and intentions. A stance can be submissive, aggressive, bored, threatened or any other emotion you can imagine.

The core posture conveys the emotion, starting with the feet, up through the stomach, reflected in the shoulders, and finishes with the head. On one extreme, a slouched, loose posture conveys apology, defensiveness or lack of confidence. If you add nervous, fidgeting gestures you'll amplify the negative energy.

On the other hand, a rigid, tense, keyed-up posture conveys arrogance, annoyance and judgment. When you add aggressive gestures like finger pointing or facial expressions like a furrowed brow, you create a very powerful and extreme energy.

Ideally, you want to be somewhere in the middle unless you're choosing a posture for a strategic reason. Whether you're standing in a corridor having a conversation or on a podium giving a presentation, start with a solid stance. In solid stance the weight is equal on your feet, no rocking or shifting weight, head up and in control.

When standing, height is a differentiator that needs to be managed in relation to others, particularly for women who fall outside 'average' height. In the man's world, height is power and we've all seen studies about the correlation between success and height. So if you're shorter than 5'4", try to level the playing field by sitting where possible or wear heels and avoid flats. If you're on the tall side, be aware you may intimidate some men so get them to sit, or if you're equal keep standing. Avoid slouching to diminish your height because you also inadvertently diminish your energy and your power.

When standing in a group, be aware of others' need for personal space. The accepted 'zones' vary by individual, but in general we each have three rings around us: the 'business zone' is for new acquaintances and professionals and we like them to stay about 6 to 4 feet away; the 'friend zone' is for people we know and trust and covers a 2 to 4 foot radius; the closest zone (1 to 2 feet) is the 'confidant zone' and only for family and loved ones. If someone steps away from you when you step in, it means you've crossed into a zone that makes them uncomfortable, so don't step in further.

If you're making a presentation, keep your posture up at all times and don't lean on the lectern. Keep your arms out and gestures intentional as you assume control. Keep your face forward and beware of turning to visuals at the side or behind you.

HOW TO GET "IT"

A cousin of standing is walking, which can also be surprisingly hard for some people. I once shot a video with a C-level executive where we needed some extra footage for editing purposes, so I asked if he'd walk down the corridor 'normally.' That was when I learned that asking someone who is not a catwalk model to walk 'normally' on camera is about impossible.

In general, be aware of your pace when you walk to notice and adapt if others are struggling to catch up or if you're always two steps behind. And remember, the more hectic things are, the slower you should walk. To walk quickly, especially in high heels making a rapid-fire click click click in a room, signals things are not in control. An appropriately focused pace without being rushed sends the right signal.

Putting It Together: Countdown to Impact

Before you head into the arena, do a pre-check:
1. Mirror check: hair neat, teeth clean, bra straps hidden, no obvious spots on clothing, shoes polished.
2. Visualize your headline: the three adjectives to describe your ideal self.
3. Stand up straight and smile.
4. Make and maintain eye contact, then extend your hand and shake hands.
5. Introduce yourself and know exactly what you want to say for your first words.
6. Take a seat and claim your space appropriately.
7. Build rapport and be gracious by accepting a beverage if offered.

CHAPTER 15

Body Language and Energy

Body Language Basics

'Mastering body language' has been around in business for decades as the secret to making deals and manipulating others. As a result, the secrets are known to all, and therefore ineffective. 'Mirroring' – the act of matching another person's gestures and posture – happens naturally when we're actually connecting with a person, but is a cliché and off-putting when forced. So, while mirroring will work to establish a bond, don't overdo it. I'll explain more about this in the 'likeability' section of this book.

Another overanalyzed body language cliché is being 'open' or 'closed.' Yes, a person may cross his arms because he's displeased, but he may also just be cold. A woman may point her feet away from another person because she dislikes him, or she could be adjusting her posture to compensate for a too short skirt.

The objective is to be interested and interesting. We mostly show if we're interested with our verbal connection, by listening and speaking. But our bodies also reveal our interest. Whom you are orienting your body toward and whom you are 'cutting out' will inadvertently reveal bias.

As a consultant I have my place in the pecking order of the client's workplace. I bring some power in the form of expertise, but mostly I'm there to make them shine, not to interfere with their hierarchy. So, I have to continually adjust my orientation to show deference to the most senior person in sometimes fluid situations. For example, if I'm with a senior client, Bob, and oriented toward him, when the bigger boss walks into the room, Mary, I need to reorient myself to include Mary without excluding Bob, particularly if there is any tension between them or if Bob feels any insecurity about his position.

To ignore this dynamic may inadvertently cause Bob to see me as a competitive threat and then he may try to block me from Mary. Now, personally, I may think it's important to get face time with Mary and make sure she likes me. But if I undermine Bob, even unintentionally, it can weaken my overall position.

Be aware of how you are including and excluding others and, without being Machiavellian, be as inclusive as possible when appropriate. To signal inclusivity, you should be:

- Orienting to others when they're speaking
- Nodding and moving your head
- Smiling
- Leaning in

For women working with men, body language can become a bit of a minefield because men can make huge interpretations about our interest and intention based on body language. 'Interested' is a fine line away from 'flirtatious' so be conscientious.

Apart from being interested, you should also be interesting. This should be obvious, but we've all been trapped in an eternally boring conversation where the other person has no clue we're completely disengaged. Yet, it rarely occurs to us that we might sometimes be the bore!

"But I'm sure they really are interested! Maybe he was just tired and that's why he was yawning?" Possibly, but people rarely fake boredom; they are more prone to fake interest by fake nodding, smiling and forcing eye contact. Pay attention to the nonverbals that indicate someone is bored when they're subtle, before the person has to actually walk away from you, and adjust. Someone who is bored or impatient will look away, disengage and withdraw and increasingly amplify the signals until the speaker notices.

Sometimes we get excited about topics that interest us and fail to notice the other person disengaging. But there is no point in continuing to send a letter that's being refused at the post box. If the topic is important, reschedule for another time or switch the energy by asking a question or diverting to a more energizing yet related topic that you can segue back from later.

Understanding Energy

About ten years ago, when I was living in Utah, I was invited to a networking event where the guest speaker was an underdog politician running for a high-profile office. I'd been following the race between these two men. The frontrunner was a Republican in a very Republican state, charismatic, handsome, dynamic. Steve, his opponent and the underdog, came from a well-known political family, so his biggest asset was his name. He was also completely brilliant, a lawyer and professor, one of the smartest people I've ever met. His ideas about government and what needed to be done for the state were logical, compelling and probably would have been exactly what was needed.

So I was looking forward to meeting this man, the quiet genius, and hearing what he had to say. It was a relatively small room, with about fifty people who were visible and influential in the community, so it was important that this man do well and connect and engage.

It was a semi-disaster. Even in this small venue, he could not project confidence and energy. He was clearly uncomfortable, with nervous energy. His face was highly flushed. He kept his head down on his paper as he read his very articulate and well-reasoned speech. When people asked questions, he answered at length. At such length that the room would start rustling and fidgeting, yet he continued talking. After the speech and Q&A, he gamely tried to work the room but by then the audience had checked out and most of them were leaving.

Instead of seeing a man who could be the future leader of the state, they saw an awkward professor. I saw a man who needed help with his presence, desperately. After the speech, I was talking with one of his aides on the campaign and offered a few insights. As a result, I was retained to help work with Steve on his presence to try and get him back on track.

The first issue, his visual facet, was relatively easy to fix. Steve's problem, I later learned, was that he had rosacea, a skin ailment that causes profound flushing. By changing the colors he was wearing to minimize the effect and using a lightly pigmented moisturizer, we were able to mitigate that issue.

His second facet, verbal, also needed work. It was a simple matter to teach him to project his words by looking up at the audience and also how to handle a Q&A. Through practice, he was able to master this and become much more effective.

The biggest issue, however, was his kinesthetic facet. His energy. Now this is a very practical and dogmatic individual. Talking to him about 'energy' was like talking to an eight-year-old about quantum physics. Yet, it was what he lacked most and was the biggest differentiator.

His opponent has an open, magnetic, very powerful energy. In a small room, he would have been a flame for moths, drawing them in like a rock star draws in groupies. Steve had a different, quieter, more introverted energy that needed to be shaped and directed.

To explain 'energy' to this very logical man, I started by drawing a diagram:

HOW TO GET "IT"

MANAGING ENERGY

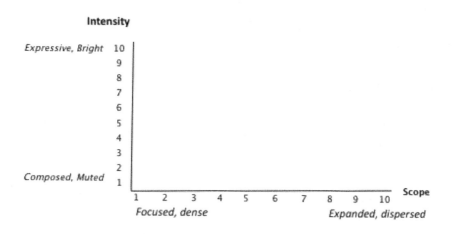

His natural energy was very composed and muted, while his comfort zone for scope was focused and narrow. He needed to learn how to intentionally 'turn up' his intensity to become more expressive and brighter. He also needed to learn how to expand his scope when needed.

Though he quickly understood the concept and even understood the issue, his concern was that he would be too 'salesy' — like a stereotypical used car salesman — if he turned up his intensity. The issue was that if he did not turn up his intensity, he could not expand his scope. A muted energy, when expanded, doesn't show up at all with an audience. It is simply being spread too thin to be noticed and make an impact. He had to turn up his intensity to a degree that was out of his comfort zone, where it felt inauthentic for him, to be able to disperse it to expand and engage an audience of 30, 300, or 3,000.

Working on this proved to be a tremendous challenge. We developed an 'intensity scale' of one to ten, where the baseline for his natural energy was around a three, and discussed how high he needed to turn up the intensity for a group. I also had to help him understand that what felt like a ten – completely over the top – to him, read like a five to most other people. He had to push himself to the point of being super intense to pick up as 'energetic' to others.

This is a difficult area to change for any leader. It takes time, practice and fine tuning. With Steve, we simply didn't have the time to move him into this slowly. He had to shift out of his comfort zone – right now – or the campaign would be lost.

We approached each speech and engagement considering two factors: the objective and the venue.

We narrowed down the 'objective' to one of two tracks: 'inspiring leader for big glorious future,' which was necessary but very close to his opponent's strengths, so we tried to use that in situations where they wouldn't be directly compared. The second track was 'intelligent and experienced problem solver' – this was an area where he excelled compared to the other candidate, who could sometimes appear superficial and therefore not as smart by comparison.

The objective track was determined based on the audience and what we thought would resonate most for them.

As for the venue, large venues require an expanded and dispersed energy, with a spotlight on individuals as needed, so he needed to elevate his intensity to the very limit to give him enough energy to work with for the group. The tone of his energy depended on the objective: 'inspiring leader' had a brighter and lighter energy while 'problem solver' had a more measured and grounded energy.

In smaller venues, the intensity could be less expanded and more muted, which worked really well for 'problem solver' objectives. He still felt like he was projecting a ten, but when coupled with the 'problem solver' strength, it didn't read as 'salesy'; it read as passionate and committed.

To understand and use your energy strategically, you need to practice and play with it like the picture and audio controls on a new television set, tweaking until you get the image and sound you want. Work on turning the intensity up and down – from muted to bright. Practice adjusting your scope from dense to dispersed.

Practice Tuning Your Energy

Use parties, gatherings and networking events as opportunities to practice playing with your energy and notice how others use their own energy. Try these exercises to learn how to use your energy with intention and purpose:

Switch 'on' and 'off.' One huge blunder is when a person switches themselves off and on like a light switch. You want to notice other people doing this and make sure you don't do it yourself. When I go to parties with 'movers and shakers' I have been on the receiving end more than once of the 'on/off' energy. Someone approaches me with big energy because they think I may be important, which I rarely am, though it pains my ego to admit that I will never be an heiress or Hollywood A-lister. Once the person realizes that I'm basically a nobody, he or she will switch off, start scanning for another target and buzz away to the next flower.

Even if they're still physically standing there speaking to me, I can feel the moment they switch 'off' and disconnect their energy. So can you, and so can others. We feel it when they aren't really listening because they're thinking about something else or what they want to say next.

Notice when you do that and break the habit. First, it's not nice. Second, you don't really know who someone is or how they can help you. Giving the gift of your energy and attention may pay off in ways you can't anticipate down the road. People can tell that you're fake listening and it means you can't make a connection.

Create an energy flow. If an energetic connection was something you could see, it would look like a wave going back and forth between two people like a current. It would have a harmonious color palette that is engaging and attractive. It should feel positive, even if the topic of conversation isn't happy or even if the two people don't agree. It should flow between you, not 'at' one or the other.

When you're in a conversation with a person, pay attention to this energetic flow. If it was visible, what would it look like? Is it a torrent coming from one person 'at' the other, who is either stoically deflecting the flow, ignoring it completely, or simply trying not to drown and get a word in edgewise? Or is it competing forces, both flowing at the other but neither being received or accepted? Does the energy flow have a color? Does each of you have a different color of energy that you're projecting, and if so do these colors harmonize or clash?

Practice lighting up and lighting up others. There are times you're just 'on' and your energy is attractive and magnetic. There's nothing more appealing than someone who brings a positive energy to a room and lights up other people. Think about the people who have helped you 'light up' your own spark. Usually they asked questions, listened well, or brought interesting ideas that inspired you. How can you light up other people by reflecting that energy in your own connections? Can you make it about them instead of being about you to genuinely be present? This doesn't mean that you don't share anything; in fact, it's quite the opposite. You're opening yourself hugely to form a connection with a person that means they walk away feeling more empowered, more enlightened, and as if you have given them a tremendous gift.

HOW TO GET "IT"

The Fit Factor: Demonstrating You're Up to the Task

One of the best investments I've ever made is my treadmill desk. Yes, I own a treadmill desk just like Victoria Beckham, though I didn't know she had one until after I bought mine. I work from home a lot and am frequently on calls or writing. In fact, as I'm writing this section of the book, I'm walking on the treadmill. It helps me keep my energy level up and helps me stay engaged and connected. It's one creative way of trying to get in exercise in the course of a busy day, and while it may seem crazy to some, it works for me.

Managing your physical health is critical to your successful rise to the top. Senior leaders have a lot in common with elite athletes. Being active affects your energy level tremendously and plays a big part in your executive performance and ability to concentrate, react, think quickly and focus. You don't need to buy a treadmill desk, but you do need to pay attention to your body and your health.

I've worked with my share of CEOs and one thing they have in common is that they're physically aware. They may not be athletic, but they understand that they have to take care of their bodies for a few reasons:

Maintaining Stamina. To have the stamina to physically do the task at hand we need to be active. Traveling and being jet-lagged, working late hours, being constantly under pressure is demanding and your body needs to be able to perform. The higher you rise up the ladder, the harder it is physically to climb. There is a physical stress to performing in the workplace.

Often we spend our days sitting in meetings, sitting at desks, and sitting in cars, planes or trains. Yet our brains are processing the stress of a day in its interactions, decisions and challenges. If you deprive your body of the opportunity to physically burn the stress your brain produces, your machine – that is, your body – eventually winds down and breaks down.

Managing Stress. Exercise helps us deal with stress. Our caveman brains are still wired to produce hormones and chemicals to deal with stress by fighting the bear that's attacking us or running away. In the board room, we usually don't flee or start swinging. So we need a healthy way to process these chemicals and channel our energy productively in a mental environment.

For women, energy levels also affect our hormones, our moods and our sensitivity to others' moods. If we're not fit and healthy, it's harder for us to deal with the demands of our jobs. The higher profile your job, the higher your stress and the intensity of your work environment – and the more energy you require. Exercise produces the endorphins we need to deal with this stress.

Sending Signals to Others. Physical health signals discipline. Looking fit and healthy signals that you're a person in control. I'm not saying you need to look like an athlete or have a perfect physique. Oprah is a great example of a woman who has publicly struggled with her weight, but is still clearly powerful and also pushes herself to exercise and be active. No matter your figure or body shape, you can still convey health and activity. If you're carrying more weight than you'd like, make sure you adapt your style choices so you convey confidence at any size.

Monitoring your exercise and your diet will help you manage your energy. People watch your energy to see if you seem tired, anxious or frenetic and then make interpretations.

Let's say you didn't get a good night's sleep and you stifle a few yawns in a meeting with superiors and subordinates. How could they interpret this? 'She must be overwhelmed – the job's too hard.' 'She's completely disengaged, she must not be following the conversation.' 'She's yawning. Clearly she can't handle the stress of this job and it's too much for her.'

Train Like an Athlete

In his book *High Performance Trading*, business coach Steve Ward, who was a performance coach for Olympic-level, elite athletes before turning his skills toward the financial trading world, helps traders improve performance. His view is that people who work in high-stress environments need to learn to manage their energy strategically to compete at work, just as an athlete competes on the field.

I'm now 45 and in the best shape of my life, but it's hard work and getting harder as I get older. When I read Steve's book about trading, I met him for a coffee and to get his insights into physical fitness for this book. I was hugely impressed by his seamless integration of physical health into mental stamina.

Because the mind and body are so inextricably linked, Steve discusses 'energy management' for individuals in business in terms of overall health that includes exercise, diet, rest, relaxation and sleep – and also day-to-day basis, particularly by being aware of nutrition and rest/recovery.

According to Steve, we all have an 'energy account' and if we make withdrawals without making any deposits, we eventually crash. One of the key strategies for keeping your energy account high is to think about and manage the four building blocks to energy:

1. **Manage your nutrition.** Food is fuel. Eat a balanced diet every day, including breakfast and a light lunch, even when you travel. Are you using caffeine and sugary snacks to get you through the day but you still get an afternoon energy crash? Avoid that by eating more whole grains, drinking more water and keeping your nutrition constant throughout the day.
2. **Exercise regularly.** Make a commitment to balance cardio and weights five times a week for at least 30 minutes. Most companies have gyms. Most hotels have gyms. If you add in the time it takes you to get to the gym, change into workout

gear, and change back into business clothes, you need to allow yourself an hour.

3. **Get enough downtime.** Rest and relaxation are required to give us time to switch off. During our day, our bodies and brains usually need to take 15 minutes 'off' for every 90 minutes of work time to maintain optimal productivity. Just like an athlete needs to take a break to rest and renew, so does the mental athlete. Manage your diary to give yourself time for breaks.

4. **Get enough sleep.** Every body is different and I know of some leaders who sleep three hours a night during the week and then have a daylong crash on the weekend. Research shows that this is not good for your body and no matter what habits you've created, going without sleep may get you through a sprint but it won't sustain you to survive the marathon. Humans need 6-8 hours of sleep a night. Manage your sleep like an account that you keep in the black at all times.

We all know physical energy management is critical, yet we continue to put it off. 'No time' is no excuse. Make a point to schedule it into your day. The CEOs I know make time to work out. I know of one who the minute he arrives, no matter how long the flight or what time of day, goes straight to the hotel gym to run for 30 minutes. He has a gym bag with shoes and workout clothes packed, has his other belongings sent to the room, and does his workout. If he goes to his room first, he says, he's inclined to check emails or change his clothes, or other tasks get in the way and then he loses his workout time. So he has his admin schedule that time in his diary as non-negotiable. As a result, he overcomes jet lag faster, feels re-energized and focused, and he is a higher performer.

About ten years ago I started focusing on my physical fitness. At age 45, it is harder to be fit, but I am in the best shape of my life. Inadvertently, I wound up following suggestions that Steve recommends for people with mentally taxing jobs and not a lot of time:

HOW TO GET "IT"

1. **Find an activity that works for you.** One day my trainer, Matt Neve, had me try a 'hang clean' and I inadvertently discovered that I enjoy Olympic powerlifting and I happen to be reasonably good at it. Now that I live in London, my trainer and nutritionist, Lloyd Chivandire, is a great motivator and I look forward to our workouts. Having a trainer is an investment in mental and physical health for me, which I consider effective management of the biggest asset and resource I have: me.

2. **Make a plan and stick to it.** I very rarely miss a workout. I had food poisoning recently and took three weeks to fully recover, and I still made it to the gym. I wasn't at 100%, but I showed up.

3. **Make a food plan.** I have a daily food schedule so I don't leave it up to chance. Especially when I travel, it's important to make sure I don't skip meals or eat a lot of carbs and fat – the easiest to come by in the corporate jungle – and know where I'm going to get lean protein and greens.

4. **Manage alcohol and caffeine.** Though Lloyd would rather I give up caffeine altogether, I allow myself one cup of coffee in the morning. I also will have a glass of prosecco at a dinner out or cocktails, but then I skip any dessert.

5. **Ten deep breaths.** Getting 15 minutes off every couple of hours is sometimes not possible. But you can make an excuse to leave any meeting to go to the ladies' room and take ten deep breaths to recharge. I try to add a meditative quality by counting from one to ten as I breathe in and from ten down to one as I exhale.

Creating a physical health plan should be just as important in creating your career strategy as developing leadership skills and technical knowledge. It requires focus, time and attention, but you need to make it a priority or it will always be put off and on the back burner.

CHAPTER 16

Taking Command – Being Leaderly and Likeable

Commanding a Room

What do we mean by 'commanding a room'? It's that energetic force field, basically, and comes from elevating and amplifying your energy so it has weight and significance and is magnetic. It doesn't have to be loud. In fact, you can be completely silent and still in command.

For myself, learning to refine my kinesthetic facet has been a tremendous boon and one of the ways I can set myself apart in business settings. This facet covers all interactions, but may be best understood in a presentation skills setting to begin.

Because I give a lot of presentations, speeches and workshops as part of my work, managing my Kinesthetic Facet is an area where I've invested a lot of time and effort. Though I enjoy the teaching-learning dynamic, I do find it very physically tiring. I'm naturally more introverted and speaking in front of large groups drains my batteries, so I have learned to be very strategic and make a plan to ensure I maintain the right energy level over the entire course.

Following the same scale I taught Steve, our professorial politician, I manage my energy according to the required intensity (being composed/muted versus expressive/bright) and the appropriate scope (focused/dense compared to expanded/dispersed). But I also add another element in how I view my energy.

This is verging into serious 'airy fairy' land, but one of my most useful techniques is to see the energy of a situation as something I can deliberately affect. In every scenario, I think of my 'energy' literally like a force field that I control. I decide what I want my force field to *feel* like to my audience — do I want them to feel empathetic, commanding, sincere, or something else? I may also think of it as a color or a shape that expands to encompass the room. If I want them to feel thoughtful and focused, I envision a massive summer-green oval that blankets the room. If I want the energy to shift to energetic and a higher tone, I may shift that to be a golden orange 'fizzy' sphere that encompasses the group. I think about how to intensify the field in certain spots of the room — say the zone where the key detractors are sitting — or disperse it so it covers a broader range for large groups.

I am also aware of each person inside my force field and if they are out of sync, I visualize changing their 'color' to match the group. If I'm in a conversation with an individual or a small group, my energy is tuned differently to consider the individuals in the group and what I want to achieve. 'Inspired' feels different than 'charged up,' for example, and to drive that energy I need to adapt my own kinesthetic approach.

When you have command of the room, you are continually reading the audience. This is when I know they're in my force field. I pick up on their tone and mood, and I adjust to match the prevailing pitch, and then take them where I want them to go. For example, if I'm on an agenda after lunch, when the group is usually experiencing an energy dip, I can't start with high-octane, buzzy energy or they'll be put off and shut me out. I have to tune into their frequency, even briefly, before I deliberately shift them up to engaged and connected.

There are two times when leaders must step up to the big leagues and manage their energy with the precision of a Formula One driver in the home stretch: moments of crisis and rallying the troops.

In moments of crisis, a leader has to diffuse panic by being muted and composed without being cold and distant. I worked for BP for many years and I knew Tony Hayward before he became a global punch line. Much has been written about this event as a case study in communication and I wasn't at the company when the Gulf of Mexico spill occurred, but I think everyone would agree it was definitely a moment of crisis on an epic scale.

In this case, Tony's natural British reserve helped to convey the appropriate muted and composed energy, but he quickly was perceived as cold and distant. Despite the scripts, his energy was not warm and lacked any ability for connection. It wasn't the only problem in that situation, but had he understood how to control and manage his energy in a crisis, it would have helped.

The second occasion for a leader to manage energy closely is when rallying the troops. A leader needs to be expressive and expanded without being melodramatic. When Steve Jobs led Apple's new product launch webcasts, his energy was spot on – huge energy without being hokey.

How to Act Like a Leader

'Being leaderly' is a challenge for women across each of the five facets, no less so in the Kinesthetic Facet. What you're really doing to be leaderly is to project confidence and convey status, which we can think of as 'body emotion.' Our bodies give off a thousand subtle clues to reveal our emotional state – strong, confident, fragile, unsettled, distracted, agitated, etc. To master the kinesthetic facet, you need to master your body emotion cues.

We project confidence when we're in a superior position and our natural body language changes. In general, the Alpha of the group takes up more physical space. The leader may speak more often, interrupt more frequently, and use more touching and pointing gestures. This certainly isn't true of every leader, but the members of the pack with less seniority will usually moderate their space, speech, interruptions and gestures to be a notch down from the top dog, even if he or she isn't particularly verbose or physically expressive.

Step outside yourself and try to see what others notice about you and if it reads as confident. Do you appear comfortable in your own skin or do you have displaced energy like fidgeting or nervous movements? How do you inhabit your body and your space? Do you feel connected to yourself, or are you watching with 'bank camera eyes'?

A lot of projecting confidence is acting. You need to feel 'on' and attractive to others – not in a physical way, but in a magnetic way. You literally need to create a magnetic pull that brings others to you so they see you as the one to gravitate toward. Acting 'as if' you were energized and confident to embody that character is often enough to help you get through your own insecurities and down moments, which we all have.

My client, Sarah, had horrible insecurities and near anxiety attacks when she would have to attend board meetings. She was petrified that she was going to be 'found out' as not knowing enough and not being good enough. I worked with her to define a character, 'Super Sarah,' for these meetings, and we discussed this persona at length – how 'Super Sarah' looked, felt and sounded.

Just like Meryl Streep physically morphs to become a Margaret Thatcher, Julia Child or the mom in 'Mamma Mia,' Sarah morphed to become the confident, capable Super Sarah executive who deserved to be at the table and be heard. Over time, 'putting on' this alter ego was less of a shift and she felt more confident naturally. She became Super Sarah who didn't fidget, projected a calm and magnetic energy, and owned the room and her space.

How do you own your space? This is particularly tricky for women. Look around the meeting table next time and see how much physical space men take versus women. Women tend to literally 'shrink' as if minimizing the space we take. Men, on the other hand, spread out, at times even taking up too much space at the table or in the room. They are claiming their territory. They will usually take up an equal or slightly smaller amount of space compared to the leader or the second in command, and they do this intuitively.

To claim your space, you need to be aware of and manage this dynamic. When I go into a meeting room, I intentionally and deliberately place artifacts on the table in front of me. My notebook, leather diary, bold pen, coffee cup, water glass, or other notes and papers, whatever I have that is appropriate to display, I do so to claim my space. There may only be one or two items, not a whole plethora, but I don't confine them to a small zone. I put them at a distance as one would in setting a formal dining table place setting to show I own this space.

Physically, I own my space by making my upper body expansive with my arm placement. While men will often own space with their lower bodies, crossing their legs with the ankle propped on the knee or widening their sitting stance, to mirror that language is uncouth for a female. However, we can put our elbows on the table widely or make sure we are using the arm rests on the chair with the elbows projecting slightly over to claim the space. We can also have a 'proud chest' – which doesn't mean emphasizing your cleavage but requires you to not shrink into yourself.

Avoid gestures that diminish yourself or cause you to 'cave in,' and deliberately expand to demonstrate your position in the pack.

Being Likeable

To be trusted, you need to be likeable. In conversation, even if you never say a word, your body language is noticed and is a decisive factor in if you'll be trusted.

One could contend that likeability shouldn't matter in promoting a leader. That is a 'head in the sand' viewpoint. You don't need to be Miss Congeniality, but no board is going to promote a woman to senior leadership who is *un*likeable. Unlikeable isn't inspiring. Unlikeable isn't relatable. And unlikeable won't get the corner office.

Countless research tells us the same thing – the nonverbals are much more believable than the words we say when it comes to being trusted for our real intentions.

In one survey, psychologists asked participants to talk about themselves for a few minutes and tracked how the listener responded and how it made the speaker feel. Of all the possible options, the most 'likeable' listeners were those that didn't say a word! What they did do, however, was gaze at the speaker, smile, and lean toward him or her. Just that was enough to convey interest and therefore, likeability.

To be seen as likeable, the other person needs to see you as 'simpatico,' or in synch. There are three 'micro' ways to make this connection with your nonverbals and when we are experiencing a genuine connection with another person, they happen automatically:

1. We smile. If you're both smiling at the same time, you're usually in harmony.
2. We mirror gestures. If your gestures are roughly similar in frequency, scale and energy, that means you're connecting.
3. We mirror gazes. Are you both looking at and away at around the same frequency and intensity? If so, that means you're in synch.

If this connection – smiling and mirroring – happens on its own, it is automatically authentic and sincere. Faking it is hard and can come across negatively with the other person as being smarmy and insincere.

That said, sometimes you need to connect with someone you don't actually like that much and you need them to like you in return. We don't always like the people who work for us, with us, or are our bosses. We still need to connect. Or you may find the other person is reluctant to make a connection for whatever reason.

One of my clients, Maria, was promoted to lead a new team and inherited a male employee, Tom, who she absolutely could not stand. He'd applied for her job and didn't get it, which wasn't a great start. Though he was a member of her leadership team, in her view he was an undermining jerk and she didn't trust him. He made no bones about his dislike of her and it was poisoning the broader team, including his direct reports. It was obvious that he would eventually need to leave the team, but in the meantime she had to try to get him onside and productive — or at least to stop attacking her behind her back. She also needed to demonstrate some coherence and connection for her extended team and demonstrate to her boss that she could manage this relationship.

My advice to Maria is the same I would offer you if there is someone you need to get on your side, with whom you are not currently connecting. You don't need to fake being best buddies with this person, but you do need to pay close attention to your nonverbals so you don't inadvertently signal that you're put off and alienate them and potentially damage yourself.

To artificially engineer a connection is challenging, but it can be done. It would be unethical, in my view, and just plain not nice to do this to manipulate the other person. But if you do need to be seen as likeable and connect, as Maria needed to connect with Tom, try the following:

1. **Identify some redeeming quality in the person.** There must be something that you respect, some talent they possess that you value, one example of when you've seen them at their best. Focus on that and amplify it in your mind's eye. Tom was technically very good at his job and was quite innovative. Every time he was a jerk, Maria would try to focus on his creativity and the good work he was delivering.

2. **Mirror without being creepy.** If Maria had been trying to win over a superior, she would try to mirror his body

language and match it. In this case, where she's winning over a subordinate who is semi-hostile, his body language was usually negative and hostile and his gaze either aggressive or disinterested. So, she needed to generally mirror his body language — sitting back, sitting forward, etc. — and then move him toward being more open, more friendly, more approachable. With gaze, she needed to hold his eye contact when he was looking at her directly so she didn't appear submissive, but not force him to make eye contact if he was looking away frequently. Instead, she worked to look at him for a few seconds, then look away, until he would eventually begin to fall in synch with her.

3. **Be very conscious of your facial expressions.** You don't have to fake smile, but you should make sure you're not frowning subconsciously. Try to keep your face relaxed and neutral. Notice the other person's facial expressions. If he or she smiles, you should smile in return. Maria noticed the subjects where Tom's mood would lighten and he would naturally smile — his dog and hiking. She didn't have a dog and she didn't like to hike, but when they had one-on-one conversations, she'd intentionally start by briefly mentioning one of those topics. Because this is a topic where he naturally has energy, she didn't even really need to be that subtle about it. She'd just say, "So, how's your dog?" or "Did you get the dog out for a hike last weekend?" or "I read a magazine on the plane the other day about European hiking trips. Have you got anything planned for your next holiday?" He'd smile, she'd smile, and they'd connect.

This is often harder for women like Maria because we're judged differently than men when it comes to being likeable. In one study, participants watched male and female speakers without any audio and were asked which ones they found most likeable. When assessing the male speakers, the observers were attracted to gestures that were 'open' or directed at the audience or listener — moving his head and hands or smiling openly toward the other person. When assessing the women, listeners found that the most likeable body cue was a spontaneous facial expression – that is, how animated her face was and how often it changed expression. So, managing your facial expressions to be open, receptive and appropriate is critical if you want to be seen as trustworthy, likeable, and therefore promotable.

Cheat Sheet to Convey Confidence and Build Trust

1. Do the Wonder Woman. According to Harvard professor Amy Cuddy, changing your posture changes how you feel and your hormone levels. By standing in the Wonder Woman 'power pose' for just two minutes, you'll raise your testosterone levels, boosting your confidence and mood, and lower your cortisol levels, which calms your nerves.

2. Do not whistle, juggle the contents of a pocket, clear your throat, wring your hands, squint, pull away, bite anything that is not a utensil – including a straw – lock your fingers in a death vise grip or touch any of the following: face, nose, crotch, bra strap, bum.

3. Manage your smile, facial expressions and body language, not your iPhone. Detach from your electronic devices (or 'The Biggest Blunder You Can Completely Control'). Even if you're in your 20s, do not check your phone or turn your back to deal with a call during a meeting. Leave it off or go out of the room. Give your attention to the people who are present.

CHAPTER 17

Climb the Ladder Gracefully – and in a Skirt and Heels

Once you make it to the top, you need to stay at the top and act like a leader. I've seen many women who get a measure of success and then suddenly have a personality transplant and wind up looking like a 'wannabe.' Poseur leaders overcompensate by clustering their power gestures – standing tall and making too many short, quick movements in bursts. They over jargon and come across as trying too hard. The result is a projection of insecurity.

Like scenes from 'Mad Men,' these are stereotypical body language cues created by men to show power and dominance. Now, they're clichéd and come across as 'old-school' – but they're seductively tempting for the woman on the rise to emulate as a way to show she's broken through the glass ceiling.

If you find yourself doing ANY of these things, step back and re-evaluate. Odds are that rather than making you appear 'in charge' they come across as insecure and will make your subordinates mock you behind your back – just like you may have done yourself or observed being done to other pompous executives while you were on the rise:

- Finger pointing. There's a line between 'Leaning In' and literally pointing.

- Distancing. Don't artificially increase your personal barrier space to keep others at arm's length.
- Looking down your nose. If you're leaning back and looking down your nose, they *will* take the piss out of you behind your back.
- Very busy, special and important. When someone is in your space, don't ignore them with your head down, or on a call.
- OTT. Exaggerated gestures, excessive touching, excessive eye contact, and condescension in speaking come across as insulting – as if suddenly the rest of them are too stupid to understand.
- Bossy Pants. I've worked for and with more than one C-level executive who rules by fear and likes to show he's the man by strutting around, angry stare, tense body language, looking sideways. Don't be that guy, gals.
- Props as weapons. Cleaning glasses, checking watches, playing with a pen, looking at a phone all signal the other person isn't important and makes a point in a power play. Not subtle, not classy.

How to Be 'Leaderly' Without Being a Bitch

Oh, the fine line between boss and bitch. Once you get on top, they want to knock you down. There are some kinesthetic cues to use to demonstrate you're the Alpha without being over the top:

- Show confidence by putting your hands palms-down on the table in a meeting. This simple gesture is more powerful than you think.
- Pat on the back, sincerely. When someone has actually done a good job, hold the physical contact a fraction longer, add in an arm-touch, and they'll feel appreciated. If you mean it sincerely, it will come across as genuine and authentic.

HOW TO GET "IT"

- Face subordinates straight on. Don't angle or 'tower' – but face them directly, with an open smile and straight posture.
- Point fingers toward them. Steepled fingers pointed up signal superiority and is off-putting. But pointing *at* the person, with lower hands, signals that you're listening and engaged.
- Slow it down. Not to the point of 'glacial' – but don't rush, project 'gravitas' and feel your weight.

The Alpha Watches the Pack's Cues

The higher you rise the more you're scrutinized and the more your energy affects those around you. If you come in with a glowering face, the room will reciprocate. Likewise, if you're light-hearted, the room will invigorate.

Notice how you affect others' body language and energy. If your subordinates are doing these gestures in clusters, consistently, it means you're dominating to the point of non-productivity and loss of affinity:

- Fidgeting, fiddling
- Covering mouth and eyes
- Breaking eye contact
- Closing eyes briefly, repetitively
- Imitating or mirroring you excessively
- Slumping
- Faltering voice
- Lowered body

If you leave this to escalate, it will result in a lack of trust and poor performance. In this case, you need to address your own body language, slow it down, open up and make them feel engaged and connected so that you can build trust and productivity.

Creating Physical Distance as a Leader

Getting to the top of the feeding chain can often be a perplexing and confusing experience for a leader, especially if you're promoted from inside an organization and stay in the same team. Now, people that were your colleagues are your subordinates. They are looking to you not just for guidance, but also for their bonus and own promotion.

So, how transparent should you be with your emotions, and how should you adapt your body language and energy? Conveying warmth and 'humanness' without being an open book is key for a leader and especially women. Too cold and you're seen as an ice-queen; too emotive and you're seen as weak.

Being overly intimate will also erode confidence in your leadership. I remember being about eight years old and going to the grocery store with my mother where we ran into my teacher from school, who was also doing her grocery shopping. Before then it had never occurred to me that Mrs. Nelson had a life outside school. As she and my mother chatted in the produce aisle, I was fascinated to see that she had Coco Pops cereal in her basket. On one hand this made her more human, on the other hand it made her more mortal.

Similarly, leaders need to be human, but they also need a distance or mystique that helps others feel confident – particularly in very large corporations. The CEO is god-like, all knowing, and we want to believe that the captain at the helm is superhuman in some way, steering the ship.

Once you reach the captain's chair, sit in your seat proudly, head held high with both feet on the ground. Assume the mantle of leadership like a cloak that you put on that gives you the right to be in that chair and make the decisions. Underneath, you are still yourself and that self is your core, but you now have an additional weight of responsibility and an accompanying energy that you have to own. You are no longer just 'one of the crew' and to continue to try and behave as if you are will only cause them to respect

HOW TO GET "IT"

you less. Carry yourself like the alpha that you are – you have earned this role, after all – and they will follow.

CHAPTER 18

Polishing Your Sociability Facet to Build Relationships

When I meet a client for the first time, I always arrive at the coffee shop or café early so I can get a seat facing the entrance and watch her arrive. Those few moments before she sees me, when she is just entering and a bit flustered and perhaps uneasy, are ideal for me to see through the façade and look at her most 'true' self. I pick up a lot about her energy, presence, and initial appearance.

I also use this as a quick litmus test for sociability, the 'fourth facet.' Sociability is the realm of manners and social graces. As my client enters the café, she will invariably need to navigate some social interaction with the hostess. Watching how she does that – is she curt, friendly, impatient, etc. – gives me a big clue as to how she treats people in service in general. This is reinforced when I observe her order a beverage from the barista or waitress. Does she acknowledge them in a sincere and genuine way? Does she handle the transaction graciously? If there's a problem, such as not having her preferred type of tea, for example, what does she do?

Kate, a new client, was running a bit late for our meeting. She was understandably flustered and when the hostess spoke to her, I could see that she was scanning the room to look for me, ignoring the hostess, as she took off her coat and put away her phone. When she spotted me, she then ignored the hostess completely and dismissively made a beeline to sit down. Then she turned on the charm and smile and apology. For me.

But of course, by this time, I've seen how she treats 'underlings' – or those people who she perceives as such. I've met a lot of CEOs in my career. I've met some that are jerks to others and some that are not. Those who have manners and social grace, particularly to those who are in a subordinate position, are more leaderly and well respected.

For a woman in business, the bar is even higher. While a man who forgets his 'please' and 'thank you' manners may be seen as abrupt, a woman is just a plain bitch. You don't want to be a bitch. You don't want others to think you're a bitch. You want to be a gracious, pleasant, professional person.

That means paying attention to manners and social graces in all your interactions. In just about every team or corporation I've worked with, there is 'the woman' that everyone fears and dislikes because she's a bitch. She's rude, condescending, unreasonable, overbearing. She may be very good at her job; she may even get promoted repeatedly. But at some point she's going to cross paths with someone who she's pissed off, who now has the power to influence her progression, and that's not a great place to be – knowing that the person you derided and dressed down four years ago is now on a panel determining your fate. Companies have long memories. Industries are smaller than you think. Your reputation as being tactless or bitchy will follow you, and it probably won't be a positive thing down the road.

The Art of the Relationship

The word 'etiquette' is loaded with connotations of which fork to use and a litany of rules that are used to make some people feel superior whilst others feel 'less than.'

In my definition, etiquette is about making connections and building relationships. It's the way we connect with others to show respect and kindness. It's being thoughtful. Sociability governs how we act and what we should do in any given situation, so that we reflect our best self and make others feel comfortable and therefore confident in our abilities.

The ability to make others feel comfortable, when you need them to feel comfortable, is an art. Now, there are moments as a leader when you should deliberately make people feel *uncomfortable*. If you want to get their attention, bite back a little, and create a level of tension to drive a desired behavior – all of those things warrant discomfort. However, none of those things give a person permission to be rude or cruel.

You can be a strong female, expect results – even demand results – but still be a lady. And I mean 'lady' in the broadest sense: someone who makes others' lives easier, who is fair and compassionate, who sees the greater good, who has her situation situated at all times.

The fourth facet gives practical, hands-on, do-it-now ways to polish your sociability and help you project the professional, gracious woman you need to get the role you want. It is a critical component for any woman who wants to rise in the ranks.

I would actually say that it's the most important and least understood facet. Yet it separates the 'men from the boys.' Women who don't get it are missing a huge strategic advantage simply because they haven't learned to leverage this important tool.

Here are my five tips for social success:

1. Be confident yet discreet. You should be the one who comes to mind for professionalism and proactivity, not for gossip and pot stirring. If you get a reputation for being indiscreet, others will never trust you. My advice: if you have a secret, keep it a secret. If you know a secret, keep it a secret.
2. Take control of making others comfortable. Own your meetings, own your office environment, make sure others are included

and comfortable and you will get the best out of them from a performance perspective, and also be a magnetic person whom people want to be around.

3. Stay in control. Don't drink too much in work situations. Don't take any substances that would impair your judgment. I spoke with a friend recently who was giving a keynote speech and she was quite nervous. She then told me about another friend who had given her an anti-anxiety prescription medication to take beforehand to 'take the edge off.' Does this sound like a good idea? Better to be nervous than to be drugged...

4. Make life easy for others. This requires noticing and being aware of how you impact other people. If you're late, you make others late. If you walk into the office talking loudly on your mobile phone, you disrupt others' concentration. If you cancel a meeting five minutes before it's meant to start, you inconvenience people who had other things to do as well.

5. Fake it until you make it. *My Fair Lady, Pretty Woman*, even *Cinderella* are all tales of unpolished girls making it into the big leagues. Pay attention to what others are doing, follow along, and try to chill out.

Sociability is one facet where I personally struggle for two reasons.

First, I don't come from a 'moneyed' background where advanced manners were de rigueur. We were pretty laid back and as a result, in high society I find myself always feeling a little on the back foot. What I've learned, however, is that people with genuinely good manners – the actual elite – want me to feel comfortable and will actually go out of their way to ensure I never feel awkward.

Over time, I've gained confidence. Being American makes it easier in the UK because it's harder for people to pigeonhole me based on my accent. I use this to my advantage. I also make sure I feel very comfortable with what I'm wearing so that I know I'm dressed appropriately and feel confident.

Second, I'm shy. People never believe this when I tell them that I'm an introvert – but it's true. Any personality profile has, indeed, revealed the truth that I am naturally introverted. That doesn't mean that I can't talk to people, but it does mean that I need to compensate for my natural shyness and put forth the effort to mingle and mix. I know the rules, tips and tricks but that doesn't make it a pleasant experience for me.

Social settings drain me. Small talk is exhausting for me. I will do just about anything to avoid a cocktail party. I know this and I have learned to make a plan for social situations: Who do I know that will be there and can I arrange to arrive at the same time? (I usually meet them there so I know I have my own transport to leave and am not then inconveniencing them if I want to leave earlier.) How long will I stay? (30 minutes, an hour, until my boss leaves?) How many people will I try to talk to? (Three new people, five?) How will I reward myself for forcing myself out of my comfort zone? (This usually includes chocolate when I get home – preferably Ben & Jerry's Phish Food.)

I wish I had the gift of natural mixing and mingling, but I just don't. I have to accept this about myself and see it as an advantage, not a disadvantage. My introversion actually gives me insight into others who feel equally awkward, and sometimes they are the biggest brains and most interesting people in the room.

Are You a Boss or a Bossypants?

As I've already said, it's not how you treat those above you that matters, it's how you treat those who are at your level and below from an economic, social, or reporting structure. So always be aware of how you treat waiters, flight attendants, restroom attendants, valets… anyone in a service role. When you are appreciative and considerate, it sends a signal that you're kind, fair, and high class. Other people notice this about you and it speaks volumes.

If you lead teams, you can be the boss without being bossy. Using questions to build connections with your team is very important, so start by understanding the difference between inquiry and advocacy.

'Enquiring minds want to know' is the tagline of the *National Enquirer* tabloid. But it's true – do you want to know what people think or do you just want to tell them what to do?

Some questions to find out if you're an inquirer or a bossypants:

1. Do you ask questions or just tell people what to do?
2. Do you ask open-ended questions that give the person space to share?
3. Do you give people your full attention and actually stop talking so they can answer?
4. Do you listen more than you speak?
5. Do you interrupt?
6. Do you 'check in' – by saying 'Let me make sure I understand what you're saying…' or 'Can you tell me more about that?'
7. Do you end interactions knowing as much about the other person as they know about you?

If you're not seeking balance, then you're missing out. People need a give and take – to listen and also be heard. I remember going on a date once with a man I'd seen three or four times that involved a five-hour drive. He'd been a conversation monopolizer in the past, which I'd chalked up to nerves, a little insecurity, and the need to impress. But it had been enough of an inequity that I decided to make this an experiment of sorts and not strive to create balance in the conversation, just to see where he would take it when left to his own devices.

The not surprising outcome is that he talked, a lot, all about himself. In that entire five hours, he asked me only three questions: had I ever had a three-way sexual experience, what did I think about interracial relationships, and was I hungry. And then he answered all three questions before I could even open my mouth. (He didn't think a ménage à trois was a good idea; he had been in an interracial relationship in university; and he was hungry.) I don't think he ever noticed that I hadn't been participating in the conversation and probably came away thinking he had come across as clever, charming and witty. I imagine he was surprised when I said I wasn't really interested in going out with him again.

A boss also needs to pay attention to the nonverbal signals you send through your sociability facet. If you close your door, it signals to all the cubicle dwellers that you have a door and they don't and they notice the disparity. It comes across as 'I'm special, you're not.' Especially if you have peers who are not in offices, you want to keep your door open so you don't signal that you think you're more important.

The rule of thumb is to close the door if there's a reason – you're on a conference call, in a meeting with a live person, or discussing confidential information – otherwise leave it open. Needing to 'focus' is not a reason. The cubicle dwellers need to focus too, and are expected to do so in an open space.

Don't take advantage of support staff or risk being labeled as a diva. Unless it's common practice in your culture, do not be the one whose PA is telling the other PAs that she has to pick up your cleaning, constantly reschedule your travel, or deal with your personal situations, because the word gets around very, very quickly.

Saying 'please' will also help you in your career. If you're a PA supporting multiple executives, each of whom thinks his or her need is the most important, whom will you respond to first? The one who demands, or the one who says 'please'? The same with your staff and colleagues. Framing your requests with a 'please' instead of an order isn't a weakness; it shows courtesy and confidence.

The Art of Saying 'Well Done'

'Thank you' goes a very long way. 'Thank you' is powerful.

I remember being around fifteen years old and getting reprimanded by my father for being late without letting him and my mother know. When I protested and said that it wasn't fair, that he wasn't taking into consideration all the times I was on time, he said to me, "It's time you realize that one 'oh shit' wipes out a whole lot of 'atta girls' in this world."

This taught me three things:

1. It's not cool to be late.
2. In the accounts ledger of manners, actions are not equal. All the times I did things 'right' were, in fact, ameliorated by the one time I messed up.
3. My father's voice in criticism was much, much louder than it was in praise. Not from a volume perspective, but from a weight and memorability.

Though it may not have been the most eloquent way to say it, my dad made his point and I have remembered it throughout my career.

You as a boss have a very strong voice. And one criticism is much, much louder than all the 'well dones.' I have the following rules of thumb when it comes to how much praise a boss should give to employees:

- Five to One ratio. You should give five positives for every negative. Make a point of it. It's hard to do, but if you don't many of your staff will eventually stop being motivated as they will believe you are incapable of being pleased, so why bother.
- End every conversation with an appreciation rather than a negative. Some are into the 'compliment sandwich – start and end with a compliment and sandwich the negative feedback in the middle. I'm not that prescriptive. But there is a power to

ending a conversation by telling the person what you appreciate about them. Even ending a team meeting by having a ritual where multiple people share a genuine appreciation. It can be something small, like "I appreciated you picking up my document from the printer and bringing it to my desk to save me the interruption to go get it," but it sets the tone.

- The Rule of Three. Thank someone three times, sincerely, when they've gone out of their way or been thoughtful on a bigger scale. That could be saying thank you, sending a note, and doing something nice in return. If they've cancelled personal plans to help meet a deadline, rescheduled their holiday to cover someone else's personal leave for a family emergency, made time to help you solve a problem, gave you a reference – thank them three times.

A close cousin of 'thank you' is 'well done.' As an American in England, the power of 'well done' eluded me for a few years. However, now I realize that a 'well done' is very high praise in this country!

A lot of people are unsure about complimenting others in social or business situations and for good reason. The fear is how will it be received by the other person – will it win others over or send the wrong message? In general, it is a good thing to do, especially when sincere. Receiving a compliment makes people feel appreciated and respected. If you never give compliments, you come across as rude and unfeeling.

To navigate the minefield of compliment versus sucking up, recognize that there are levels of 'compliments.' Safe compliment areas include:

- Personal accomplishments (Congratulations on running the marathon! I heard you completed that course – well done! I saw that you got that keynote/award/article – very well deserved!)
- Talents (You have such a gift for languages, I really admire that. That's great that you are into sailing – what a skill. I hear you're in a choir? That's such a wonderful talent to have.)

- Style and taste that avoid appearance (That's a great suit – is it new? I love those shoes. What an interesting necklace – it looks great on you.)

Awkward compliments:

- Appearance/body. Never say, "You're so thin!" or "You've got such a great figure!" At best it feels like an inappropriate come-on, at worst it makes the other person feel uncomfortable as they attempt to equalize.
- Flat compliments. Don't just say, "You are so smart!" Use the compliment to further the flow of conversation. Don't say "You speak Chinese? Wow." Say, "That's great that you're studying Chinese. I imagine it takes a lot of focus?"

Learning to give compliments without being smarmy is important. The world's top CEOs, executives and board members have typically mastered the art of subtle flattery on their rise through the ranks. The premise is simple: people want to believe the best about themselves and even if the compliment is intended to suck up, they'll still roll with it and feel more positive toward the other person. You actually don't need to be overly concerned that people will take flattery as manipulative, unless it's your boss, where the agenda is more obvious.

Like it or not, flattery is a necessary part of building relationships and climbing in the ranks because it helps engender trust and begins to position you as the 'heir apparent' to the upper echelons. They are looking for the right person to pass the baton to, the person they can visualize in the post or who they think they can trust to carry on their work.

Women struggle in this area because we tend to be very direct in compliments – and equally direct in rejecting them so as not to appear that we feel superior to another person. Women 'level' themselves, making flattery challenging for us.

HOW TO GET "IT"

If you think that flattery doesn't matter, I'd urge you to try a six-week experiment. Start by identifying one person you need to influence in your rise to get your next job. Now, you're going target him/her with a six-week campaign using the steps below.

(Remember, if this person is male, be sure you do not give any flirtatious signs with your body language, or your compliments could be seen as a come-on. So when you're in your 'flattery campaign' make sure you moderate the five facets: keep your distance physically, don't touch or lean in during conversation, avoid wearing tight/revealing clothing, don't draw attention to your mouth with bright lipstick, wear lower heels or flats, and try to carry a body-blocking accessory — like a notebook that you can hold in front of you as a barrier.)

Over six weeks, employ these seven techniques in meetings and conversations to build a better relationship:

1. Preface a compliment with a disclaimer. Disguise the goal of the compliment and also help the person look modest by starting with "I don't want to embarrass you, but…" or "I know you won't want me to say this, but…" or "You're going to hate me for saying this, but…" and then toss out the compliment freely. You have, in effect, pre-leveled so they don't need to be embarrassed and they won't feel overly flattered. Again, don't have any physical contact and be aware of looking through your lashes or anything that could be construed as flirting or it will have a reverse effect.

2. Ask for advice as a way of showing deference. Couching a compliment by seeking advice is actually very clever. You may get good advice, but what you're really doing is showing that you want to learn from the person, that you admire and respect them. The subtle backhand is that you're paying them a compliment by asking them for their advice. And by saying that you see them as wise, they will think you are wise, too. Make sure the subject you're asking about is gender neutral and not personal — you don't want to highlight that you're not 'one of

the boys' or ask advice on something that makes you seem like a weak damsel in distress. Instead, make sure you're asking for advice about a serious business concern.

3. Give back-door compliments. Good things and bad things always get around. It's much more effective for someone else to say you've complimented a person than it is to do so directly. When we speak glowingly about someone behind their back, knowing they're likely to find out about it, it tells the person that you hold them in regard and it comes over as sincere and genuine. Again, make sure you're not complimenting their physical appearance or it will sound like a crush – compliment their leadership style or specific achievements.

4. Deliberately push back so you're not seen as a pushover. When the individual you want to flatter is pushing you to do something or get on board, don't agree straight away. It's best to argue a little first and then go along. This validates their sense of being smart and logical and they feel that you are discerning and worthy of trust. Ask good questions before you yield with the "OK, you've convinced me, I'm on board." This is important for women because it shows you're not a pushover and you have 'teeth.'

5. Do your homework. Find out what he or she thinks about a topic in advance by gathering information – then express similar views before they have a chance to introduce what they think. When done appropriately and not stalker-like this comes across as very sincere and you get credit for agreeing with the person without coming across as 'kissing up.'

6. Make what's important to them important to you. Learn about the other person's values. Are they supporters of a charity, do they have a specific religious conviction, are they committed to the environment? Establish early in the conversation that you have the same value – before they have a chance to declare their position. When we believe that others share our values on things that are important to us, we're less likely to doubt and more likely

to trust what they say next. Avoid talking about things that make you appear weak or as if you're looking for sympathy – focus on values that are shared and strong.

7. Establish common denominators. What do you have in common with this person? Do they like you? For men, they'll refer to a club or alma mater without thinking twice. Women need to do the same. This may mean joining a club that you know they belong to or another shared organization. Perhaps you have family that are in the same club or school? By mentioning the connection, you are raised in their estimation. Look at sports connections – golf clubs, tennis clubs – and education.

Now, I realize this seems manipulative and will be very uncomfortable. Get over it. There are men and women in your workplace who are doing this very thing, consciously or not, and doing it very well. And when it comes time for promotion, those in power to make the decisions will tip their way. If you look at it objectively, none of these steps toward flattery is actually 'wrong' or insincere. You can find common ground and give compliments without being a jerk or a manipulator.

The Trust Equation

Being a leader means being discreet. If you can't be trusted to keep confidences of those who work for you or with you, how can you be trusted with most confidential information? If you are asking others to behave unethically, what does it say about your own ethics? If you agree to behave unethically, can you be trusted?

I once had a client who put me in a very awkward situation. I was retained to work with this company on a project that required me to have access to the CEO and leadership team with frequency while reporting to a woman, Doreen, with accountability for the overall project. When Doreen needed to go on leave to undergo fertility treatments to conceive a child, I understood her feeling that this was a personal matter that she didn't want to share with her boss and colleagues.

The problem was that Doreen was expected to attend a company conference on the dates she needed to have the treatment. Of all her options of response, she chose to tell me the truth (she was skipping the conference to get the treatment) and that she was going to lie to her boss and tell him she had had a cycling accident and had to skip the conference. This is something I did not want to know. Even worse, Doreen then tried to enlist me in her lie by saying, "So, if he asks you, you need to tell him that I was in an accident."

So, what do we have here? First, I now know that Doreen is a person who is comfortable with lying and asking others to behave unethically. This does not inspire me to want to work with her. Second, I am now about to become complicit in her bad choice and if she's caught in the lie, so am I.

I had two options – to either go along with it or to tell her no. I chose a 'soft no,' saying, "Doreen, I understand you have your reasons for not wanting to tell your boss about your treatments. And I'm sure you understand that it would be difficult for me to lie about it. So, if I were asked, I'd prefer to just say that I don't know where you are. That's also a lie, but I really just want to stay out of it."

Her response was one of concern that I was going to 'out' her and our relationship was never quite the same after that incident. Eventually, I moved on to another project with another company. But I did learn that a colleague who was also on the team had ended up suing the company for unethical work practices, largely stemming from choices Doreen had made, and when the emails around the event were subpoenaed, more of her lies and unethical behavior came to light.

Top Ten Things Women in Business Should Never, Ever Do

1. Don't cry in meetings or in front of an audience. You may get choked up with genuine emotion, and that's fine, but don't open the waterworks or you'll seem insincere and make every man in the room uncomfortable.
2. Don't tell off-color jokes, ever.
3. Don't swear or use bad language. This is my downfall – every year my resolution is to curse less. But I know that women are judged more harshly than men and it lowers the tone rather than making you more included.
4. Don't flirt at the office.
5. Don't gossip. Remember: is it true, necessary, and kind? If not, keep it to yourself.
6. Never complain. Nobody likes a whiner.
7. Never explain. Nobody likes excuses.
8. Never blame. Throwing others under the bus just makes you look foolish.
9. Never send an email when you're angry. Give it 24 hours to cool.
10. Don't brag, and don't point out your flaws. Let your accomplishments speak for themselves and focus on your strengths.

CHAPTER 19

How to Be Gracious

We all know those people who make others feel instantly comfortable. They are warm, genuine, and sincere. They are interested and interesting. They express appreciation for others and they make you feel good just being around them.

We also all know those people who are awkward and uncomfortable to be around, who make others feel 'less than' or create a tense energy. They make people feel unsettled, anxious, or bad about themselves. They bring up the bad stuff at the worst time. They backbite and talk badly about others. So we avoid them.

Being an attractive person isn't about being physically pretty, it's about being a positive person to be around. How do those gracious people do it? Charismatic people shift between different tactics. Don't get stuck in just one, or you won't genuinely engage the other person – but think of this as a menu to choose from in your social connections:

1. Be interested and interesting. Ask questions and genuinely listen. Bring a subject to the conversation that others will be interested in as well, not just because you want to show off knowledge or make yourself look good.

2. Appreciate others. Let them know you understand and appreciate their good qualities. Tell someone directly or

indirectly that she is talented, funny, smart or attractive so she feels good about herself.

3. Connect by finding where you overlap. Ask about common interests, similar experiences, feelings, or friends. Making a connection helps people feel understood and creates a sense of belonging.

4. Elevate the conversation and the energy. People are drawn to others who are uplifting and buoyant in spirit. This doesn't mean being a comedian, but elevating the mood and the tone to be in the moment, smile, highlight the positive, and bring levity and lightness.

5. Enlighten without being arrogant. People like to learn. If you have something to share that relates to the person, then share it. Beware of being a know-it-all and notice if they check out, but it's great to share information and also learn yourself.

6. Shine the spotlight on others. My job is to help others shine. That can be your job, too. Whether it's your boss, a colleague, a friend, or someone who reports to you – in a social setting if you 'tee up' another person to let them shine, especially someone who may not be as socially adept, it makes you feel great and generates a good vibe.

I was invited by Jenifer, a friend and client, to go with her to a very posh London society event because she was working on her networking skills. My role was to help Jenifer shine and feel the power and positivity of a successful event.

We started by joining in the same conversations and I modeled drawing others out by asking questions and connecting. In one group, there was a woman who happened to have a home in Utah, where I grew up. Rather than diving into that conversation, which would potentially exclude Jenifer, I asked about frequent flying – an area where we could find more common ground and then leverage other topics.

HOW TO GET "IT"

The woman mentioned she'd recently flown back from Turkey, and I knew Jenifer had lived there as a child. That gave Jenifer a chance to elevate by talking about the beauty of the country, enlighten by telling the woman about some places she might visit, and opportunities for Jenifer to feel appreciated and have the spotlight shine on her.

Mixing and Mingling Made Simple

What if you feel awkward in social settings, but you don't have a friend to help you ease into the situation? It's very common to have to attend events alone, which can be daunting.

So don't be embarrassed to introduce yourself to someone, especially if someone is also standing alone. If you're introducing yourself into a group, it's slightly more challenging, particularly if you don't know anyone. Be aware before you join in – this ensures you're not jumping in inappropriately.

I was listening to a radio program where they were talking about people meeting their rock star idols. One man they interviewed was a superfan of Bruce Springsteen and had seen him in countless concerts. Somehow he was given or won backstage passes and was obviously excited. Having never been backstage before, he didn't realize there was a lot of alcohol, and it was free! Being nervous, he had several drinks and then plucked up his courage to approach The Boss and introduce himself. Unfortunately, he picked a time when Springsteen was crouched down intently engaged in conversation with another person sitting on a sofa.

When he came up behind and interrupted, looming from above, he was given a dismissive look, a 'hello,' and a cold shoulder. To his credit, the man didn't seem to harbor a grudge against the star, saying, "I should never have interrupted Springsteen in a crouch!"

I think that's a good rule of thumb for us all: 'Never Interrupt Springsteen in a Crouch.'

The best bet is to approach a group that seems to be in general chit-chat, not an in-depth discussion, wait until there's a break in the conversation, then make eye contact with anyone and simply reach out your hand and introduce yourself: "Hi, I'm Coni Judge from Eden Communications." Et voila. You can also join the conversation by extending the topic: "That's so interesting. Sorry, I overheard your conversation and that's really fascinating. I'm Coni, by the way."

If you're on the flip side – in a social setting where you know others, be gracious and welcome in the loners who may not know anyone. When making introductions remember, "Mr. President, I'd like you to meet…" You should always use the name of the most senior or important person first. If you're welcoming a customer or client, he or she is always the most recognized person – even above a CEO,

Taking initiative to introduce yourself and others shows that you are engaged, socially skilled and comfortable. If you sit back and wait for an introduction, you will appear distant, uninviting, and passive. This sounds simple, but personally I find this very challenging and have worked to overcome my trepidation and shyness. People who are naturally extroverted or social butterflies don't have the same issues and find this natural, but until I have a personality transformation, I have to fake it!

Some of the tips I use to make mixing and mingling in new settings easier for myself:

- Remember to smile. Smiling makes us seem likeable and pleasant, but if a woman doesn't smile, she seems uninterested or cold. Try to fit in by adapting and being similar to others. This doesn't mean being a Stepford Wife. However, if you choose to focus on your individuality rather than your commonality with others, you will appear interesting and eccentric at best, inaccessible, self-involved and socially awkward at worst. You want to be safe, comfortable, nonjudgmental.

HOW TO GET "IT"

- Look the part by being well groomed. This makes me feel more confident that I fit in, and in general good grooming demonstrates that you are a thoughtful person, healthy and confident. Lack of attention to your grooming and style comes across as socially unaware and careless.

- Be nice but not brilliant. I don't need to wow everyone with my amazing knowledge and genius and brilliance. I just need to be nice, engaged, and thoughtful.

- Your first sentence positions you, so keep opening lines simple, positive and pre-planned within reason. I usually know the first sentence I'm going to say so I don't get tongue tied, but I keep it simple and related to something going on: "Hi, I'm Coni. Isn't that view amazing?" Getting too 'smooth' can come across as shallow, aggressive or calculating. If you open the conversation by being in the moment – talking about the immediate situation, you show you're safe, socially aware and easy to engage.

- Start with a positive. If you open with a casual negative opinion you will at best seem straightforward, but more likely to be unlikable and unpleasant. So avoid criticizing the food, venue, host, or just having to be there. "Hi, aren't these things awful?" is not the best opener. If someone opens with a negative to you, it's fine to acknowledge and then shift to something positive. It's the difference between "Wasn't traffic awful today?" and "How did you manage the traffic today?"

Trips and traps to avoid when you're mixing can sometimes be a little hard to see. Make sure you don't stay in one topic too long or in one conversation too long. You don't need to latch on to someone like a life raft at sea. As soon as they shift their body language or look around, end with, "There's someone I have to speak with, but it was really nice meeting you!"

Accepting Gentlemanly Behavior as a Woman

Yes, I can open my own door. Yes, I can take off my own coat without help. Yes, I can carry a box. When a male colleague offers to help with my door, coat or parcel, I choose not to take it as a way of diminishing my capabilities or competence. I choose to accept that he's being chivalrous and helpful.

Being gracious means accepting his help in a polite way. What is the other option? To assert my competence, refuse his help, and make him feel foolish or offended. What could possibly be the strategic advantage of offending anyone who is attempting to be kind?

Even if an offer of chivalry is put forth in a patronizing or diminishing way – as I experienced the last time I was at a client office in Texas and a man held open the door and said "After you, darlin'" while he clearly checked out my derriere – this is not the time to make a feminist stand. It's the time to be a lady and accept the help.

In turn, you should be chivalrous to male and female colleagues:

- Whoever gets to the door first holds it open for others.
- The person closest to the elevator door exits, holding it open for others who may be slower or encumbered.
- If a man or woman is having a difficult time with a jacket or scarf, offer to help.
- Stand when you great a man or woman, particularly if he or she is of higher rank, a client, or elderly.
- When someone is carrying a heavy parcel or awkward package, offer to help.

One tricky area for women in business is that of chairs. The general rule is to not hold chairs for men or women, unless there's a physical need. However, men of a certain age, and a certain class, were raised to always hold out a chair for a woman when she is sitting down for a meal. Sometimes this extends to business dinners, lunches, or breakfasts. Men get confused in this situation because they don't want to be sexist, but they also want to be polite. What to do? The objective is to avoid confusing, awkward moments and focus on building a positive business relationship.

So, when you approach the table, if a man moves to pull out your chair, simply allow him to do so and say, "Thank you." If he asks, "Can I get the chair for you?" you can accept or refuse. My rule is to always accept courtesy when it's offered, regardless of gender. If someone offers me water or a coffee, I accept graciously. If a man offers to pull out my chair, I accept.

Another gray area is revolving doors. Etiquette, again, dictates that the man should enter the door first to exert the energy for the woman to enter with ease. Modern men just find this a confusing and awkward moment. If a man looks like he knows the revolving door rule and is going to propel it for me, I accept. It may also mean he's just going to go first, which is also fine. If he hesitates and allows me to go first, he's trying to be a gentleman, so I also accept and go through first – even if it means muscling the inert door – because his intention was to be chivalrous.

Managing Motherhood Graciously

I have three sons. I've been a single mother for most of my career and my youngest son has severe autism. This means that I need to balance my life thoughtfully to be the mother I need to be, and also do a good job and provide for my family. So when I have a child who's unwell, or a meeting at the school, or a childcare emergency, I explain the situation with minimal drama, do what needs to be done, and make sure I deliver on my commitments.

Becoming a mother was a pivotal moment in my career. Despite every woman's intention to 'have it all,' it doesn't 'all' come without compromise or sacrifice in large and small ways.

I have had more than one conference call from inside my bedroom, inside my closet, with every door imaginable shut, to avoid my client or boss hearing a crying child in the background. Every time I felt like a terrible mother. And every time it turned out fine. As a mom, we make dozens of judgments every day. I may sequester myself for a conference call, but then I hold firm on never missing an important school event because I'm working late or traveling.

In general, I try to separate mothering from working as much as possible:

- When I'm at work, I'm a worker first. I'm there to do my job. So pictures of the kids on my desk are fine, but classroom artwork and other artifacts go at home on the fridge. Look at your male colleagues' and senior executives' offices. They aren't decorated like a preschool classroom.

- Most people at work don't care about your children's lives. This means schools, illnesses, social dramas, or other minutia of life. Save those newsflash conversations for your family or girlfriends.

- If I need to miss work due to a 'kid thing' I minimize it as much as possible and don't make a big deal of it. I work with a lot of people who don't have children, and it's not fair for me to get a 'get out of work free' card because I do. I still go to my kids' events; I just don't announce it to everyone.

- I keep what's private, private. My youngest son has profound autism that is an ongoing concern with a lot of educational, medical and emotional issues. I don't talk about it very often because my issues are not any larger or smaller than anyone else's. Everyone's child has his or her own concerns, and the last thing I want is to come across as expecting pity or dominating conversation with my personal life.

- If someone, usually a female colleague, asks about my children, I tell them "They're fine, thanks, and how are yours?" Usually it's because they want a conversation opener to talk about their own children. I'm happy to listen, keep my parenting thoughts and commentary to myself, and try to move the conversation to something more gender neutral than mothering, particularly if male colleagues are nearby. I don't want to create the 'mommy club' at work that alienates my male counterparts.

- If I'm with my kids and run into a colleague, client or boss in a social setting, which has happened, I introduce the children, chat briefly, and then we leave. I don't want to prolong the conversation to be awkward or potentially have the kids become impatient and act out. Most bosses will be understanding and actually appreciate not having to engage with your kids for too long.

- If I'm working from home, my office is a no-kid zone. When I'm on the clock, my kids know that I'm not to be disrupted. I try to schedule conference calls for naptimes or avoid when they'll be coming home from school or babysitter handover times. We've all been on conference calls where you can hear kids in the background crying or arguing, the doorbell rings and someone has to drop off the call to open the door to hear the kids come bounding in from school. It's at best unprofessional, at worst a reminder that you're working from home and potentially distracted or skiving off.

Romance and Friendships

The quote 'If you need a friend, get a dog' has been attributed to Harry Truman and Ronald Reagan, and is said by Gordon Gekko in *Wall Street*. It's true that friendships and relationships in the workplace don't need to be excluded, but they need to have boundaries, particularly if you're in leadership and have access to confidential or sensitive information.

With friends at work, be cautious about what you reveal to your work friends when it comes to personal issues – dating, marriage, children, divorce, sexual preference, death, or personal finance. Information can be misconstrued or used as gossip fodder later on. So be sure anything you don't want known stays private.

As your career is propelled, your friendships will likely become more formal and less friendly. Most leaders find out the hard way that as they rise up the ranks it's best not to form friendships with subordinates. When you know people too personally, it can make the tough decisions — like layoffs, performance reviews, and other interventions — gut wrenching for you both.

Socializing also becomes awkward as you rise through the ranks. You don't know if people are joining you for the drink after work, or the second one, because they want to or because they think that saying 'no, thanks' will insult you. Socializing in a business setting is fine, or during away days or holiday parties. But choose your real friends outside of work.

With colleagues, bosses, or clients, don't let friendship be the reason you make promises or commitments that you shouldn't or can't keep.

Office romances are common and it's inevitable that people will meet at work and fall in love. Before you open up the office pool to romance, know the policy at your company and consider the ramifications of CEOs who have resigned due to what was deemed an inappropriate relationship at work: Stryker's Stephen P. MacMillan, Best Buy's Brian Dunn, and Hewlett-Packard's Mark Hurd.

If you do decide to date a colleague, keep it mum on social media, make the office a non-PDA zone, and don't talk about the relationship with the office. If you decide to date a subordinate or your boss, change the reporting relationship and notify Human Resources as soon as you both agree that this is a real relationship.

If one or both of you is married, proceed at your peril and consider the 'bulletin board rule' — would you want this action to be posted on the bul-

HOW TO GET "IT"

letin board for everyone to see? Then it's likely that no good will come of it and you probably shouldn't do it.

HOW TO GET "IT"

letin board for everyone to see? Then it's likely that no good will come of it and you probably shouldn't do it.

CHAPTER 20

Basic Business Etiquette

When you're mixing business and entertaining, certain rules apply, particularly if you're entertaining a boss or client. If you invite the boss to a social setting, particularly if he or she is old school or very senior in ranking, try to include a few other guests with similar interests to smooth it over. Act normally and address your boss as you would at work, either as 'Mr. Jones' or 'Bob' – don't change just because you're in a social setting.

When dining out, the guest orders first, regardless of gender. If the waiter comes to the table and you are the host, you should say, "Oh, please take my guest's order first." If you're at lunch or dinner with your boss, defer to him or her to order first. If he or she asks you to order first, go ahead.

When it comes to paying the bill, the person who did the inviting pays the bill. Sometimes the guest insists on paying. In this situation, it's most important to avoid an awkward conversation or tension. If it's a meal with the boss and you did the inviting, offer to pay but then let him or her pay if he or she insists at all. If it's a client, I first say, "Oh, no, let me pick that up. It's on the company." If they still insist, I just allow them to pay and say, "Next time, it's on me." So, the next time I go out with that person, I will arrange to pay the bill away from the guest, either by arriving early and telling the hostess my intention, or excusing myself to use the ladies' room, and then asking the waiter to give me the bill after my guest leaves.

How to Host a Meeting

Hosting a meeting means actually being a host. If you don't have a personal assistant, it falls on you to ensure the meeting prep goes smoothly. Even if you do have a PA, it never hurts to check, especially if it's an important meeting involving senior executives.

1. Go early and make sure the room is ready and the technology works.
2. Make sure there's a defined purpose for the meeting and you know your definition of 'success' for the time.
3. Start on time.
4. End on time. If you need to run over, ask permission as soon as you realize the situation and allow those who need to leave a gracious exit.
5. Acknowledge latecomers graciously but without derailing.
6. Keep on track by dealing with off-agenda items and problems off line. Knowing how to deal with someone who wants to dominate the meeting, a know-it-all, or a devil's advocate is the mark of a leader. Showing you have command of a meeting shows your superiors that you have what it takes.
7. Always end with a thank you.
8. Follow up with a summary and next steps.

Etiquette in the Office – Ten Women You Don't Want to Be

1. The Loud One who is taking conference calls at her desk in an open plan, disrupting others from doing their jobs.
2. The Personal Caller who is talking to her kids, husband, mother, sister at the office.
3. The Primper who is putting on nail polish, hairspray or makeup at her desk.
4. The Drama Queen who has a new dilemma every day and wants to share it.
5. The Tipsy One who gets just a little too drunk at business events and doesn't seem aware.
6. The Eavesdropper who listens in on conversations in open plan environments and then brings them up.
7. The Dominator who has to chime in on every conversation or meeting, even if she has no real point to make.
8. The Judge who is quick to identify any flaw and makes a point of 'helping' others by revealing their weaknesses in public.
9. The Whinger who is never happy, always negative, and finds a reason to share it.
10. The High Maintenance One who needs a special meal, a special car, a special everything. If you do have dietary requirements, such as allergies, discuss it with the waiter quietly and privately. Make sure your special requests don't inconvenience others.

Technology and Social Media Etiquette in Business

The little electronic devices that we use to connect ourselves to each other bring with them a host of etiquette issues and are seductive tools for bad behavior. How many people around you, right now, wherever you are in the world – on a train, subway, plane, or coffee shop – are looking at a device rather than a human?

It should be a no-brainer, but how many politicians have we seen on the dais behind a speaker checking their phone rather than paying attention? How many times has someone 'dismissed' you by taking a call during what you felt was an important conversation? How often are you taken aback by what other professionals post on their social media accounts and think less of them?

It matters. And mastering how to stay on the right side of technology and social media separates the girls from the women.

- Pay attention to the person in front of you. Talking on a cell phone while with a colleague or acquaintance signals that you think they are less important. However, visibly turning off your phone or silencing it while it's ringing, combined with "Oh, I'm sorry, let me turn this off. Now back to our conversation…" can send a positive message.

- Don't text or check your device during meetings unless it's absolutely necessary. Even then, it's safest to mention at the beginning of the meeting, "I may need to keep an eye on my mobile as I'm expecting an important email that I need to forward."

- Remember that anything you put in writing – email, text, and instant message – can be copied and forwarded. Make sure you think about what you write and if it's sensitive, just assume it will be forwarded. If that's a problem, don't write it down.

- Keep it polished. Don't use girly fonts in wacky colors for your emails. Don't have silly ringtones that distract. Don't bedazzle your phone or get a Hello Kitty cover for your tablet. This is not your high school bedroom, so don't put stickers on your laptop.

- Don't be the person that forwards jokes and other 'humorous' emails in the workplace. If it's a professional article, fine. Otherwise, keep it to your friends.

Social media is ubiquitous, growing and fraught with pitfalls. Every week it seems that there is another platform. YouTube, Pinterest, Foursquare, Vine, Instagram, and there will be something else tomorrow. The most frightening thing about social media is that it never goes away – your missteps remain forever.

Keep a boundary between personal and professional on your social media. The lines get blurred quickly when colleagues become Facebook friends and clients are Twitter followers. Make a conscious decision about whom you will friend in your social media domains because once you include professional acquaintances, you can no longer treat it as a personal channel.

This means if a business associate sends you a friend request, you need to decide how to handle it. Your LinkedIn profile is an appropriate place to network with colleagues. If someone sends you a friend request on Facebook or other account you use for family and social friends, it's fine to ignore the request and then send them a contact request via LinkedIn. Don't decline them; just let it drift. If you do accept colleagues, make sure you have the privacy controls on your page set up, and keep in mind that that is no guarantee to keep something from going viral.

So, keep the following in mind:

- What you post can get you fired. Don't express controversial opinions. Don't curse or use offensive language. Make sure the 'sensitivity' filter is switched on. It will go viral. It will live forever.
- Social media can be a great tool to be accessible – when you're the CEO or in a very senior role. Until then, make sure you

- know why you're blogging, tweeting or posting and be sure it aligns with your career objectives and personal brand.
- Photos make an impression. Be conscious of what you post and who tags you in photos. Avoid pictures that show too much skin, show you intoxicated or impaired in any way, or show that you were out partying instead of at home sick like you told your boss.
- Have a good photograph that is recent, flattering, simple background, wearing professional clothing and appropriate makeup and hair.
- Decide what social media to promote on your business cards and email signature and what to eliminate. I include a link to my LinkedIn www.linkedin.com/in/conijudge and my company website www.coni.london.

Cross Cultural Awareness

The world is actually very small when it comes to big business. Having worked in multinationals for most of my career, I've worked in dozens of countries and with colleagues from more cultures than I can count. Growing up in a small Utah town, I never imagined I'd have such a well-used passport and the opportunity to work with people from around the world.

I've learned to accept that other cultures have a way of doing things, and to be successful I need to adapt and abide by them. It's up to me to understand and change, rather than to be arrogant and assume they'll adapt to my American style.

Corporate cultures also vary dramatically. What is rewarded? What is allowed? How do things get done? It changes from company to company and before you rush headlong to make your mark on a new company, it's wise to sit back for a bit and see how things work. I'm reminded of a man who came into a long-vision oil company culture from the fast-paced technology sector and absolutely bombed as he tried to make over the company. He was seen as being out of touch and didn't last long.

How to get on in any culture:

- Prepare. Before you travel to a new country to work, go to a new company, or if you get a boss or team member from another culture, do a quick Google search to learn more about the culture, dining traditions, clothing expectations, and ways of doing business. Read up on local news so you can carry on a reasonable conversation.
- Identify important people, learn how to pronounce their names, know their titles. Use formal titles and don't address others by their first name unless invited.
- Adapt your pace. Americans are known for being assembly-line driven. That doesn't always go down well in other cultures where there's a prelude to business, such as having rounds and rounds of tea in the Middle East before they get down to brass tacks. Their work start and stop times will also differ. Before you set an 8 a.m. breakfast meeting or a midday lunch meeting, find out what's appropriate.
- Learn how negotiating works in that country. In China, the art of negotiation is quite different than in England. There are norms, expectations and countless ways to blow deals.
- Make sure you're on the right side of your company policies. If you work in a country where 'incentives' are basically bribes to get things done, you need to protect yourself and your career.
- Avoid hot topics like politics, religion, and sex (gender and sexuality) by all means in any conversation. Steer it away immediately to safer ground.
- Know the business card etiquette for your first impression. Make sure you have cards with you at all times, just in case.

- Learn a few words of the local language: please, thank you, good morning, good afternoon, good night, hello and goodbye.

You should also know how women are seen in a country or culture and adjust your style and approach. I usually adapt my clothing and my style to fit in and ensure I don't offend. If in doubt, find other women who are also working in that culture and ask them for guidance. They can tell you what to expect from that company in that setting.

This is a tricky area. Once I was traveling in India and wore a traditional sari to a dinner. The Indian people present were delighted and I got many compliments. One American man, who was rather competitive with me, took it as offensive and made a point to tell my boss and my boss' boss that he thought it was inappropriate. I learned the lesson to err on the side of being conservative. And I also learned that it's unwise to give your competitors bullets to shoot you with…

As a woman traveling abroad, there are also safety considerations. I've more than once found myself in an awkward position where I've realized, maybe it wasn't the best idea for a blonde American woman to be traipsing out and about alone. So, make sure you're conscious of your surroundings, check in with the consulate before traveling, and ensure you're following company policy at all times.

If negotiations are critical, it is likely that you'll use a translator of some kind. Even if the other party speaks English, or you speak their language, you'll want to ensure the subtleties aren't lost. While you don't want to offend, you also want to be sure the translator is neutral. Make sure you use a company-approved translator rather than accepting one from your client. Arrange to meet the translator beforehand to review the agenda, have you review your visual aids, and ensure you feel confident with his or her capability. If you have reservations, find another translator if possible.

Gift giving is another cultural area to ensure you understand. In Japan, gifts are given and expected on numerous occasions and the presentation is very important. In some countries bringing wine is expected where in others it would be seen as an insult that you think the host might not have enough. So ask a colleague who is familiar with that country and culture what is appropriate before you dive in.

To Gift or Not to Gift

Gifts are expected at key points in a professional relationship, to mark a milestone or a holiday, but the key is to ensure they are appropriate: not too personal, not too pricey. Otherwise, they can backfire.

If you're giving gifts outside the company to vendors or clients, make sure you're in line with your company policies. Usually branded items such as pens, paperweights, etc., are okay, but stay on the right side of policy and don't get into a sticky situation.

If an employee has gone above and beyond, first use the formal internal reward systems provided – whether it's a financial bonus or another type of acknowledgment.

There may be times where you want to give a personal gift to a colleague. If you're giving a gift inside the company, follow these guidelines:

- Gifts for your assistant depend on the length of time they've worked for you. Ensure the gift is not overly personal. Books, theatre tickets, gift certificates are all good ideas.
- Gifts to the boss should be given with caution and may be seen as sucking up and a way to curry favor. A group gift from the team is the safer bet.
- Gifts for colleagues should be professional and set in the workplace: pens, letter openers, travel items. Temporary gifts like flowers (apart from roses, which have a romantic connotation), foodstuffs, candy or beverages are also appropriate.

- Ensure it's presented thoughtfully and modestly. Be proud of giving the gift and always attach a card.

If you receive a gift, it goes without saying that you should be appreciative. It's usually expected to open the gift in front of others, unless it's a formal occasion. And don't forget to send a thank you note, written on real paper rather than a text or email. Also make sure the gift doesn't violate company policy, especially if it's from a vendor or customer. You don't want to get in trouble for accepting an ugly paperweight. If it does violate the guidelines, regretfully return it and explain why it's not allowed by your company. Ensure the process is documented in the event it's ever questioned later.

What about regifting? While it's on the verge of tacky, we've all found ourselves in a pinch, needing a gift and having our own homes or offices to 'shop' from. Eek. So, consider it a form of recycling:

- Don't leave evidence of past gifting, such as a card or wrapping paper, and make sure it's in good condition.
- Don't give the same gift back to the giver.
- Tell the person it's a regift if it's really special – like tickets you were given that you know they'd appreciate more. That actually is more thoughtful.

Handling the Worst Case Scenario

There are times when we all find ourselves in trouble and in danger of being inconsiderate or rude.

1. Being Late or No-Showing

If you're going to be late for a business meal or appointment:

- Advise as soon as possible with an expected arrival time by calling the other person's cell phone or the restaurant.

HOW TO GET "IT"

- Apologize when you do arrive, without making excuses. A simple and sincere 'I'm so sorry to be late' will do.

- Don't dilly-dally in menu selection. The other party has had a lot of time to look at the menu waiting for you, so either choose the first item from the salad menu or let him or her order first and then just order the same thing.

- Make absolutely certain not to take calls or have any other behavior during the meeting that could be considered rude or inconsiderate.

If you're going to be late for a meeting or conference:

- Decide if it's best to wait for a break or to enter immediately.

- Before you enter the room, get what you need out of your bag and have yourself completely situated so you can sit down and immediately engage. You don't want to take off your coat, scarf, put down a handbag, get out a pen, find a notebook, rattle papers and folders, get out a laptop, etc.

- Find the door that is the least noticeable to enter, and if possible, identify an open seat before you make yourself known.

- Be unobtrusive as you enter, apologize without interrupting anyone and take your seat with minimal fuss.

If someone no-shows on you, send a text or call his or her assistant after fifteen or twenty minutes. A simple, "I'm at the restaurant and I'm wondering if I've got the wrong date or time? Please ring me back."

After thirty minutes, send a text or leave a note with the maître d': "Bob, I waited nearly an hour and hope everything's all right? Please give me a call at the office." If you're leaving a restaurant without eating, give the maître d' a tip to acknowledge you've held a table. When Bob does appear, accept his apology without making a big deal of it, and if it was your error, apologize for the misunderstanding.

2. Forgetting Names

What's in a name? Everything. Yet, I am the first to admit that I totally stink at remembering names. I can remember what the person was wearing when I met them, the stories they told me about their family, and where we met, but the name eludes me. The more I try, the more it flees my mind. I've tried associations – which never work because every man seems to be named Simon, Dave or Jon.

I so envy people who have name recall, as it's a skill I wish I could develop. But, as I don't have that wiring in my brain, I have to cheat:

- When I go to a meeting, I make a map of the names on a piece of paper while people are introducing themselves. Then I try to be as unobtrusive as I can when I refer to it.
- I've become accustomed to just saying: "Oh hello! I remember meeting you, we had a lovely conversation about India, but I can't believe I've forgotten your name. I'm so sorry!" or "My mind has gone blank. I'm so sorry that I've forgotten your name."
- If it's hard to pronounce, I admit it. "I'm sorry, I didn't quite catch your name?"
- If someone mispronounces my name – which is very, very common – I try to help him or her out as soon as I see him or her struggle. With a smile, I say, "I've probably heard my name pronounced twenty different ways, but it's Mah-see-ahv. A challenging name to say!"

3. Awkward Introductions and Disabilities

If you frequently encounter the same awkward moments, have your one-liners memorized. Like my 'I've forgotten your name' line – I have it memorized so it makes an already awkward moment more seamless. Or, for example, if you're very tall, have a response that is non-offensive that you can use in every setting, like "Yes, I was always chosen first for basketball!"

Disabilities are another potentially awkward moment.

- If you have a physical disability, you should have a prepared line that helps get people past it simply and quickly and moves the conversation on.
- If you are introduced to someone with a disability, don't bring attention to it. Just be aware and let the disabled person lead.
- Don't use the disability as a conversation starter to ask personal questions, particularly if you've only just met the person. It's not their responsibility to educate you on what it's like to be blind, deaf or in a wheelchair.
- Don't condescend or pity. "I just don't know how you do it" or "I could never do what you do" or "I find you so inspiring" are not positive ways to start a conversation. Having a disabled child, I hear these things quite often and I'd much rather talk about shared interests or business rather than deflecting notions that my life must be horrible. Because it's not.

4. Being Found Out

So you applied for the internal job promotion without telling your current boss, and you've now been found out. You've sent an email to 50,000 people and misspelled your boss' name. You've had a moment of indiscretion where you spilled the beans on a secret, and now it's come back to bite you. You forwarded an email without noticing at the beginning of the trail that it said something disparaging about the person to whom you've sent it. You've pocket dialed someone's voicemail and they now have overheard a sensitive conversation. You sent a text or email that autocorrected to a curse word.

These things happen. The best you can do is to acknowledge without blaming others, apologize sincerely, try to make reparations where possible, and take it like a lady.

Early in my career I was convinced that Flash was the hottest new technology and we should use it for our annual message from a C-level executive. We wrote a script and came up with a futuristic theme that ended up with him being in a spaceship. Honestly, I don't know what I was thinking in hindsight, except that I got swept away in the moment. It was a disaster.

As I was licking my wounds, my wonderful boss took me aside and told me not to be so hard on myself. "If we all had to wear our mistakes like anchors, none of us would be able to move," he told me. So now, whenever I screw up, and I do, I try to remind myself to unshackle the anchor from my ankle, do my best to make it right, and keep moving on.

5. Dealing with Rejection

The reality is, sometimes we win and sometimes we don't. As you climb the ladder, the jobs get more scarce and the competition more fierce. You won't get every job.

Nobody likes to be rejected or turned down for the job or promotion. When you are on the losing end, try to reframe and realize it didn't work out this time, but it doesn't mean that it won't next time. Send a brief note to say thank you for being considered for the job to show you're a person of class and good manners. You can also send a note of congratulations to the person who got the job if it was an internal hire and you know the individual.

Never burn a bridge in a moment of having your feelings hurt. You never know when you'll need it on another day.

Practice: Polishing Your Sociability Presence

Social graces are evolving, not static. As technology changes, new rules emerge. As you rise through the ranks, navigating social waters becomes more complicated and fraught with issues.

The more senior you become, the more the microscope becomes trained on you and every misstep has potential serious ramifications. When you were at the beginning of your career and less noticeable, it was perhaps easier to let your personality shine through and be forgiven for saying or doing something potentially offensive. Now, that can be career suicide.

Being 'politically correct' gets a bad rap, as if it's selling out. And to some extent, yes, it is about editing yourself. But it's also about recognizing that you have a responsibility to consider how you are viewed as a representative of your company and yourself. Don't go out on a yacht race when your company's oil well is leaking and destroying an ocean. Don't use defamatory or racist language as a 'joke.' Don't have sex with your co-worker or boss and expect there to be no consequences. Don't write and send that email that you'll later regret.

You have the skills, tools, and resources to make changes in how you present yourself in the workplace. Use this as a way to polish and refine your facet to project your best self, build successful relationships, and make your way to get the job you deserve and have earned.

CHAPTER 21

The Fifth Facet - Can You Create a Star?

'Star quality.' 'It.' *'Je ne sais quoi.'*

The indefinable something that makes one individual stand out from the crowd.

We may not be able to define 'It' very well, but we know it when we see it. And It separates the stars from the rest in every field – politics, theater, music, athletics, science, and corporations. In the business world, 'executive presence,' 'image,' and 'gravitas' are used to describe that 'It' factor that elevates one individual ahead of the pack.

'It' is elusive. Some perceive it as something you're born with or you're not. Did some people get sprinkled with the 'secret ingredient' at birth while others missed out? And if you missed the sprinkling, does that mean you're basically screwed?

Countless surveys show that the person with the highest IQ or most impressive degree isn't necessarily the one who succeeds. Executive presence appears to be the critical element that tips the balance one way or another for career acceleration.

Presence also apparently comes more easily to men than it does to women based on research. In my mid 40s and American, I am from a fortunate generation. I have never faced a true glass ceiling because women before me splintered it. Yet, women in every industry and age category are still at a disadvantage when it comes to gravitas. Worse still, we hamper our own ability to improve because we find it awkward to discuss, afraid of causing

So we are faced with options: to dismiss and ignore this area as inconsequential; to accept defeat and decide you are powerless to get the job you really want and deserve; or you can take control and tackle it head on.

Along with elevating your skillset, working hard, and managing your career, taking control over your executive presence is one tool to achieve your personal and professional objectives.

Those people who appear to have executive star quality and been sprinkled with the elusive 'It' are often successful simply because they have worked to understand how others perceive them. They recognized that they need to deliberately reveal their blind spots, faced them head on, and made progress rather than getting hung up on 'perfect.' They carry on and keep their spine straight in the face of setbacks and challenges. They allow vulnerability to shine through, galvanizing people to follow and believe in their leadership. That's how you become a corporate star.

A Matter of Mindset

So what? Why bother defining it if you can't get it? Why would you want to know there's a pot of gold if you can never have it? It's one thing to have the problem defined, it's another to believe something can be done about it.

I continue to be wholeheartedly convinced that it is possible to teach Executive Presence because I have seen it and I have done it. The root is a question of mindset. Those who believe that the X factor or executive presence is a magical 'dose' have a 'fixed' mindset while I believe that it absolutely can be taught if one is willing to be open to change. 'Mindset' is a term coined by renowned psychologist Carol Dweck. Basically, Dweck developed the theory that there are two types of mindset – fixed and growth.

According to Dweck, 'In a fixed mindset, people believe their basic qualities, like their intelligence or talent, are simply fixed traits. They spend their time documenting their intelligence or talent instead of developing them. They also believe that talent alone creates success – without effort. They're wrong. In a growth mindset, people believe that their most basic abilities can be developed through dedication and hard work – brains and talent are just the starting point. This view creates a love of learning and a resilience that is essential for great accomplishment. Virtually all great people have had these qualities.'

So maybe all these great people didn't have the secret sprinkling. Perhaps these people just realized that they needed to become aware of how they projected themselves, turn up their own wattage strategically in key areas, and use their power to get people to listen to their ideas and seize opportunities. And then they did it.

Mapping the Minefield of Presence

The Fifth Facet has three elements: Gravitas, Politics, and Positioning.

- Gravitas is your general ability to project competence and confidence by understanding and leveraging the first four facets: Visual, Verbal, Kinesthetic, and Sociability.
- Politics is recognizing the social and political dynamics of an organization and developing a personal strategy to play the game without selling your soul.
- Positioning is how you frame yourself and your career to be both authentic and aspirational and how you tap into your resilience and personal strengths to be seen as a leader.

CHAPTER 22

Understanding Gravitas

According to CTI, 'gravitas' is the most important pillar in executive presence. What you say, how you look, and how you act contribute to your gravitas and underscore that you're the 'real deal' and worthy of being heard and followed. Women walk a fine line in projecting gravitas without triggering negative responses from both men and women. Your presence or gravitas needs to be constantly retuned and refined depending on the situation and audience.

I would describe myself as a 'confident introvert,' which can easily be perceived as 'snobby' if I don't pay attention to the cues I'm giving verbally and nonverbally. So I was surprised when I recently got feedback from a British colleague that I was coming across as an 'American cheerleader' in a meeting. I was talking about an area where I feel particularly passionate, and I switched to 'On' – which meant my voice raised a few octaves, my smile wattage amplified, my gestures got bigger, and it tipped me over the edge of credibility, in her perception.

Given my concern about being cold or snooty, perhaps I was overcorrecting with friendliness? In some situations, mostly in America or with audiences that require high energy, this would be an asset. But in a small room of English people, this was not a good thing.

Feedback can be hard to process, especially when it's about style instead of skill. I could've been offended, defensive and resistant to this feedback, and, in fact, it was my first instinct to reject it and rationalize it as being her issue, not mine. And though it did sting a bit, rather than pushing it away, I shifted into neutral, actually listened to what she was saying, and accepted it as a well-intended and potentially valuable gift. I appreciated her bravery to step out and give me input and chose to listen and accept it. Because this was new feedback for me, I asked a few other people that I trust if they had seen this behavior as well, and started to get a feel for this insight – my 'cheerleader' knob on my Executive Presence mixing board. My energy level is an asset but it can also be a blocker with some people.

Now that I am aware, it's no longer in my blind spot. I can pay attention to the response I'm picking up from audiences, particularly British females, and instead of turning up the friendly factor – which is what I would have done in the past to create connection – realize that it could be having a counterproductive effect. So I need to turn down the Cheerleader and lower my tone, gestures, and energy to appear and be more calm and thoughtful. I can activate Cheerleader when I need her and turn her down when she's getting in the way.

What is getting in your way? Are there aspects of your personality that may be off-putting or sending the wrong signal? Maybe you think you are projecting 'knowledgeable' but really you come across as 'know-it-all'? There are many fine lines for women and awareness is the starting point to becoming strategic about how to navigate them.

The Low Hanging Fruit of Gravitas

In their study on Executive Presence, CTI found that 67% of the senior executives surveyed thought that 'Gravitas' was what really mattered in getting promoted. Their research also found that gravitas was an area where women are more harshly judged than their male counterparts, particularly when it came to five specific gaffes:

1. Sexual impropriety
2. Indecision

HOW TO GET "IT"

3. Arrogance
4. Superficiality
5. Lack of impact

The first time I read this list I wasn't particularly surprised that they were issues; I was more intrigued as to why these would be the top five because they are such rookie mistakes and easily avoided. If cracking Executive Presence is advanced physics, these 'Gravitas Blunders' are addition and subtraction.

How to avoid the obvious traps:

1. Don't mix sex and work. The higher you are, the greater the spotlight. The issue isn't the conduct itself as much the lies. And while a man embroiled in a sex scandal can claim he's a sex addict, go to rehab, and then be forgiven, women get stigmatized. Remember Bill Clinton's love triangle: who got forgiven, who got to be Secretary of State, and who got the scarlet letter?

2. Develop a poker face to avoid appearing indecisive. If you're ever unsure, commit to commit. This move to decide later lets you have your conflict out of sight of your boss and subordinates, preferably with a thinking partner you trust.

3. Balance visibility with horn-tooting. Own your space but don't overinflate. This is hard for women because we tend to diminish our achievements and are then overlooked. The answer, however, is not to overcompensate with arrogance and excess or it will be seen as masking insecurity.

4. Be three questions deep. You can never afford to be seen as shallow in your knowledge. If you have an opinion, give it thoughtfully, but remember that it's better to be quiet than to speak if you have nothing to say just for the sake of making sounds.

5. Give people what they want – a compelling vision that touches, moves, and inspires. Check to be sure there's something in your vision for everyone: a view of the future, awareness of the practicalities that must be addressed now, a reflection of the past and what's been learned, and an understanding of how people will benefit or be impacted.

Being Yourself – On Purpose

'Authenticity' is a word much bandied about and a concept that I believe is the foundation of executive presence. If a leader is inauthentic or has the air of an 'imposter,' we can sense it intuitively and we are confused and distrustful. If, however, a leader is connected to herself, we see this authenticity as a manifestation of sincerity and vision, and we are inspired and touched.

Being authentic does not mean baring your soul to the entire office every single day. There is a balance to be found between being your authentic self without being a poseur and being selective and strategic about what you share with your staff and colleagues. Playing a role at work does not mean you are unnatural, calculating and superficial. It does mean that you stay true to yourself and project that best 'work self' as a leader while you're in the office. You can be transparent in making decisions and in your leadership style but you do not need every thought and motivation to be completely transparent to be considered 'authentic.'

This is where the concept of managing one's executive presence raises questions about a potential authenticity paradox and why authenticity is a struggle for many leaders, especially women rising through the ranks and stretching beyond their comfort zones. Some may think that the entire concept of managing your executive presence is about playing a part, which is the opposite of authenticity. To the contrary, being authentic is fundamental to your executive presence. If you're not being authentic, you're not actually present. There is no 'model' of the perfect executive woman – you don't need to be anyone but yourself. You do need to be aware of the impact you have on others and how you're perceived, but you still need to be authentic and true to yourself.

Authenticity begs the questions: Who am I, really? Do I allow others to see the real me? Am I being my real self consistently? And to be authentic also requires bravery and confidence.

Scientifically, the idea that each of us has a 'true self' that is reflected in actions and emotions is difficult. Ultimately, we are authentic when we are acting in a way that is harmonious with our true self.

So, the first question is, do you really know yourself? British researcher Alex Wood and his colleagues have become the leading figures in the scientific exploration of authenticity. Wood says there are three aspects of authenticity: 'self alienation,' or limited knowledge of one's beliefs, emotions, and purpose; 'authentic living,' or the degree to which a person lives in accord with her values; and 'accepting external influences,' or being influenced by beliefs and desires of others.

The other side of the coin – that searching for 'self' is like seeking a unicorn. Gender studies expert Peg O'Connor claims that there is no authentic self as identity is always a work in progress, and that the trend in seeking this authentic self so aggressively is unsettling and potentially destructive. We can get stuck in navel gazing to the point of paralysis.

I believe there is a middle ground. We are always evolving and a work in progress as a person. We have life experiences, unanticipated circumstances, and external influences that force us to constantly react and re-evaluate. It's like waves continually crashing onto the shore day after day. To me, the interesting question is are you responding to these incoming waves from a strong center that feels real or true to you, or are you gulping breaths and simply hoping to survive?

When you're a new leader finding your feet or when you're entering a period of rapid growth or identity transition such as a career or life change, you may feel like the waves just keep crashing and you're only reacting. The question is: are you reacting based on your authentic beliefs or because you think it will be popular?

In his work on authenticity, Wood and his colleagues created an authenticity scale where they ask people to rank their agreement with twelve statements:

1. I think it is better to be yourself than to be popular.
2. I don't know how I really feel inside.
3. I am strongly influenced by the opinions of others.
4. I usually do what others tell me to do.
5. I always feel I need to do what others expect me to do.
6. Other people influence me greatly.
7. I feel as if I don't know myself very well.
8. I always stand by what I believe in.
9. I am true to myself in most situations.
10. I feel out of touch with the 'real me.'
11. I live in accordance with my values and beliefs.
12. I feel alienated from myself.

If you rank yourself high on statements 2, 7, 10, and 12 it signals 'self alienation,' which means you may have limited understanding of your own beliefs, emotions, and purpose. This can also mean you have higher stress and are less happy than other people. How you responded to statements 1, 8, 9, and 11 indicates how authentically you're living – if you're living a life in accordance with your own values. The remaining statements – 3 through 6 – reflect how strongly you're influenced by the beliefs and desires of others, or your willingness to accept and succumb to external influences. Again, the more influenced we are by outsiders, the higher our stress and dissatisfaction with life.

What surprises you about your answers? What will you do to live more authentically?

Having Courage to Be You

While we can argue whether or not there is a 'real self,' what we do know is there is some voice inside us that says we're either in sync or out of touch with our core. Showing our real self to others requires being vulnerable, which is not always comfortable. But the act of being strong enough to knowingly reveal our own weaknesses is perceived as courageous by others and is the mark of a leader.

The most important window is the first 90 days in a new role. These are your first impression days and where you set the scene for your authentic work self – authoritative yet approachable. You need to adapt to the new situation without feeling fake and continue to tweak and adapt until you find an authentic self that meshes with the culture and feels sustainable. This requires finesse. If you put on an act, you'll eventually be found out and seen as a fake. If you just lay yourself bare without any thought to your initial impact at all, you may not just miss an opportunity to grow into your next leaderly version of self, you may also damage your standing by oversharing without having knowledge of whom to trust, getting a sense of the culture, and finding your feet.

Women are yet again held to a different standard in this realm: being too vulnerable is weak while overcompensating and being perfect is alienating. This is a personal journey that each woman has to navigate on her own.

The first step is to really know yourself. I know my Achilles' heel(s) and over the years I've learned three things when it comes to being my authentic self:

- First, I have to let go of perfect. I know I am a perfectionist, but sometimes good enough is still pretty damn good. Every day is an opportunity to grow and get better, rather than feeling bad about not being 'good enough.' I resist the urge to judge myself harshly every day, and see that what I'm doing is more than enough.

- Second, I have to not let my insecurities make me appear standoffish and judgmental. I have earned everything I have achieved. Therefore I deserve to own my space without artifice or defensiveness. I come from a small town and I was the first in my family to attend college and earn a degree, by no means Ivy League. My first real brush with elitism was when I worked in Silicon Valley with a guy who tried to use his degree from Cornell as a way to make others feel inferior – and having graduated from Weber State College in Ogden, Utah, it often worked on me. It took time to learn to embrace my roots and not try to minimize or apologize for it.

- Third, if I'm in doubt about how to connect with someone, rather than close down and retreat, I force myself to speak the emotional truth. An early mentor told me this and it's become my mantra for authenticity. When things get woolly and confusing, I ask myself, 'What is my emotional truth?' Am I scared, angry, overreacting, avoiding? How can I express this emotional to myself? Do I need to express it to others? No matter how frightening or daunting it may be, the emotional truth is usually the best course.

Becoming Mindful

A close cousin of authenticity is mindfulness. Leaders who are mindful convey groundedness, centeredness, and inspire confidence from others. Initially a Buddhist concept that has become popularized as a psychological practice and self development tool, mindfulness is essentially a way of

HOW TO GET "IT"

non-judgmentally paying attention to your emotions, thoughts and sensations in present moment.

Learning to be mindful is an ongoing practice; like strength training or doing cardio, you have to work at it and practice becoming situationally aware, sustaining your attention, and developing empathy and control to manage yourself and your thoughts.

For a woman who wants to improve mindfulness and succeed, I can think of no better source of inspiration and wisdom than Brené Brown. In Brown's book *The Gifts of Imperfection: Let Go of Who You Think You're Supposed to Be and Embrace Who You Are*, she lists ten 'guideposts' to cultivate and what behaviors or thinking you need to let go of to become more mindful:

1. Cultivate authenticity… and let go of what people think
2. Cultivate self-compassion… and let go of perfectionism
3. Cultivate a resilience… and let go of numbing and powerlessness
4. Cultivate gratitude and joy… and let go of scarcity and fear of the dark
5. Cultivate intuition and trusting faith… and let go of the need for certainty
6. Cultivate creativity… and let go of comparison
7. Cultivate play and rest… and let go of exhaustion as a status symbol and productivity as self-worth
8. Cultivate calm and stillness… and let go of anxiety as a lifestyle
9. Cultivate meaningful work… and let go of self-doubt and 'supposed to'
10. Cultivate laughter, song and dance… and let go of being cool and 'always in control'

If you read through the list and all the attributed you'd want to cultivate: authenticity, compassion, resilience, creativity, calm — that's the type of leader that people follow and trust. If you're perpetually preoccupied with perfectionism, fear, comparison, self-doubt and anxiety it comes through in your behavior and energy with others and causes them to question your abilities.

Reading the list above, which ones resonate for you as the areas you need to work on most? Choose two or three that you want to work on and begin my noticing how often your thoughts go to the areas you should be 'letting go.' Which one is the biggest area for you?

Now, how can you rewire your thinking? A technique that's helped me over the years comes from Dr. Lynn Johnson, an expert in positive psychology. Start by visualizing what it is you're letting go and then transform it into what you want to cultivate. Let's say you want to overcome number eight — anxiety as a lifestyle. Close your eyes, take a few deep breaths, and then visualize a path with 'Anxiety' in front of you. Does it have a color? Does it have a shape? Can you 'see' it?

With each inhalation visualize inhaling 'Anxiety' into your body — and then the alchemy takes place where you transform 'Anxiety' into 'Calm and Stillness.' Try to visualize what 'Calm and Stillness' looks like. Does it have a color or a shape? When you exhale, you project 'Calm and Stillness' into the path ahead of you.

Every time 'Calm and Stillness' dissipates and 'Anxiety' comes back into focus in front of you, inhale and transform it again. Practice doing this for a long as you can until you start to feel the 'Calm and Stillness' triumphing over 'Anxiety.'

With practice, when you notice 'Anxiety' creeping into your thoughts and with a few quick breaths you should be able to calm it and transform it into 'Calm and Stillness.' That's mindfulness — mastering your thoughts so that you are being and projecting your best self as often as possible.

Top Tips for Achieving Gravitas

1. **Know thyself.** Use personality profiles such as the Myers Briggs Type Indicator (MBTI) to expand your blind spot into how others can perceive you. Particularly pay attention to Introversion/Extroversion and see how you can not just embrace, but leverage your natural tendency to help you succeed.

2. **Cover your bases.** Take one tip from each of the first four facets to project Gravitas for an important meeting: Visual – wear colors to emphasize your eyes and draw attention to your face; Verbal – measure your pace of speech and use pauses to effect; Kinesthetic – focus on projecting a calm, stable energy; Sociability – consider how you can be more gracious.

3. **Know your own strength.** Do you know which strengths energize you, help you shine, and feel fulfilled at work and in life? Strengthsfinder 2.0 by Tom Rath is a survey I give each of my coaching clients and at workshops along with the Values In Action (VIA) Character strengths assessment. Take the online surveys, identify your top strengths and make a plan for how you can use these strengths every day to be your best, authentic, happiest self.

CHAPTER 23

Polished Politics

I don't think I've ever met someone who says, 'I love corporate politics!' More often people profess to disdain politics – sometimes because they actually do and sometimes because it's a good political tactic to pretend you don't care about politics. To ignore politics simply because you don't think it should matter or because you don't want to play the game is a decision made at your peril. Politics happen – it's a fact and pretending otherwise is foolhardy. That's how you look up one day and find you are on the ice floe alone, with a polar bear that isn't going to play nice. And then it's game over.

Companies are like families – interwoven, complex, unique, and potentially dysfunctional. The politics of a company is reflected in its culture, which is evidenced by:

1. What's said. These are the conversations that are allowed and disallowed. How do people speak to each other formally and informally? Is it open and honest or is it like the movie *Mean Girls* with grown-ups? In some companies the people who challenge and speak up are rewarded and in other companies those people are penalized as being naysayers.

2. What's done. Forget the policies and procedures, how do things really get done? Are decisions made in the boardroom or in the smoker's area? Who are the decision makers and who are

the figureheads? Who gets left out or undermined when the rubber hits the road and who's still standing?

3. What's valued. Every company has a mission, values, behaviors, and stated standards. But what behavior is actually rewarded with promotions, bonuses, and favor and what is punished by being passed over? A company may say they value treating people with integrity, and then promote the guy who regularly makes unwarranted unreasonable demands and makes people cry.

The key is how to play the game without selling your soul. That starts with being aware of what's really going on and noticing what's said, what's done, and what's valued. For women this is absolutely critical. You don't need to be a dude in a skirt, but you do need to know how the men are playing the game so that you can create your own strategy.

Gender studies have told us that men approach work like they're going to battle and women often approach work like they're going to a social gathering. Simplistic, but I see it in evidence every day. Men aren't there to make friends; they're there to get ahead. Men typically don't say 'I want them to like me.' Women often do. Not all men and not all women, to be sure, but enough to make the generalization warranted.

To get the promotion you don't need to play politics like a man, but you need to observe his game and choose your responses strategically. Make choices with intention and purpose and from a vantage point of awareness.

The critical times to be aware of politics are during times of change – such as a leadership change or a restructuring – and during the performance cycle when it's time for your review. This is the time to go on high alert and pay attention to the entire chess board. Others will make big moves, alliances will shift and people will leapfrog or get jumped over.

A mentor or thinking partner is very helpful in these situations. Having someone with a neutral viewpoint who can help you see the mines planted in the field and plot your course is invaluable. This may be a colleague, a consultant, or a friend and confidante.

Proactively Managing the Game Board

Politics is a game. The idea of 'playing a game' may repel you – but the game is going on whether you want to admit it or not. Refusal to observe the game and its effect on your career won't help you. If your career is a chessboard, do you have a game plan and do you know the key players? There are a lot of players on the board and while it may seem Machiavellian to think you're in control, it's important to understand the real ranking of the players, their patterns of movement, and their motivations. Then you can make decisions about how to play your own game.

Start by recognizing that you need to devote some of your resources to this area in the form of mental energy and time. If 80% of your time on the job is about the work itself, 20% is about managing the politics. The best way to marshal your resources is to identify where to target your energy so you're efficient and effective, and that means identifying the players.

Create two stakeholder maps – one for your short-term career and a second for long term following the same steps you would do for a project stakeholder exercise:

1. **Who matters?** List all the key stakeholders for your career – the people who can help you or hinder you. Be thorough and specific. It may be a group such as 'industry headhunters' or an individual 'Bill.' Anyone who may be a lever to propel you or a blocker to impede your progress should be on this list.

2. **Who matters most?** For each individual or group consider their level of interest and influence. How interested are they in your career? Do they have a vested interest in your success, have they established a mentor role, does their success rely on your success? And then how much influence do they actually have in your current organization or field? Give them a score

from 1-10 in each area. You want to focus on the people with the greatest influence and interest – these are your advocates. This should be about 20% of the entire stakeholder group – so you're going to focus effort in the right area.

3. **How can they help – or at least not hurt?** Your next step is to create a plan for how you're going to connect with these key stakeholders to manage them and hopefully get them on your side, perhaps as a mentor or at least an advocate in key conversations that impact your future. For each key stakeholder, think about how they perceive you now and where you want them to be in an ideal world (desired state).

Before you engage with a key stakeholder, a board member, for example, you should create a communication roadmap so you can ensure an effective conversation:

- What do I want him/her to know, feel, and do? *(I want him to know what I've accomplished this year, feel that it was important to our success, and ideally mention it in the next board meeting.)*

- What's in it for him/her that I can leverage or consider? *(He's a new board member who wants to be seen as being influential and making a difference on this board. If I share an article that has some useful information and let him take it to the board, he'll look good and appreciate my help.)*

- Looking at his/her past behavior, what has been helpful that I can reinforce and what has been detrimental that I can redirect? *(He isn't afraid to speak up in meetings, so I'll share that others have told me they appreciate his being forthright. Sometimes he hijacks the conversations if he doesn't have a formal agenda, so I'll offer to share a preview of the agenda in advance.)*

HOW TO GET "IT"

When You're Under Siege – Grace Under Fire

The documentary *Blackfish* is a powerful view on SeaWorld and other performance aquarium experiences that has had a tremendous impact on the company's perception and brand, ultimately contributing to the resignation of SeaWorld's CEO.

While it's a compelling documentary from a content perspective and an interesting case study on how social media and film can impact perception, there was one chilling moment that I remembered long after the film ended.

In one scene, the documentarians show footage of a seasoned trainer, Ken Peters, being attacked by an orca. As the camera rolls, the whale seizes Peters' foot and repeatedly takes him to the bottom of the pool before surfacing briefly and then taking him under water again. Watching the recording is horrifying as you realize what's happening to this man and how helpless he is in face of this massive animal that seems intent on killing him slowly.

What is amazing, however, is Peters' reaction. At each interval on the surface, he doesn't appear to panic. He doesn't look like a man being murdered. He manages to keep his cool and overrides panic, engaging his skills as a SCUBA diver to breathe deeply while activating his knowledge as a trainer to try and soothe the whale by stroking and speaking calmly. All this just before being plunged to the bottom again.

At one point, the whale briefly releases his foot. Peters uses this moment to slowly move himself to the tail of the whale, and then, when he's clear, swim like hell over a net that's been raised, and reach the edge of the pool. He then staggers to stand on broken feet and ankles before being rescued by his shocked colleagues even as the whale continues to pursue him and then circles slowly in the water.

So why am I telling you about a whale trainer? Regardless of one's views on animal captivity and social responsibility, there's a lot to learn about grace under fire from this extreme example. The key is to not panic and keep your head. Peters activated his training, became calm and focused, and reacted with bravery and purpose, saving his life.

While most of us don't experience such dramatic events on the job, we still face onslaught attacks from time to time. Not from whales, but from colleagues and competitors. In one of the most challenging periods of my career, I found myself under siege by a female with a grudge. I was getting divorced from my husband, who also happened to work at the same company, in Human Resources. The divorce turned out to be amicable, but as with most divorces we had our ups and downs and we each had turned to friends for support. In his case, he turned to another HR professional for counsel. I also suspect that there were moments where he wasn't feeling particularly charitable or positive toward me, and he told her what a heinous bitch I was, how I was ruining his life, and all the emotional things someone may say when in the process of dismantling a marriage.

Fast-forward about nine months, my relationship with my soon to be ex was on an even keel, he had moved to another department, and, as ever, the company politics had changed. My head of HR, with whom I had a great relationship, had moved on to another role. Sod's Law: my now ex-husband's former confidante was promoted to be my new HR manager. She didn't like me much. I think perhaps she greatly disliked me (which is an understated British-ism for 'she hated my guts') and thought I deserved some sort of comeuppance.

Her perception and vendetta became very clear when it came time for me to negotiate my terms to leave the organization and move to another country, and she did everything in her power to make my life hell. At first I didn't understand what was happening and I thought I was being paranoid about her behavior. I was unaware of what my ex had shared with her and I expected that she would behave professionally. She'd not been particularly friendly to me in the past, but I hadn't had much dealing with her. So I missed all the signs and I didn't have her on my radar as a possible blocker.

HOW TO GET "IT"

I was a single mother, moving three children back to America, with no work prospects lined up. I was tired and as this woman began making my situation difficult, I allowed my emotions to be hijacked and I didn't manage the politics well. I alienated key allies who could have helped me resolve the situation and everything I did seemed to make it worse.

Talking with a thinking partner helped me regain perspective and make an action plan to get back on track. I looked at the resources available to me and decided to approach my ex and ask for his help. He responded favorably and helped to defuse the situation. I then activated some of my remaining allies back in the company who were very supportive and though it eventually all worked out, it was a stressful time and incredibly draining.

What did I learn? Keep a cool head even when you're drowning. Stop and breathe. Then figure out what's happening, what you can do, who can help, and keep it contained. I also was reminded of the dangers of enemies. You don't need to fake friendship, but you also rarely benefit by alienating someone or making an enemy. When your knee-jerk reactions can be emailed or posted and then last forever, pause before you write or speak and consider that these axioms exist for a reason: Keep your friends close but your enemies closer. Sugar catches more flies than vinegar. Be careful who you step on on your way up, they will be there on your way down. And never burn a bridge.

Top Tips for Polished Politics

1. **Tooting your own horn.** It may feel artificial and political to 'sell' your ideas at work – shouldn't your work just stand on its own merit? Get over it! If you're not willing to push yourself to sell it, who's going to recognize and help you drive your brilliant idea? Identify three people who can help you bring your great concept or plan to life and make a strategy to enroll them and get it going.

2. **Climb down the ladder.** 'The Ladder of Inference' by Chris Argyris is a key concept that every leader should understand and manage. Be aware of your actions and if they're based on reality or assumptions. Also recognize when others are acting from atop their own 'ladders' and adjust your reactions accordingly.

3. **Take a page from Musashi.** A way of looking at conflict and finding your own advantage, *The Book of Five Rings* can help you identify which approach you usually take (earth, water, fire, wind, and void/neutral) and which approach your opponent is taking and rather than reacting instinctively, to choose a response intentionally. If your tendency to lash out with fire isn't working, maybe shifting into neutral and then choosing another approach, like water – moving sideways to move forward – will be more successful. This is a great way to think about how to get out of sticky 'groundhog day' situations with key individuals whom you tend to clash with again and again.

CHAPTER 24

Positioned for Success

Sheryl Sandberg was on the cover of *Time* magazine with the headline 'Don't Hate Me Because I'm Successful.' Can you imagine any male senior executive being labelled with that headline? The world can be cruel to ambitious, successful women, deeming them less likeable than their equally ambitious male counterparts. That means women need to learn to withstand a great deal of criticism to succeed.

In Joseph Campbell's book *The Hero with a Thousand Faces,* we learn that the Hero's Journey is a classic plotline seen in countless films where the 'everyman' becomes a hero. Campbell himself pointed out the discrepancy between the male and female perspectives of mythology, saying "All of the great mythologies and much of the mythic story-telling of the world are from the male point of view. When I was writing *The Hero with a Thousand Faces* and wanted to bring female heroes in, I had to go to the fairy tales. These were told by women to children, you know, and you get a different perspective. It was the men who got involved in spinning most of the great myths. The women were too busy; they had too damn much to do to sit around thinking about stories."

We have so many archetypes for men, yet only four for women: the Mother, the Battle-axe, the Pet, and the Seductress, as identified by Rosabeth Moss Kanter in 1983.

The Seductress turns quickly into the villainess and is inappropriate and disliked. (Basically, avoid being the Seductress!) The Pet is the favorite but ultimately her need to be loved and favored means she won't be taken seriously and won't make it to the top. The Mother is a cousin of the schoolmistress and while she commands authority, she is too stiff to be a leader. The Battle-axe is scary and though she can make it to the top, she is rarely beloved or liked. Sometimes a woman cast as the Mother and the Battle-axe doesn't want to seem difficult or be disliked, whether it's negotiating a higher salary or making a decision that's unpopular with staff, so she'll hold back. Then she appears inconsistent and wishy-washy.

So how do you win? You win by writing your own story that feels real to you, by not taking things personally, and making sure you hold your ground. You win by recognizing that at times you play all four of these characters in the minds of your male and female colleagues, and that you need to do so with intention and purpose.

Hannah recently sought my advice about how to deal with her new boss, a male, who had cast her as the Mother and put her in charge of his office refurbishment – something clearly outside her scope of work and far below her pay grade as a VP. As we talked about how to reframe the situation and get back on track (e.g., doing her real job) it became clear that the guy sort of saw 'décor' as a female thing and as Hannah happened to be in his office when he was thinking about his office, he somehow attached it to her.

She, wanting to please and not be seen as being obstructive and therefore a bitch, said 'Okay' and fell right into a female archetype of Mother with a dash of Pet. She had to reposition herself with this man, and fast. By identifying who should really be doing this work, and sending a series of very carefully worded emails, she was able to get herself off the hook, use it as an opportunity to frame herself as adding value in her real job, and get back on course.

But if she hadn't repositioned, she'd be the one making sure the pictures were hung and the rug delivered. Not a place you want to be.

When we talk about positioning, it's about how you show up in the eyes of those who are important to your career and how you're positioned against your peers and others in your organization. Nothing happens in isolation, so a strong person sat next to a weak person appears stronger; an attractive woman in a team of men will have to beware of being cast as the flirt; two women who don't get on can be framed as being 'mean girls' in their own drama, and so on.

Ultimately, you write your own story and define your own moments. Intentionally craft your tale and change it over time as you grow and evolve. My story was 'high achiever reaching for the brass ring,' then 'young mother balancing big corporate career and family,' then 'single mother and entrepreneur,' now as my sons are grown and my life enters a new chapter, I'm in the process of redefining my own story again, and I'm excited to see where it takes me.

What is your narrative? Are you updating it to reflect not just who you authentically are but also who you aspire to be? Are you steering clear of clichés and harmful archetypes as you live your tale?

The Motherhood Conundrum

It's one thing to be forced into the 'Mother' archetype at work and another thing to be an actual mother trying to have a career and family.

This begs the question, can a woman actually have it all, and what is 'it'? It's rare to find a professional woman who feels completely satisfied with her personal life and career. We seem to always be torn and seeking to be more, do more. Balancing life choices across the career and family spectrum is individual to every woman.

Harvard Business Review recently asked 4,000 executives worldwide to explain how they reconcile their professional and personal lives. Of the leaders surveyed, 88% of the men were married, compared with 70% of the women. And 60% of the men had spouses who don't work full-time outside the home, compared with only 10% of the women. The men had an average of 2.22 children; the women, 1.67.

According to the study's authors, Boris Groysberg and Robin Abrahams, some intriguing gender differences emerged when they looked at the data:

> "In defining professional success, women place more value than men do on individual achievement, having passion for their work, receiving respect, and making a difference, but less value on organizational achievement and ongoing learning and development. A lower percentage of women than of men list financial achievement as an aspect of personal or professional success. Rewarding relationships are by far the most common element of personal success for both sexes, but men list merely having a family as an indicator of success, whereas women describe what a good family life looks like to them. Women are also more likely to mention the importance of friends and community as well as family."

It seems that managing the tension between work and family was primarily the woman's problem. As technology makes it possible to be multipresent, some women need to completely separate their work and home lives. Others, like me, have a blended approach. Neither comes without upsides and downsides. We still live in a world where partner-wives are praised for making positive contributions to achievement yet partner-husbands are mostly appreciated for not interfering with the woman's career trajectory.

While nobody discounts the difficulty of balancing work and home, women often underestimate the impact that mothering has on their image as a professional. According to the HBR article, "Many women keep their networks separate for fear of harming their image. Some never mention their families at work because they don't want to appear unprofessional. A few female executives won't discuss their careers—or even mention that they have jobs—in conversations outside work."

But again, not all women reported such conflict between their professional and personal 'selves,' and several suggested that the tide is turning. One pointed out, "The more women have come into the workplace, the more I talk about my children."

How does being a mother impact your executive presence? My advice is to model the male behavior in your organization and look at the senior leaders' positioning. Do they have photos of their kids on their desks and drawings from day care on their bulletin boards, then you can too. If it's common for the guys in your office to talk about their kids and take time away for school activities, then by all means follow suit. If, however, you're the only one talking about ballet recitals and daycare woes, and your office looks like a kindergarten classroom, then you're positioning yourself as a mother first and signaling that you're not fully engaged on the job. When they think about who to promote, even if they don't say it out loud, they will wonder if you have the capacity to take on more responsibility given your role as a mother. This isn't fair or right, but it's a reality.

Also look at your boss's orientation toward family. If your senior leader is older with grown children or no children, he or she isn't likely to empathize with your need to take time off for school meetings. That doesn't mean you don't go to the meetings, it means that you just say you need an afternoon for a personal appointment and leave it at that. Don't hide being a mother, but don't highlight your mothering or your obligations as a parent if the culture may penalize you for it.

I have successfully worked for bosses who never asked me my children's names, if they were boys or girls, or how many I had – and I never volunteered the information. I have also worked for leaders who would often start a conversation by asking 'So, how's your eldest son getting on now in university?' and remembered thoughtful details. I still wait to be asked and don't initiate conversations about my kids. Usually if they initiate a family conversation they want to talk about their kids, so I share a little about my family and then ask about their kids and let them roll on to tell me what's happening in their world.

The point for me is that when I'm working, I'm not there to show everyone that I'm a great mom. I'm there to show them that I'm a great worker and leader. 'Mom' is my full-time job, 24/7, and the most important role in my life. I am always aware of my kids and where they are and what's going on, like blips on my mental air traffic control screen. But there is no upside to sharing that in the workplace. When I'm at work, I need to project focus, competence and that I'm committed to the job I'm being paid to do and do it well.

Status: One-Up, One-Down or Equal

An integral element of positioning is status – actual and perceived. This has little to do with your actual position in the hierarchy of an organisation and more to do with your bearing and attitude. It's the difference between being seen as arrogant instead of competent. As humble rather than 'whipped puppy.' As friendly or a sycophant.

It's a delicate balancing act for any leader, and especially for women. When we start working with a new person – whether it's a new boss, colleague, or subordinate – our insecurities tend to come to fore and wreak havoc with our positioning. Any area where you may feel deficient (talent, appearance, intelligence, finances, education, or other achievements) can trigger the need to overcompensate and the result is that it will amplify our insecurity.

When we're coming from a place of insecurity, we can sometimes try to inflate ourselves in relation to the new person, which actually makes us look weak. In many cases making others look good and showing generosity actually makes us appear stronger.

HOW TO GET "IT"

When I was facing a challenging personal issue, Dr. Lynn Johnson introduced me to Leary's Interpersonal Circle Model of Personality as a way to objectively see how I needed to position myself to get the desired outcome with the other individual.

Using the Leary Circle, the first step is to understand your options of positioning: one-up, one-down, or equal. The second is to consider how 'warm' or 'cold' you need to be perceived to get your desired outcome.

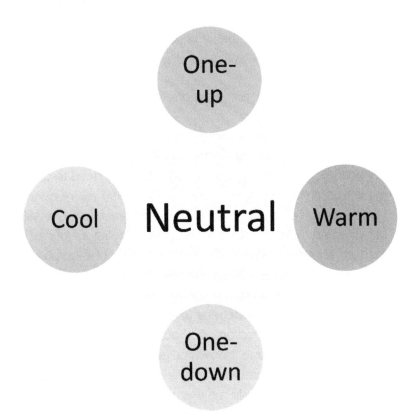

I'm aware that this sounds a bit cold and Machiavellian, yet our brains are hard wired to continually understand how we are oriented toward others. To choose a position with intention doesn't mean you aren't being your real self, it means that you're deliberately orienting yourself toward others to increase the likelihood of the desired outcome.

In this case, I'd been assigned to a project and partnered with a new, very junior consultant, Heather, who was an absolute mess. She was young, lacked basic skills and knowledge, and was not strategic. I had no idea why she'd been hired but unravelling that decision wasn't my priority. I had a project to deliver. My first tactic was to tell the consultancy that I needed a different associate, but that was not an option. So, I had to decide how to orient myself against her to get the best outcome: a successful project delivered with us working together. I had to be completely committed to Heather's success because it was actually the only route to my own success.

To manage the Heather Situation, step one was to determine my position – one-up, one-down, or neutral:

- **One-up**: One-up comes from a place of superiority or dominance. You want to be one-up when you need to be the expert or in command. The downside is that if you're using it to overcome insecurity or to make others feel inferior, it will backfire and make you appear arrogant or needy of affirmation. It's hard to make a positive connection from a one-up position. If you need to impress, you don't have to be one-up – you can subtly weave your status, position, and rank into your conversation without appearing to dominate. What if you have a naturally dominant personality? You need to be aware of this and know when to tone it down or else be perceived as overly bossy – not a good tone for a female. Choosing one-up against Heather could have made me seem like a bully and would have made the client wonder what was going on, actually pulling me down.

- **One-down**: One-down comes from a place of deference or modesty. It's easy to think of one-down as being weak, but it's actually a very strong position in many cases where you benefit from the other person feeling superior. If you're unintentionally putting yourself one-down it may be because you feel inferior or less-than. That's not the same as making this a strategic choice and it will ultimately make you appear incapable and unconfident. You can be self deprecating to elevate the other person, but do so without shaming or making yourself look inferior. When you're one-down, the warm/cool tempering is critical to balance or you won't be seen as leaderly. You also can't spend all your time in one-down or you're just a pleaser, never a pioneer. As a woman with aspirations to lead, you don't ever want to be seen as the submissive female. I couldn't go one-down against Heather or it would've been inauthentic and suicide for the project.

- **Neutral**: When in doubt, go for equal or parity position. In this state you're seeing each other eye-to-eye even while you take measure of how the other person is positioning himself or herself against you. Picking up on cues around if he sees himself as superior can then influence if you want to allow that to happen and amplify it by showing deference, level yourself by finding common ground, or position yourself to push to one-up.

In this case, I decided to be neutral even though naturally I had more experience and was actually one-up compared to Heather. However, by treating Heather as equal, it served to give her confidence and also helped us appear united for the client. I did this by balancing how frequently I took the lead and how often I asked her opinion or credited her for ideas in front of the client. This helped them see her as being more credible and made us stronger.

The second aspect in Leary's model is cool versus warm. I view this as a seesaw. Once I know where I am and where I want to be on the one-up/one-down axis, I decide if I want to be warm or cool.

Cool is more calculated, realistic, and controlled, but can also be seen as being negative or 'glass half empty.' On the other side, warm is more positive but can become a Pollyanna and appear shallow and unrealistic if left unchecked.

- **One-up/Cool:** This is the shark eye, the ultimate in superiority – aggressive, competitive, and narcissistic. This is boastful, arrogant, and dominant. If you want to be a very strong leader with no room for questioning, with complete authority, this is your position. Unless you're the most senior person in the room, use this with caution. But if you need to show teeth, this is the stance to adopt to defend your territory. You can be firm but avoid being seen as exploitative.

- **One-up/Warm:** This is strength with affinity. The responsible leader who advises, offers help and support, manages fairly, cares about people, and is firmly in control. This is a strong, sustainable position for a leader of a team and a great position with parallel colleagues that you want to differentiate yourself against. If you position yourself as one-up/warm against your competitor for the promotion, you are seen as preferable and collegial.

- **One-down/Cool:** These are the rebels, the skeptics, the complainers, and the slightly suspicious. Now, if you want to be seen as an unconventional thinker, one-down/cool is the way to go. You're a non-conformist who doesn't need to follow the pack. Temper yourself, however, so you're seen as realistic and modest rather than disruptive or distrustful. If that's not working for you, you need to warm it up from time to time to be trustworthy.

- **One-down/Warm:** The friendliest position, this is cooperative, dependable, and participatory. It's also dangerously close to suck-up. While you may be admired and respected for your ability to toe the line, you're also seen as very conventional, dutiful, and obedient. This may make you seem weak, clingy, or dependent if it's not occasionally tempered with a little one-up as needed.

Heather was a very energetic, extroverted personality. I wanted to be friendly but I didn't want this to become a stand-up comedy show or be her best friend. I needed her to defer to my authority and respect me, so I chose to be on the cool side. Because I had chosen to adopt a neutral stance, I could make sure I wasn't dominating her and I wasn't deferring to her. Instead, I was keeping her at an appropriately detached distance but showing that I valued her contributions and didn't see myself as superior or inferior.

The outcome was that we survived the project and did a good job. I found ways to subtly coach Heather on skills and concepts out of the client's view so that she looked good and therefore made us both look good. I did it in a way that wasn't patronizing or diminishing, so I wasn't seen as being her mentor or having any control at all. We appeared to be a cohesive team on the surface, though I was pulling most of the weight underneath.

Controlling Your Universe

How much control do you appear to have over your life or others? 'Taking' control versus 'having' control are two completely different arenas. There are three options: overcontrolling, out of control, or in control. This is a minefield for women to manage as men, in particular, can often get triggered by the controlling level of a woman and harken to other interpersonal relationships such as their mother or wife.

Overcontrolling: If you're blatantly controlling, it doesn't matter how good you are at your job, people will resist you. A woman who is overcontrolling can be seen as being bossy or motherly. Take the example of Carmen the control freak who's meeting a new consultant for lunch:

> *Carmen: Hi, so nice meet you. So, tell me about yourself. Where are you from?*
>
> *Consultant: I'm from the States originally, but now I live in Sweden.*

Carmen: I have friends who are Swedish. I'm from the Netherlands but I've never been to the States. So, excuse me, but I think we should order now so we can get started as quickly as possible. I've been here before; I think the salads are good but most of the other dishes aren't that great. I suggest the chicken Caesar or the Cobb salad.

Consultant: Um, well, I haven't seen the menu yet.

Carmen: We could get menus but like I said the best things are the salads, the chicken Caesar or the Cobb.

Consultant: I think I'll just ask to see the menu.

Carmen: I'll find the server; but you know that table over there just opened up and it's closer to the window where we'll be able to see the traffic and get an idea of when we should get ready to leave to avoid any post-lunch rush.

Consultant: Really, I'm fine here.

What is Carmen doing? She probably thinks she's being helpful and efficient. In reality she's being a control freak and dominating. This also comes up in conversations where leaders talk about how they must micromanage everything their team does in great detail. If you're doing everyone else's job, what does that say about your ability to lead?

Out of Control: The other side of the control coin is complete abdication and indecision. This is a killer for women who need to be seen as decisive in work and in life. This is an example of an actual conversation I overheard a few weeks ago at a corporate off-site between Wendy the wishy-washy wannabe leader who's talking to a senior leader, Stephanie:

Stephanie: Where are you from, Wendy?

Wendy: Well, I live in Surrey now but that's because my ex-husband had a house there and I can't afford to move until he gives me the

HOW TO GET "IT"

money that he owes me. So I'm a little stuck but I hope I can move but I need to find a place that's close to commute but I don't know where yet.

Stephanie: Oh, well, good luck finding someplace new.

Wendy: Yeah, he took me for a ride. And then there was a contractor who was supposed to do some work so we could sell the house but then he took off with the money and didn't do the work so that's been really bad.

Stephanie: Sorry to hear that. So, how long have you been with the company?

Wendy: I wanted to get a different job but my boss wouldn't let me apply for anything new because he wants me to stay in this job so I've been stuck for a while now. People make promises and then they don't follow through.

Stephanie: Well, I hope that works out for you, I'm sure he values what you do. What sort of work are you doing now?

Wendy: Well, right now I'm really overwhelmed. The team just doesn't come through and I can't depend on anyone to do their job so if they don't do their jobs I really can't do mine. And until I get a good boss who can really lead there's not a lot I can do in the company.

Stephanie: You know, there's someone over there I need to speak to quickly. It was nice to meet you.

Wendy: Oh, you too. I'm just waiting for my colleague who's supposed to meet me but she hasn't texted me yet so I'll just wait here, I guess. But I'm sure you're busy.

We all have disappointments, frustrations, betrayals, and setbacks. But think about if you're positioning yourself as being a person who is in control of her life, career, and destiny. The stories you tell about yourself shouldn't be sugar coated, but they also shouldn't portray you as the victim. Victims aren't leaders.

In-Control: Somewhere in between control freak and out of control is the perfect balance: someone who takes charge and is independent without being domineering. Notice your position and make sure you're demonstrating that you're a woman in control of your life and destiny, who doesn't feel the need to control or micromanage others along the way.

Drama Free Zone

"Oh, we used to call her Scary Sarah," said Caroline, a client who was describing a former colleague who had had an affair with a senior leader and when it all went awry, found herself needing to leave the company.

"You called her what? Why?" I asked, a little shocked at this gossip coming from an otherwise very level-headed leader.

"Well, she took no prisoners. So once we realized that they were having a fling then everyone just turned on her and it was really horrible," she recalled. "I mean, I think it all turned out all right in the end but it was just such a drama."

Would you ever want to be 'Scary Sarah'? I've also heard of 'Loony Libby,' 'Crazy Catherine,' and 'Witchy Wendy.'

Oh, the drama. How many corporate dramas have you seen unfold in front of your eyes? It's easy to get sucked into drama at the workplace and it rarely ends well. Whether you're an active participant or an observer, drama derails you from your objectives and depletes your energy. As a woman in a corporate environment, the 'catfight' cliché comes from drama situations that escalate.

The key is to either stay clear or know when you're in a drama and get yourself out of it as quickly as possible. To do that, you need to under-

HOW TO GET "IT"

stand 'The Drama Triangle,' defined by Dr. Stephen Karpman in the late 1960s and still commonly used in psychology and psychotherapy. The drama itself may just be a game, based on nothing tangible or real, but the players can be tenacious and intense – and I guarantee there are drama triangles all around you at your workplace.

The drama triangle is composed of three actors or roles: the Victim, the Rescuer, and the Persecutor. In a nutshell a Drama Triangle is really simple: the Victim feels sad self-pity because of what the Persecutor does and the Rescuer tries to help the Victim recover. I don't think it's a coincidence that these three roles are closely related to the four female archetypes with the Pet being the Victim, the Mother being the Rescuer, and the Battle-axe and Seductress being the Persecutors. It's Real Housewives at the office every day.

Remember that these are roles people play, not real people; the real person is much more complex than the role. In life, people who engage in the drama triangle tend to have very 'dramatic' personal *and* professional relationships, but they function and rise to power and lead teams and have families just like those who don't participate in drama triangles.

It is impossible to be contented, productive, fulfilled, and genuinely happy when you're engaged in non-stop drama. A person who lives on the drama triangle will automatically bring that behavior to the work setting if it's not mitigated. First, the individual needs to understand the triangle. Then, he or she can be retrained to create a new relationship pattern in the workplace to be effective and productive.

The triangle is exhausting and never ending. Because there are no limits or ethical boundaries you don't know when you are 'done' with the drama. This lack of boundaries or an ending means you become exhausted, but can't quit the drama. A drama ends when a player refuses to be involved and quits, or in extreme cases when the drama escalates to the ultimate level and in extreme situations can even result in death, as in the case of the Astronaut Love Triangle in the United States that made headlines around the world. Many of the homicides and accidental deaths we see in the news every day are actually the end result of a highly evolved drama triangle that has gone out of control.

If you play one role in this drama you play them all. While each person may have his or her favorite role, the demands of drama require that each person will move through all the roles, like people playing musical chairs.

How does this unfold in three acts? Let's start with Act One:

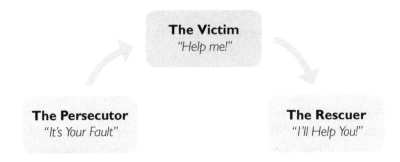

With a Persecutor in place, Victim continues to cry for help and Rescuer repeatedly responds. However, Victim will not let the Rescuer make him feel better because there is secret pleasure in continuing to be the Victim. As the drama unfolds, the Rescuer tells herself, "You must try harder" and redoubles her efforts to make the Victim feel better...

Eventually, the Victim becomes annoyed at the Rescuer's persistence and moves to a new role – Persecutor. The Victim is now set on punishing the Rescuer, saying, "You are a bad rescuer. You obviously failed and I am justified in punishing you for failing me." Now we have a new Persecutor to refuel the drama and set the stage for the next act.

HOW TO GET "IT"

Act Two:

The Victim
(formerly the Rescuer)
"I'm so helpless and depressed. I was only trying to help."

The Persecutor
(formerly the Victim)
"I'm angry. Leave me alone. You can't help."

The Rescuer
(former Persecutor or a new player)
"I'll Help You!"

The new Victim has to recruit a new Rescuer to complete the triangle and help her feel better. However, the Victim will never allow the Rescuer to really help. The Rescuer tries repeatedly and becomes frustrated.

Act Three:

The Victim
(returning to his original role)
"Help me!"

The Persecutor
(former Rescuer)
"It's Your Fault"

The Rescuer
(returning to his original role)
"I'll Help You!"

The Rescuer becomes angry with the original Victim/new Persecutor and does something that puts the Persecutor back into the Victim role. With the original Victim in the role once again, the original Rescuer can now return to her original role and no longer needs to be the Victim. The Rescuer who was recruited in Act Two is now in the role of Persecutor.

What drives the drama? When it comes to drama, each person has a favorite role based on our motivation and ego.

The person's motivation is usually anger, helplessness, or anxiety and tends to be driven by our childhood experiences and family dramas. The Persecutor is motivated by overt anxiety and subtle helplessness; the Victim is motivated by helplessness with an undercurrent of anger; the Rescuer is motivated by anger with some anxiety.

The individual's ego goes back to being Childlike, Parental, or Adult. None of the roles involve thoughtful problem solving, which is the adult ego state. So, no one is a full human being – they are all living in a restricted range. The Persecutor is an angry, disciplinarian parent that fits in with the seductress or battle-axe; the Victim is childlike and links to the pet archetype; and the Rescuer is a concerned and overly indulgent parent like the traditional mother or schoolteacher.

Ideally we can all be childish and fun, adult-like and problem-solving and parental in caretaking and holding others accountable at different times. We should be flexible and adapt to different situations. People who are rigidly in one or another role are not whole. They have a limited range of flexibility. And they are unhappy.

Are you playing in drama triangles at home or at work? Take a long, objective look at the relationships that cause you stress and tension. Odds are there is a drama going on underneath that you might never have noticed.

To end your role in the drama, you have to back away and require that each person deal with his or her own issues. You must call the behavior what it is and leave the person to sort out his own feelings and bounce back. But that's not enough; when the drama ends, the various players will respond with a burst of behavior that may be new to the drama.

The Victim will get very angry and then very helpless. Having been rewarded for being a Victim, she will at first be very angry when she is told it is her own responsibility to recover. She will then shift to extreme helplessness and exaggeration, trying to get the Rescuer to participate in the Drama again.

The Rescuer is going to be very afraid and despair, "What will the poor Victim do?!?!" and reinforce the Victim. To get through this burst, you must help the Rescuer focus on her own feelings and deal with them.

The Persecutor will have an anxiety burst, convinced that "No one is getting it! We need to do the right thing or else!" and step up persecution and blame. To get through this burst, you must help the Persecutor focus on how to cope when things aren't going well and determine what she will do to help herself cope rather than controlling others.

Managing the Trust Equation

When we make a first impression, we instantly size up the person's intelligence, likeability, competence, and trustworthiness. Trust is therefore not just earned over time; it's also instantly perceived and part of your executive presence.

Because one of the core attributes of a senior leader is trustworthiness, you need to build trust with stakeholders inside and outside your organization to get to the next level. So how can you manage others' perceptions of your trustworthiness? Communications expert Charles Green has broken down 'trust' for leaders into an equation: Trust = Credibility + Reliability + Intimacy / Self-Orientation. Over time, the way you communicate and present yourself equates to an increase or decrease in your trustworthiness in these four dimensions:

1. **Be Credible.** Telling the truth is the simplest way to not get caught in a lie. Mark Twain said, "I always tell the truth, because then I don't have to remember what I said." Once you've been shown to be untruthful, you become untrustworthy. So rule number one is to be truthful even if people may not like what you have to say. It's also important to know what you're talking about. People will trust you if they respect and rely on what you have to say. People should believe "I can trust what she says about…"

2. **Be Reliable.** People notice what you do. It's true that actions speak louder than words. People watch and take signals from your behaviors and decisions. If you make a promise, keep it. If you can't keep it, you need to explain it. People need to feel confident that if you say something, you'll do it. If you say one thing but do the opposite, you lose trust. This isn't always obvious because we often imply our word – and then don't understand when people perceive that we've broken it. If you say you value spending one to one time with your direct reports, but then you always have a reason for canceling your meetings with them, what are they going to believe? You want people to say, "I can trust her to…"

3. **Be Discreet.** Green calls this 'Intimacy' in his trust equation, which essentially means that if someone tells you something in confidence, you won't repeat it. They need to feel that you're human and have a sense of empathy. We've all seen this go awry. I recall having lunch with a senior leader who started telling me about another colleague who had misused his corporate credit card and named the person. She was completely indiscreet and my first thought was that if she was willing to divulge something about this guy today, tomorrow it could be me. That doesn't build trust. You want people to feel "I can trust her with…"

4. **Be Selfless.** Yes, you want to succeed. Yes, you care about your career and your family. But to be perceived as a leader people need to know that you care about them, not just yourself. Listening is an important part of this aspect. Leaders have conversations that are dialogues, not monologues. When they listen, they give their full attention and show people that their motives aren't completely selfish. You want people to believe "I can trust that she cares about…"

Top Tips to Position Yourself for Success

1. **Don't allow interruption.** If you're consistently talked over in meetings, find a male or female colleague to interrupt the interrupter on your behalf and say, 'Wait a minute – I wanted to hear what Helen was saying first." If you're guilty of interrupting a colleague, stop yourself. And if you notice another woman being interrupted, intervene on her behalf.

2. **Show generosity and share the glow.** Research shows that if you give credit where it's due, you will actually look better and appear more leaderly. Conversely, men are more forgiven for taking credit for another person's ideas, but women are discredited if found out. So resist the urge to take the glory and make allies while making yourself appear stronger.

3. **Get in your boss's brain.** Learn about the Herrmann Brain Dominance Instrument (HBDI) – a system to measure and describe thinking preferences in people – and identify which quadrant your boss uses most. Every time you email, speak, or interact with your boss, start by answering the questions in his quadrant. An Analytic boss is in the here and now – she wants to know the facts and logic; an Innovative boss is a future thinker – she wants to start by seeing the big picture vision; a Relational leader wants to know how it impacts people and feelings; and a Procedural thinker is always looking to the past first – she wants to know the steps and process you'll follow.

CHAPTER 25

Navigating The Blind Spot

Actively revealing your blind spots – what others know and think about you but you don't know yourself – is a never-ending, somewhat terrifying process that you must revisit throughout your career. These are the 'Jaws' moments where we know something's underneath the water, but we are afraid to look. The trick is knowing it's a shark that can eat you *before* you see the dorsal fin approaching.

The Johari Window is the standard for understanding how blind spots work. Basically, there are four 'realms':

1. **The Arena** is what is known to others and known to you. If you look at my photo, you know and I know that I am a Caucasian woman with blonde hair in her mid-40s.

2. **The Façade** is unknown to others but known to you. So, I know that I have had my hair colored since I was in my late teens and I'm mostly grey in reality. If my colorist does a good job, you won't know that I'm not a natural blonde!

3. **The Unknown** is what you don't know and I don't know, so it doesn't really matter. Maybe I don't know that I have a spot on the seat of my skirt, but you can't see it because my jacket covers it anyway. It exists, but it's irrelevant.

4. **The Blind Spot** is what is known to others but unknown to you. This is the area we need to shine a bright light on and see what there is to see. If you don't take important things deliberately out of your blind spot and into the arena, you cannot succeed and are setting yourself up for failure.

One example of a Blind Spot in the Visual Facet is Victoria Beckham's breast implants. She had implants, fairly obvious ones, put in a long time ago – probably because she wanted them and liked them. She was a pop star married to a football/soccer star. She wanted cleavage so she bought some. There's nothing wrong with that and I have implants myself, so I understand the reasoning.

The problem came when she started her own fashion line and wanted to be taken seriously as a designer. The 'Playboy' aesthetic of an hourglass figure is not the same as the 'Vogue' aesthetic of a rail thin model. She found she couldn't wear her own designs without looking overly sexy. She found when she looked overly sexy, people didn't take her seriously as a designer and businesswoman.

This must have existed in her Blind Spot for some time before she acknowledged it, brought it into the Arena, and then decided to have the implants removed. You don't need to do something so extreme, but it illustrates the point.

Blind Spot reveals require bravery and grace when they're pointed out to you for the first time. The executive who fails will do so because she has a knee-jerk reaction to reject the 'reveal.'

I realize this is easier said than done sometimes. A few weeks ago I was running a workshop with a group from Procter & Gamble for around a dozen participants. All the participants knew the very professional and lovely Irish woman who'd organized the course, but I'd not met her before the event. We'd exchanged multiple emails, however, about my travel and logistics.

HOW TO GET "IT"

On the day, she introduced herself to me and I thought she said 'Claire' when in fact her name was Cleo. I'm American and the accent threw me, plus I'm terrible with names and always have to employ tricks to remember names, such as writing notes. After she introduces herself, I wrote 'Claire' at the top of my notes for the day, completely blanking that I'd been corresponding with 'Cleo' for weeks.

For the first three hours of the course, I referred to her repeatedly as 'Claire' – as in "Thanks, Claire," "Claire, do you know when the lunch break is scheduled?" "Claire was so helpful in sorting out all the arrangements for today."

Eventually, I referred to 'Claire' when she was out of the room and a participant in the front raised her hand and said, "Did you know she's called Cleo?" I was embarrassed, of course. But when Cleo came back into the room I said something like, "Oh, my gosh, Cleo – I'm so sorry I've been calling you 'Claire' all day. I need to work on my Irish! You're all on task to correct my pronunciation throughout the day." I then apologized again in private and it was fine.

When it came to the Blind Spot discussion in the workshop, I used this as an impromptu example of how Cleo's name was in my blind spot. It was awkward for everyone, every time I said it, until we brought it into the Arena. How I dealt with it, in this case a relatively benign issue, sets the tone for the rest of the course.

For you, you may think you are open to blind spots being revealed, but I guarantee some of them will be a bit bitter. Pay close attention and make sure you don't shut down the giver.

Finding a 'Blind Spot Buddy'

I love to SCUBA dive and it's something I've been lucky enough to do around the world. When you learn to dive, you're taught that one of the keys to diving safely is having a buddy, someone to help you out of a situation, share air if needed, or get help. In return, you help them if they find themselves in a bind.

I would advise you to get a 'blind spot buddy' to help you bring things that may be blocking you into the Arena. As you think about who you may recruit for this role, you're looking in your social and professional network for someone who's mutually dependent – that is, if you drown, they drown. Ideally, your buddy would be more than an acquaintance, so you know them well. Your relationship shouldn't be professional only, so someone who you just know at work but haven't connected with emotionally at all isn't a good choice. Similarly, you don't want a buddy who's purely social. While you may be able to trust and share with this person, he or she doesn't know you in a professional context and can give a limited perspective.

Your buddy needs to know you professionally and also be someone supportive, who you trust and respect. You should also both have some sort of dependence that binds you – possibly being on the same team, having the same targets, working in the same field, etc.

I've had multiple buddies over the years. My friend Robin Marrouche is a longstanding blind spot buddy who knows me personally and professionally. She gives great advice and insight and accepts the same from me. I know I can safely give her any feedback and she will still like and love me. I also know that I can hear anything from her and I will still like and love her.

Early in my career I was a grant writer for a non-profit Catholic hospital. My blind spot buddy came from an unusual place, Sister Stephanie, a nun who was about 20 years older than me and the only nun on the Board of Trustees. She told me when my skirt was too short or when I talked too much in a meeting. I told her when she came across as too emotive in leadership meetings and needed to add more data instead of stories. For some reason, she listened to me. It was a great relationship and she was a pivotal person in my development as a professional.

HOW TO GET "IT"

When Carla, the prestigiously educated, young Public Relations director at this rural hospital, was painfully self-sabotaging her career with an arrogant attitude and crazy crying jags at the copy machine with all the lights off, Sister Stephanie used these as teachable moments to illustrate what a more effective response would have been in the situation. Sister Stephanie also tried to talk to Carla, who responded by arguing with her about how everyone hated her and then brought her Cornell mug to her office so that people would take her seriously.

When I realized my first real boss was a complete idiot and sinking the small ship that we were on together, Sister Stephanie, who had a vested interest in ensuring the successful voyage of this ship despite this man's incompetence, strategized with me about what to do and how to handle it. I remember her telling me that she was praying for him to get fired. When I said that didn't seem very Christlike for a nun, she replied, "God wants everyone to succeed and do their best. This is not his path so I'm not praying for him to fail, I'm praying for him to find a place where he can do some good."

When Sister Stephanie had to give presentations to all 500 employees about the Mission of the hospital, "To care for the sick as if they were Christ in person," she would ask me to read her speeches and make sure they didn't sound too 'nun-ish' as many of the staff were Mormon, not Catholic, or not religious at all, and would resonate with the younger staff.

It was a successful, mutually dependent relationship that worked very well for us both.

Another option is to hire a blind spot buddy. I've hired two people to help me with my blind spots over the years, MJ Ryan, a noted author and thinking partner, and Dr. Lynn Johnson, also a writer and prominent psychiatrist. I pay them to tell me the hard truths that no one else will. Even if it isn't pretty.

Nose Blowing and Other Problems

As a presence coach, people hire me to basically be their 'blind spot buddy.' Sometimes this is simple, and other times it's a little surprising what we find in the blind spot. I worked with a female CEO who had a problem in her Sociability Facet. When I started working with Laura, I did a series of interviews with some of her team members, colleagues and external stakeholders – an Executive Presence 360 of sorts.

The first thing her PA said to me was, can you get her to stop blowing her nose in public? I was a bit surprised that this had come up, and asked for clarification. According to the PA, Laura would regularly get out a tissue and blow her nose very loudly in the middle of meetings. Not just staff meetings, meetings with people from outside the company, with senior leaders, with the Board of Directors, with the Chairperson. So, yeah, that's a bit of a problem.

The next issue was how to deal with it. Taking that from the Blind Spot to the Arena was delicate. The PA didn't want to do it and it's something that Laura was unlikely to do by herself because if she knew it was inappropriate, she'd have done something about it already – a bit like Sierra not writing on her arm anymore.

I thought about how to bring this into the Arena quite a lot. I couldn't tell her that her PA had mentioned the nose-blowing as that would betray confidentiality. I also felt like telling her that someone in her 360 had raised it as an issue would rattle her and shake her confidence because it's a bit embarrassing and she could potentially get a little paranoid about it. We were in a delicate place, new to the coaching relationship, so caution was paramount.

My moment came when we were shopping for outfits for her to wear in a corporate photo. She was in the fitting room and I was waiting outside. From inside, I heard her blow her nose. This was not genteel. This was loud. This was seriously loud. Like when someone has a really unusual laugh that reverberates, Laura's nose blowing was really, really, really loud. I

HOW TO GET "IT"

suddenly realized why her PA had raised the issue as it was not something that would go unnoticed in a public setting.

"Laura, what was that?" I called out into the fitting room. "Oh my gosh, do you have a flock of geese in there with you?"

"No, why? Was it loud?" she said as she opened the door to show me the suit she'd been trying on.

"A little loud," I said. "Good thing it's just me. You'd never do that in front of 'real' people so I'll take it as flattery that you feel comfortable with me. Now, let's look at that jacket."

As we carried on, I could see her processing my comment about the nose blowing: (1) it was loud enough for me to comment on; (2) it wasn't appropriate with people who aren't friends or family. Immediately, it went from blind spot into Arena.

Later in the day, she said, "Sorry about blowing my nose earlier. I think I have allergies."

I laughed and reiterated that I took it as a sign that she and I were getting along well, but, yes, as long as her 'allergies were acting up' she would of course excuse herself from a meeting and go to the ladies room if she ever had to make that sound again.

That's what a blind spot buddy does and what you do for them. You carefully and directly reveal things that could be blocking them from being their best self. You show them the flaws in their facets as caring and compassionately as you can, with no malice or judgment. What they do with it is up to them. Your job is just to tell the Empress that she has no clothes.

In general, I only give feedback when asked for it. People are usually a little paranoid or overly aware when they meet m.e, so I'm aware that my comments can come across as having more weight than usual. So I try to restrain myself and not offer unless asked.

How to Reveal the Hidden Truth to Someone You Think Needs It

The second element here is the giving of feedback. I so wish that I had a silver-bullet answer to give when people ask me how they can tell others about their executive presence 'issues.' Later on I'll talk about getting a 'feedback buddy' and how to give/receive feedback for yourself. But the truth is, you can't give someone feedback who doesn't ask for it and expect them to listen. Even if they do ask for it, you have to tread lightly or they may not hear it at all, anyway.

You also need to consider why you want to give the person feedback. Does this really come from a genuine place of wanting to help them? Is there any whiff of competition, or one-upwomanship that could taint the input, anyway? If you're not sure, I recommend taking that feedback, writing it down in excruciating detail, and then giving it back to yourself. Odds are, you're trying to tell yourself something in the guise of 'feedback' to someone else.

Kate (the woman who blew it on the podium in front of everyone with her short skirt, etc.) didn't ask me for feedback. I tried to give it to her anyway, and even with my skill and expertise in this area, she didn't want to hear it.

I think of giving input as similar to therapy, where you have to have your own breakthroughs, or like an addict who has to hit rock bottom before they can address the problem. You can point out areas for improvement, but these elements are so touchy, tender, and raw, that it is like navigating a minefield. There are land mines, barbed wire, and a host of issues that have nothing to do with a woman's work or her job and everything to do with how she sees herself or what she's ignoring.

Giving Personal Presence Feedback: When It's Not About You

According to CTI, 81% of women, when given feedback on are personal presence, not always clear on how to correct for it. Similarly, 81% of women surveyed are willing to make the changes, if only someone would tell them. The issue is being told and being brave enough to be the one who opens up another person's blind spot.

One time I was dating a guy who was a senior executive at a nameless company, but it basically is the concert juggernaut and dominator of all events in the universe. He negotiated contracts. He was a fairly important dude. He wanted to be an even more important dude. He also had a weird white scar across his front teeth from being hit by a hockey puck when he was younger. It didn't help that his front teeth were crooked and slightly pronounced, making it the one thing you couldn't help but look at when he spoke. So, when he was talking, part of your brain was looking at the teeth, trying not to, wondering where else to look, and wondering just how that happened.

I knew that he was sensitive on the subject and it didn't bother me, so I didn't mention it. Until he was asking for my professional advice on a video he was going to give, and I said, as gently as I possibly could, 'Have you ever thought about veneers?' He got very offended, said I was superficial and rude, and broke up with me.

So.

The truth was that ignoring this was holding him back. The CEO of a big company can't have scarred teeth. She can have bad teeth, can have a scar on her face; that would be better – we can work with that and it's understandable. But this is something so easy to fix that it's odd for it *not* to be fixed. And that little question niggled away and detracted from his Executive Presence.

But the point is that he didn't want to hear about it. Maybe he didn't want to hear about it from his girlfriend, but the reality is he knew it and he knew others knew it – it was in the open domain – but he had a host of other issues around it that made it a sore spot.

In hindsight, I also found this a really interesting case study about strength and weakness. I am terrible at Excel. Truly awful. I do my invoices in Word, much to my accountant's shock and dismay. This guy was an Excel genius and I asked for his help to put together a worksheet for a company called Boart Longyear that had asked me to help them create a branding process for newly acquired companies. It was complicated for me, easy for him. He helped me and the results were great. I had no problem admitting that I lacked a skill where he excelled (literally) and could help me grow and succeed. Yet, when my area of expertise was brought into the equation, he couldn't accept my help because it was too sensitive to admit a 'failing' in this arena.

Don't be that person who can't get feedback. Also, don't be that person who wanders into the minefield, uninvited, without a flak jacket.

If you do want to give feedback to someone who is not your blind spot buddy, these are the basic steps to follow for success. Let's imagine we have Hannah, a great gal who dresses too sexy and isn't going to get promoted. What to do:

1. Ask if you can give feedback and wait for permission. They have to say yes. So say, "Hannah, I know making a good impression is important to you, do you mind if I give you some feedback?" Then listen to her words and her body language and her entire vibe. If she says "Yes" and seems genuine, then proceed. Frankly, it's unlikely that she's going to say "No" – so your listening is important. If she says "Yes" and crosses her arms and legs and clenches her jaw and sits back in her chair and looks at you with daggers, you need to do damage control and say "I think you've got a lot of potential and I just have noticed that you're on a good path for success. If there's ever anything I can do to support you, I'm happy to help." If she asks about the feedback, that means she really does want it. If she shies away, then let it drop.

HOW TO GET "IT"

2. If she said "Yes," then offer an honest observation and try to be specific. Don't say: "I've noticed you dress a little sexy in the office." Do say: "The skirt you wore yesterday was short."

3. Explain the impact of the observed behavior. This is the 'So what?' moment. "When you wear shorter skirts than most of the other women, it stands out but not necessarily in a good way. You don't want people to look at your legs instead of listening to your ideas."

4. Suggest actions and an alternative – and the 'What's in it for you' factor. "So, you know, I always look at Mary who dresses very classy and had a great style when I'm not sure about what to wear. She seems to wear longer skirts and trousers, so that's a good guide. You can see how people listen to her and respect her."

This is hard, isn't it? It's hard to say and hard to hear. I know, because Sister Stephanie, my wonderful blind spot buddy, had to tell me when I was 22 that my very cool skirt was two inches too short, and showed me the fingertip rule (if it's shorter than your fingers when you're standing up with your hand by your thigh, then it's too short to sit down in like a lady – the nuns know these things from years of Catholic school corrections!) I'm so glad she told me that at 22 so I didn't have to learn it ten years later. It was embarrassing, but it was also true and it came from a place of generosity and support.

Some other guidelines to keep in mind before you dive in:

- Don't say it in public – find a private moment.
- Find the right messenger. Maybe it's not you? Who will they be most receptive to – ideally someone they trust and have a connection with is best.
- Be honest and specific about the behavior.

- Lead with sincere compliments, knowing that the negative will likely be the only thing they remember or hear, but still give them anyway.
- Use humor and smile if you can and it feels sincere.
- Give a boost at the end so it ends positively.
- Be an example. Before you throw a rock, make sure your own house isn't glass in this Facet.
- Be gentle and monitor their body language – your voice is 'loud' in this moment. If they back away, shut down, or start resisting, you need to pull back. You may not reveal everything at once and choose to just give some feedback.

'She Might Cry' – or Why Women Don't Get as Much Feedback as Men

One of the biggest issues with women and executive presence is that they are less likely to have received feedback incrementally over the span of their career. Whereas one man will say to another man "Dude, your breath reeks. Here's a mint" before the big meeting, women and men are reticent to give feedback to a woman.

Why? For men, there's a fear that she may become emotional and cry or something really awful. For women, there's a fear that the other woman will think she's being rude and will dislike her for her it. The 'why' doesn't necessarily matter, because either way, the woman with the bad breath loses.

After I wrote my first book, *Beauty Rehab*, to address confidence and self-esteem for women, I met with a very smart man and writer who heads up one of the UK's biggest PR and communication firms. I gave him a copy of the book and we talked about my work. He could not wrap his head around how he would ever advise a woman to use my services, even though he believes Executive Presence matters and is, in fact, critical to success. This is a man who advises CEOs, royalty, and public officials on what to say when they do horrible things like embezzle money, cheat on their wives, or get caught with hookers.

He asked me to write down words to use to introduce the need for executive presence coaching for a woman – a sort of 'cheat sheet' script. This is what I wrote:

"Is there anything that you think may be holding you back from getting the job/result that you want?"

If you ask that question of senior woman, someone who you know has a Presence issue, I guarantee that on some level she is aware of the gap. What you are testing is if she's ready to do something about it.

If she says "Yes" and then raises something that has do to with how she looks, sounds, acts, behaves, or relates to others, that's your 'in' to guide her toward feedback.

If she says "Yes" and then raises issues of competence or qualification, either she is unaware or unwilling to approach the presence issues at this time. You may want to probe a little and see if she expands and leads the conversation toward Presence, but do so gently and thoughtfully.

If she says "No" and shuts down the conversation, then you have no room to move and anything you say will not only not be heard, but could cause damage to your relationship whether it's personal or professional.

Why Giving Unwanted Feedback Isn't Such a Great Idea

What if you feel really strongly and you really want to give her feedback? In just about every workshop I teach, someone asks me this question. They see someone amazing, talented, smart who is holding herself back, but isn't receptive to feedback.

My answer is: "You can't be more committed to someone's success than they are." If they aren't open and ready, you can't make them change. It simply won't work. If you do try, you may create a 'hydra effect,' where you attempt to cut off one head by giving well-intentioned feedback, but you then create a whole host of new problems as new heads pop up because she resents your input or otherwise acts out.

About the only thing you can do in this situation is to attempt to correct the issue behaviorally without giving insight directly. After you witness the behavior, try to determine what precedes it (the antecedent) and what follows it (the consequence.) If you have any influence or control over either the antecedent or consequence, that's the place to apply an intervention.

For example, what do you do if an otherwise qualified, intelligent and talented woman is continually droning on in meetings and is seemingly unaware that her behavior is boorish or inappropriate – and is doing herself no favors?

If you don't get any open footing with the initial inquiry and have to go the behavior route, you would want to observe her before and after she speaks (drones).

For an antecedent approach, consider: Is she usually filling in silence? Is she usually talking over other people? What is usually happening just before she speaks? Use that moment before, to shift the energy and flow. If she's filling silence, you fill it first and then hand over to her saying, "Pam, do you have anything to add, given that we only have a few minutes?" If she's just trying to prove herself because she's insecure, try to pre-empt her speaking with "Pam, I know you have a lot of knowledge on the subject. If you want to give a quick overview I'm sure others would want to connect with you afterward to hear more."

For a consequence approach, consider: What are the others usually doing while she's speaking – ignoring, being hostile, avoiding? What usually happens after she speaks – everyone goes on and ignores what she's said, the

HOW TO GET "IT"

meeting ends, someone says something snarky? Then find a way to shift the energy to something very opposite when you're with her one on one and she rambles.

You can choose to simply give her no feedback at all – just say "Huh" and then go to the next topic. You can also choose to change the dynamic to interrupt her flow and then reward her for a shorter answer – so say "I'm sorry, I dropped this thing," bend down and hold up a hand to silence her, then when you come back up and reconnect, say "I think I've got that, thanks for explaining it so succinctly when we're all so busy." Every time she gives a short answer in a meeting, make sure she's rewarded for being brief, something like "Thanks, Pam, that was really spot on."

It's very important that you recognize her other strengths and amplify them, or you will shut her down or isolate her. So find other ways to give a lot of praise and she will hopefully be more receptive to your suggestions for blind spot improvements as she comes to trust you.

Of course, it may be easier to just say, "Pam, you talk too much and lose the entire group." And maybe you should and maybe she'd be receptive. But if you're reticent and think you'll alienate her or cause her to withdraw, you still have an obligation to try and help her, to give her the feedback and input she needs to succeed as best you can.

CHAPTER 26

Pulling It All Together for the Long Haul

Every journey takes its toll and a career is a marathon, not a sprint. To stay on course requires getting and sustaining your momentum, developing your resilience, and not just recognizing, but actively embracing your vulnerabilities.

How to Get and Sustain Momentum

We all have dreams, but sometimes the first step is the hardest one. I remember the first time I heard of the book *The Secret*, a philosophy that claims if you believe in something strongly enough, it will happen. While it's good to be optimistic, to believe that things will 'just happen' is a recipe for disaster. Things don't miraculously manifest because you want them to happen. The reality is that while there is power in positive thinking and self-belief; there is also a lot of hard work, planning, persistence, and effort involved.

How do you activate practical optimism to help you achieve your goals? It's about creating tension. Think about a rubber band on just one post. It has no energy or tension. Now, imagine stretching it to a second post. There's immediately tension and things start to activate as point A moves toward point B.

First, define your point A by recognizing where you are today, really. Unflinchingly avoid the tendency to sugar-coat your current reality and ask yourself honestly: "What results do I have now? What truth am I living now? What are my current circumstances?"

Look at your answers. Make sure you're not:

- Describing only what you do or don't like
- Making things better or worse than they really are
- Minimizing how bad or good things actually are
- Imposing how your life should be
- Analyzing how your life got to be the way it is

Really think about this statement. Make certain that your answers represent the results you are getting now, not what you think you need to do about them. Observe your current situation from a place of non-judgment, acceptance, and compassion.

A genuine 'current reality' could sound like: "I am a vice president at Company X. My career options are thinning out and the competition is increasing for available roles. I am qualified and have deep expertise in my field. I do not have a strong sponsor or mentor currently. I am unsure of how others perceive me. I enjoy managing teams and am good at it. I have options to grow in this company and I am also willing to look at other companies."

It does not sound like "I am unappreciated in my role and have no opportunities for growth because my company doesn't value women. I work really hard but it isn't valued. I can't rely on others in my team to back me up so the weight falls on my shoulders. If I continue to work hard things will happen – they just have a way of working out."

Second, define your point B, your desired result. Your vision of the future needs to be something that really matters to you and answers the questions "What do I want to create? What do I want to bring into existence?" It may seem counterintuitive, but a genuinely effective result is a stable state – it's the level where you're meant to settle.

Look at your answers to the questions above. An effective result:

- Focuses on results, not how to achieve them. Otherwise you're limiting what is possible.
- Is motivated by 'I want it because I want it,' with no obligation to actually achieve it. You do not have to make this a reality. You just have to believe that you want it.
- Is affirmative, descriptive, and specific.
- Is situated in the future, yet you can see yourself in it right now.
- Reflects your thinking when 'the sky's the limit' isn't constrained by what appears to be 'possible' or 'doable.'
- Is inspired; inner-directed from your mind, heart, body, and spirit.
- Is driven by curiosity, passion, wonder, and aspiration.

Third, create tension. If you're honest about where you are today, without judgment, and you're committed to where you want to be, you'll begin making choices, big and small, to move yourself toward your future. You may not achieve your big vision of the future, but you have to visualize yourself in the corner office, making a difference, influencing others, leading well or it's never going to happen.

Cultivating Resilience

The strong survive in all aspects of life, if only because they refuse to give up. Success isn't what you achieve; it's what you overcome and leaders with gravitas are resilient. Why do some leaders stay on course despite setbacks while others falter and fail? I believe it's their innate resilience that sets a real leader apart from the pack.

When I worked for National Semiconductor, I had to advise leaders on communicating layoffs. A lot. It was a time and an industry that was short-term driven and management by layoff was common. One layoff cycle meant cutting two very senior leaders, Bill and Jim. Both men were called in, asked to clear out their desks, and escorted from the property in a ritual of shame that is longstanding.

Bill was a transplant from California and hadn't been in the area for long. He didn't have a wife or kids. He had a specialized, highly marketable skill-set in a competitive environment. It may have taken a few weeks for him to find another job, but it would have happened relatively quickly.

Jim was the older of the two. He had a wife and children in college that he needed to support. He was from the local area and had been with the company a relatively long time and was in a specialist field. The odds of him finding an equivalent job without having to relocate to another state weren't great.

Their responses were different and showed how you can never predict who will be resilient and who won't. Jim was deeply religious and a devout Mormon. After he was laid off, he went to the LDS temple and sat and prayed. Then he went home, assessed his savings, and planned a trip with his wife. It took about four months before National hired him back as a contractor and he was pulling down double salary.

Bill had a different reaction. He just got stuck and became very angry. I've seen a lot of layoffs and I'd never witnessed such a blow-up from such a senior leader. He roared out of the building and it was like a cyclone had passed through. The next day we were advised that after he'd left the office, he was in a motorcycle accident caused by speeding and sustained serious injuries, and was lucky to be alive.

Two different men, both disappointed and facing uncertainty, and with different reactions. One showed the ability to be grounded and resilient while the other was hopeless and reactionary. For both of them, life went on, but with consequences.

Every person, male or female, who has achieved success has had a journey that others cannot understand completely. It's full of setbacks, achievements, compromises, and courage. People who are resilient seem to get knocked down and come back stronger. Failure doesn't drain them; it recharges them. Positive attitude, optimism, and downright dogged determination see them through.

Women require more resilience than men because we are told 'no' more often, we are judged more harshly, and we have to prove ourselves more often and with greater consistency and veracity.

Resilience doesn't have to be something you're just born with – no magic 'resilience dust' to be had. Resilient people feel depression, anxiety, and fear just like people who are less resilient – but they don't just recover, they find a way to change their situation and be better off than they were before the trauma.

You can strengthen your resilience and develop the thick skin you need to make it in any situation. If you are not resilient, you will fail because every woman who 'makes it' has to walk through the fire at some point. If you have a Teflon resilience to bounce back, you demonstrate your determination and grit and prove that you have what it takes to lead.

Martin E. P. Seligman, considered the father of positive psychology, has spent years developing ways to teach resilience to help people work through times of failure and stagnation successfully, turning difficult experiences into catalysts for improved performance, including a $145 million initiative for the US military.

The key seems to be learning a three-step process:

1. Understand the setback is temporary. Nothing lasts forever. Not even pain, frustration, anger, or fear. No matter how bad things are, it will change eventually. This is not the end of the world. If you say to yourself, "This will go away quickly. It's a temporary setback," you are going to activate resilience.

2. Recognize that this is just one event. It's an isolated incident and not a universal conspiracy. "It ain't nothin' but a thing." I had an aunt who superstitiously believed that bad events come in threes. As a result, she was always waiting for the next bad thing and keeping an internal scoring system that somehow related random events. Realize that this is just one situation and you will activate resilience.

3. Figure out what can be changed. Everything is changeable. There are actions you can take, no matter how dire the situation. You can do something about it. You are not helpless. This also requires perspective. What's the best case? What's the worst case? What's the most likely case? And what can I do about it?

Improving your resilience lowers symptoms of burnout, reduces depression and anxiety, improves your health and sleep, and reduces dependence on coping mechanisms such as smoking and alcohol. It also shows that you're a leader and dig deep to rise and face the challenges of your position and your life head on.

That doesn't mean that each of us doesn't need a 'reboot' sometimes. U2's song, 'Stuck in a Moment You Can't Get Out of,' was inspired by a fictional conversation Bono had with his friend Michael Hutchence, the INXS lead singer who committed suicide. As Bono said in 2005, "It's a row between mates. You're kinda trying to wake them up out of an idea. In my case it's a row I didn't have while he was alive. I feel the biggest respect I could pay to him was not to write some stupid soppy song, so I wrote a really tough, nasty little number, slapping him around the head. And I'm sorry, but that's how it came out of me." It's a good song to listen to when you feel like you're overwhelmed, because it has some tough love elements.

When I've been stuck in a moment, I've benefitted from very smart people who have helped me out by reminding me of the three steps to perspective. Practice these yourself whenever you get knocked down or feel less-than:

1. Become aware of the moment. How do you feel in your body? What thoughts are you having and can you put them into words? What are your feelings or emotions? What do you hear? What do you smell?

2. Find your center. Go to ground and focus on ten slow breaths. Count up to ten on each inhalation and back down to one on each exhalation. Control intrusive thoughts and images by visualizing them getting smaller and disappearing.

3. Expand your awareness. Resist the urge to withdraw and contract. Instead, intentionally expand. Release tension. Remember that this is temporary, local, and changeable.

The Final Lesson: Vulnerability

Employees don't trust leaders anymore. A 2013 Gallup poll found that only 13% of employees worldwide are engaged at work. Only one in eight workers—out of roughly 180 million employees studied—is psychologically committed to his or her job. In study after study, frustration, burnout, disillusionment, and misalignment with personal values are cited among the biggest reasons for career change. At a time when public confidence and employee morale are so low, the leader who is authoritative yet relatable is the one who will inspire.

When I'm coaching a client, the final lesson of Executive Presence is that vulnerability is the strongest, bravest position she can take to achieve gravitas and make an impact. Vulnerability is not weakness; it unleashes an atomic power where you ultimately achieve success and feel fulfilled. You don't have to confess every weakness, fear or insecurity – in fact, you need to project that you are at the helm and capable at all times. But you don't have to be perfect all the time. If you're outside your comfort zone, you don't have to pretend that you have all the answers if the truth is that you need to bring in additional thinking or get more information before you make a decision.

Each of us, from time to time, has to don a mask to get over a bad day or 'fake it until we make it.' The problem is, if you're trying to wear a mask every day to be someone you're not, you cannot ultimately succeed. I can tone down my 'American Cheerleader' but I can't kill her and pretend to be "Serious Brit" because it is not sustainable. In this case, the mask would become too heavy a burden to uphold because it's not who I am.

According to transformation guru Dr. Peter Fuda, there are two ways in which leaders use a mask. "One is to conceal perceived inadequacies and flaws to preserve the polished facade we have come to expect of 'great' leaders. The other, subtler way is to adopt a certain persona at work that the leader feels is necessary for success. Both uses undermine trust and effectiveness if they are completely detached from reality. They also create inner conflict, as leaders struggle to align their work and home lives. By dropping the mask, a leader can craft a more meaningful and congruent identity, which enhances relationships and business outcomes."

You may have developed some masks or 'rackets' that worked for you early in your career – being the smart girl, the good girl, the overprepared girl. Now, as you've grown to become a woman and a leader, it's okay to be a little less polished and more vulnerable. You can be more vulnerable in certain cultures, when you've established yourself, and with people you trust because showing humanity from a position of gravitas is both authentic and a great way to disarm others who are trying to put you down. Now, being vulnerable doesn't mean you cry at staff meetings and share all your innermost thoughts; it does mean that you don't need to be a Stepford Exec to get ahead.

HOW TO GET "IT"

I've taught many workshops over the years and have, a bit lazily, come to rely on my PowerPoint to remind me of what's next, infused with video clips at key moments to energize the group and make them laugh, or to illustrate a point, and it has pictures to reinforce key points. Recently I gave a six-hour workshop to a group of thirty leaders, and discovered that the projector was broken and therefore no PowerPoint. I had to wing it.

What could have been an epic failure turned into a great success because we were in it together. The participants felt for me and were generous. I was less 'polished' and therefore more vulnerable. It was one of the most engaging, fun, and positive workshops I've ever done and the feedback was astoundingly positive.

There was nothing fake about this success. I wasn't bluffing anything. I was able to handle it, be vulnerable, and go with it because I knew that I knew my stuff, that I had the ability to make it work, and I rose to the challenge not by faking it but by being my real self, inviting others into my world, telling stories as they came to my mind, and letting people see that I was human, imperfect, and still, hopefully, inspiring and able to make our time together valuable and meaningful.

I recently read a leadership trends blog that dismissed executive presence as a method by which imposters might take power, but would ultimately be 'found out' because it's all surface rather than substance. I hope that I've managed to shed light on this relevant, growing and evolving field for women and show that there is nothing artificial at play. Executive Presence is about revealing your genuine brilliance, not manufacturing a façade.

Great artists, musicians, poets, and leaders learn the rules, master the rules, and then break the rules. As a woman working to achieve her career aspirations, when you polish, practice, and master your executive presence, you learn to follow your own course and show your own vulnerability. This is how you find your voice, your signature, and allow your confidence as a leader to fully shine and be recognized.

Made in the USA
Middletown, DE
28 June 2023

34064053R00169